# 1st Workshop on Applying NLP Tools to Similar Languages, Varieties and Dialects 2014



**Held at COLING 2014**

## Dublin, Ireland
## 23 August 2014

ISBN: 978-1-63439-221-1

**Printed from e-media with permission by:**

Curran Associates, Inc.
57 Morehouse Lane
Red Hook, NY 12571

CURRAN ASSOCIATES INC. proceedings.com

**Some format issues inherent in the e-media version may also appear in this print version.**



Printed by Curran Associates, Inc. (2014)

For permission requests, please contact the Association for Computational Linguistics at the address below.

Association for Computational Linguistics
209 N. Eighth Street
Stroudsburg, Pennsylvania 18360

Phone: 1-570-476-8006
Fax: 1-570-476-0860

acl@aclweb.org

**Additional copies of this publication are available from:**

Curran Associates, Inc.
57 Morehouse Lane
Red Hook, NY 12571 USA
Phone: 845-758-0400
Fax: 845-758-2634
Email: curran@proceedings.com
Web: www.proceedings.com

# Introduction

The interest in language resources and computational models for the study of similar languages, varieties and dialects has been growing substantially in the last few years. The first edition of the Workshop on Applying NLP tools to similar languages, varieties and dialects (VarDial) confirms the interest in the topic.

Within the NLP community, the impact of language variation in the development of language resources and NLP applications has been explored in recent years with experiments in different directions. For example, automatic classification or identification of closely related languages such as in Huang and Lee (2008) and Tiedemann and Ljubešić (2012); corpus-driven studies focusing on lexical variation between varieties such as the one by Piersman et al. (2010) or Ljubešić and Fišer (2013); and finally, the adaptation of language models in the context of machine translation such as in Nakov and Tiedemann (2012).

Together with the VarDial workshop we organized the Discriminating between Similar Languages (DSL) shared task. Discriminating between similar languages and language varieties is one of the bottlenecks of state-of-the-art language identification and it has been topic of a number of papers published in the last years. The DSL shared task provided a dataset to evaluate system's performance on discriminating 13 different languages in 6 groups of languages.

The 18 papers that appear in this volume deal with different NLP tasks and applications such as parsing, morphological analysis, part-of-speech tagging, language identification and speech recognition. The VarDial workshop received 18 submissions and 12 of them are published in this volume. The DSL shared task received 22 inscriptions and 8 final submissions. Five system description papers plus the DSL shared task report appear in this volume.

We take this opportunity to thank the VarDial program committee who thoroughly reviewed all papers; the DSL shared task participants for valuable feedback and discussions; and the COLING organizers for their support, specially Jennifer Foster who replied promptly to all our inquiries.

Marcos, Liling, Nikola and Jörg
VarDial Organizers

**Organizers**

Marcos Zampieri, Saarland University, Germany
Liling Tan, Saarland University, Germany
Nikola Ljubešić, University of Zagreb, Croatia
Jörg Tiedemann, Uppsala University, Sweden

**Program Committee**

Željko Agić, University of Potsdam, Germany
Jorge Baptista, University of Algarve and INESC-ID, Portugal
Francis Bond, Nanyang Technological University, Singapore
Aoife Cahill, Educational Testing Service, USA
Paul Cook, University of Melboune, Australia
Liviu Dinu, University of Bucarest, Romania
Stefanie Dipper, Ruhr University Bochum, Germany
Sascha Diwersy, University of Cologne, Germany
Tomaž Erjavec, Jozef Stefan Institute, Slovenia
Mikel L. Forcada, Universitat d'Alacant, Spain
Binyam Gebrekidan Gebre, Max Planck Institute for Psycholinguistics, Holland
Nitin Indurkhya, University of New South Wales, Australia
Jeremy Jancsary, Nuance Communications, Austria
Marco Lui, University of Melbourne, Australia
Preslav Nakov, Qatar Computing Research Institute, Qatar
Santanu Pal, Saarland University, Germany
Sebastian Padó, University of Stuttgart, Germany
Reinhard Rapp, University of Mainz, Germany and University of Aix-Marsaille, France
Felipe Sánchez Martínez, University of Alicante, Spain
Kevin Scanell, Saint Louis University, USA
Yves Scherrer, University of Geneva, Switzerland
Serge Sharoff, Leeds University, United Kingdom
Kiril Simov, Bulgarian Academy of Sciences, Bulgaria
Elke Teich, Saarland University, Germany
Joel Tetreault, Yahoo! Labs, USA
Francis Tyers, UiT Norgga Árktalaš Universitehta, Norway
Cristina Vertan, University of Hamburg, Germany
Torsten Zesch, University of Duisburg-Essen, Germany

# Table of Contents

# Conference Program

**Saturday, August 23, 2014**

9:15–9:30 Opening Remarks

09:30–10:00 *Corpus-based Study and Identification of Mandarin Chinese Light Verb Variations*
Chu-Ren Huang, Jingxia Lin, Menghan JIANG and Hongzhi Xu

10:00–10:30 *Diachronic proximity vs. data sparsity in cross-lingual parser projection. A case study on Germanic*
Maria Sukhareva and Christian Chiarcos

10:30–11:00 *Pos-tagging different varieties of Occitan with single-dialect resources*
Marianne Vergez-Couret and Assaf Urieli

11:00–11:30 Coffee Break

11:30–12:00 *Unsupervised adaptation of supervised part-of-speech taggers for closely related languages*
Yves Scherrer

12:00–12:30 *Morphological Disambiguation and Text Normalization for Southern Quechua Varieties*
Annette Rios Gonzales and Richard Alexander Castro Mamani

12:30–14:00 Lunch

14:00–14:30 *The Varitext platform and the Corpus des variétés nationales du français (CoVaNa-FR) as resources for the study of French from a pluricentric perspective*
Sascha Diwersy

14:30–15:00 *A Report on the DSL Shared Task 2014*
Marcos Zampieri, Liling Tan, Nikola Ljubešić and Jörg Tiedemann

15:00–15:30 Coffee Break

**Saturday, August 23, 2014 (continued)**

**Poster Session**

15:30–17:00 *Employing Phonetic Speech Recognition for Language and Dialect Specific Search*
Corey Miller, Rachel Strong, Evan Jones and Mark Vinson

15:30–17:00 *Part-of-Speech Tag Disambiguation by Cross-Linguistic Majority Vote*
Noëmi Aepli, Ruprecht von Waldenfels and Tanja Samardžić

15:30–17:00 *Compilation of a Swiss German Dialect Corpus and its Application to PoS Tagging*
Nora Hollenstein and Noëmi Aepli

15:30–17:00 *Automatically building a Tunisian Lexicon for Deverbal Nouns*
Ahmed Hamdi, Nuria Gala and Alexis Nasr

15:30–17:00 *Statistical Morph Analyzer (SMA++) for Indian Languages*
Saikrishna Srirampur, Ravi Chandibhamar and Radhika Mamidi

15:30–17:00 *Improved Sentence-Level Arabic Dialect Classification*
Christoph Tillmann, Saab Mansour and Yaser Al-Onaizan

15:30–17:00 *Using Maximum Entropy Models to Discriminate between Similar Languages and Varieties*
Jordi Porta and José-Luis Sancho

15:30–17:00 *Exploring Methods and Resources for Discriminating Similar Languages*
Marco Lui, Ned Letcher, Oliver Adams, Long Duong, Paul Cook and Timothy Baldwin

15:30–17:00 *The NRC System for Discriminating Similar Languages*
Cyril Goutte, Serge Léger and Marine Carpuat

15:30–17:00 *Experiments in Sentence Language Identification with Groups of Similar Languages*
Ben King, Dragomir Radev and Steven Abney

15:30–17:00 *A Simple Baseline for Discriminating Similar Languages*
Matthew Purver

# Corpus-based Study and Identification of Mandarin Chinese Light Verb Variations

**Chu-Ren Huang**[1] **Jingxia Lin**[2] **Menghan Jiang**[1] **Hongzhi Xu**[1]

[1]Department of CBS, The Hong Kong Polytechnic University
[2]Nanyang Technological University

churen.huang@polyu.edu.hk, jingxialin@ntu.edu.sg,
menghan.jiang@connect.polyu.hk, hongz.xu@gmail.com

**Abstract**

When PRC was founded on mainland China and the KMT retreated to Taiwan in 1949, the relation between mainland China and Taiwan became a classical Cold War instance. Neither travel, visit, nor correspondences were allowed between the people until 1987, when government on both sides started to allow small number of Taiwan people with relatives in China to return to visit through a third location. Although the thawing eventually lead to frequent exchanges, direct travel links, and close commercial ties between Taiwan and mainland China today, 38 years of total isolation from each other did allow the language use to develop into different varieties, which have become a popular topic for mainly lexical studies (e.g., Xu, 1995; Zeng, 1995; Wang & Li, 1996). Grammatical difference of these two variants, however, was not well studied beyond anecdotal observation, partly because the near identity of their grammatical systems. This paper focuses on light verb variations in Mainland and Taiwan variants and finds that the light verbs of these two variants indeed show distributional tendencies. Light verbs are chosen for two reasons: first, they are semantically bleached hence more susceptible to changes and variations. Second, the classification of light verbs is a challenging topic in NLP. We hope our study will contribute to the study of light verbs in Chinese in general. The data adopted for this study was a comparable corpus extracted from Chinese Gigaword Corpus and manually annotated with contextual features that may contribute to light verb variations. A multivariate analysis was conducted to show that for each light verb there is at least one context where the two variants show differences in tendencies (usually the presence/absence of a tendency rather than contrasting tendencies) and can be differentiated. In addition, we carried out a K-Means clustering analysis for the variations and the results are consistent with the multivariate analysis, i.e. the light verbs in Mainland and Taiwan indeed have variations and the variations can be successfully differentiated.

## 1 Introduction: Language Variations in the Chinese Context

Commonly dichotomy of language and dialect is not easily maintained in the context of Chinese language(s). Cantonese, Min, Hakka, and Wu are traditionally referred to as dialects of Chinese but are mutually unintelligible. However, they do share a common writing system and literary and textual tradition, which allows speakers to have a shared linguistic identity. To overcome the mutual unintelligibility problem, a variant of Northern Mandarin Chinese, is designated as the common language about a hundred years ago (called 普通話 *Putonghua* 'common language' in Mainland China, and 國語 *Guoyu* 'national language' in Taiwan). Referred to as Mandarin or Mandarin Chinese, or simply Chinese nowadays, this is the one of the most commonly learned first or second languages in the world now. However, not unlike English, with the fast globalization of the Chinese language, both the term 'World Chineses' and the recognition that there are different variants of Chinese emerged. In this paper, we studied two of the most important variants of Chinese, Mainland Mandarin and Taiwan Mandarin.





*Proceedings of the First Workshop on Applying NLP Tools to Similar Languages, Varieties and Dialects*, pages 1–10, Dublin, Ireland, August 23 2014.

## 1.1 Variations between Mainland and Taiwan Mandarin: Previous studies

The lexical differences between Mainland and Taiwan Mandarin have been the focus of research in Chinese Linguistics in the recent years. A number of studies were carried out on lexical variations between these two variants of Mandarin Chinese, including variations in the meanings of the same word or using different words to express the same meaning (e.g., Xu, 1995; Zeng, 1995; Wang,1996). Some dictionaries also list the lexical differences between Mainland Mandarin and Taiwan Mandarin (e.g., Qiu, 1990; Wei & Sheng, 2000).

By contrast, only a few of such studies were corpus driven (e.g. Hong and Huang 2008, 2013; Huang and Lin, 2013), and even few studies have been done on the grammatical variations of Mainland and Taiwan Chinese. Huang et al. (2013), the only such study based on comparable corpora so far, suggested that the subtlety of the underlining grammatical variations of these two dialectal variants at early stage of divergence may have contributed to the challenge as well as scarcity of previous studies.

## 1.2 Light Verbs in Light Verb Variations

The study of English light verb constructions (LVCs) (e.g., *take a look, make an offer*) has been an important topic in linguistics (Jespersen, 1965; Butt and Geuder, 2003; among others) as well as in Computational Linguistics (Tu and Dan, 2011; Nagy et al., 2013; Hwang et al., 2010; among others). Identification of LVCs is a fundamental crucial task for Natural Language Processing (NLP) applications, such as information retrieval and machine translation. For example, Tu and Dan (2011) proposed a supervised learning system to automatically identify English LVCs by training with groups of contextual or statistical features. Nagy et al. (2013) introduced a system that enables the full coverage identification of English LVCs in running context by using a machine leaning approach.

However, little work has been done to identify Chinese LVCs, especially between different variants of Chinese (cf. Hwang et al., 2010). Chinese LVCs are similar to English LVCs in the sense that the light verb itself is semantically bleached and does not contain any eventive or contentive information, so the predicative information of the construction mainly comes from the complement taken by the light verb (e.g., Zhu, 1985; Zhou, 1987; Cai, 1982). For instance, 進行 *jinxing* originally meant 'move forward/proceed', but in an LVC such as 進行討論 *jinxing taolun* proceed discuss 'to discuss', 進行 *jinxing* only contributes aspectual information whereas the core meaning of the LVC comes from the complement 討論 *taolun* 'discuss'. Chinese also differs from English in that many of the Chinese light verbs have similar usages and thus are often interchangeable, e.g., all the five light verbs 從事 *congshi*, 搞 *gao*, 加以 *jiayi*, 進行 *jinxing*, and 做 *zuo* can take 研究 *yanjiu* 'do research' as their complement and form a LVC. But Huang et al. (2013) also observed that differences in collocation constraints can sometimes be found between different variants of Mandarin Chinese. For instance, constructions like 進行投票 *jinxing tou-piao* proceed cast-ticket 'to cast votes', where the complement is in the V(erb)-O(bject) form, usually can only be found in Taiwan Mandarin. Hence, Chinese LVCs are challenging for both linguistic studies and computational applications in two aspects: (a) to identify collocation constraints of the different light verbs in order to automatically classify and predict their uses in context, and (b) to identify the collocation constraints of the same light verb in order to differentiate and predict the two Chinese variants based on the use of such light verbs. The first issue has been explored in Lin et al. (2014): by analyzing Mainland and Taiwan Mandarin data extracted from comparable corpora with statistical and machine learning approaches, the authors find the five light verbs 從事 *congshi*, 搞 *gao*, 加以 *jiayi*, 進行 *jinxing*, and 做 *zuo* can be reliably differentiated from each other in each variety. But to the best of our knowledge, there has been no previous computational study on modeling the light verb variations, or other syntactic variations of Chinese dialects or variants of the same dialect. Therefore, this paper builds on the study of Lin et al. (2014) and will adopt a comparable corpus driven approach to model light verb variations in Mainland and Taiwan Mandarin.

# 2 Data and annotation

Our study focuses on five light verbs, 加以 *jiayi,* 進行 *jinxing,* 從事 *congshi,* 搞 *gao* and 做 *zuo* (these words literally meant 'proceed', 'inflict', 'engage', 'do', and 'do' respectively). These five are chosen for two reasons. First, they are the most frequently used light verbs in Mandarin Chinese (Diao, 2004); second, although the definition of Chinese light verbs is still debatable, these five are considered the most typical light verbs in most previous studies.

The data for this study was extracted from the Annotated Chinese Gigaword Corpus (Huang, 2009) maintained by LDC which contains over 1.1 billion Chinese words, consisting of 700 million characters from Taiwan Central News Agency (CNA) and 400 million characters from Mainland Xinhua News Agency (XNA). For each of the five light verbs, 400 sentences were randomly selected, half from the Mainland XNA corpus and the other half from the Taiwan CNA Corpus, which results in 2,000 sentences in total.

Previous studies (Zhu, 1985; Zhou, 1987; Cai, 1982; Huang et al., 2013; among others) have proposed several syntactic and semantic features to compare and identify the similarities and differences among light verbs. For example, while Taiwan 從事 *congshi* can take informal or semantically negative event complements such as 性交易 *xingjiaoyi* 'sexual trade', Mainland 從事 *congshi* is rarely found with such complements (Huang et al. 2013).

In our study, we selected 11 features covering both syntactic and semantic features which may help to identify light verb variations, as in Table 1. All 2,000 sentences with light verbs were manually annotated with the 11 features. The annotator is a trained expert on Chinese linguistics. All ambiguous cases were discussed with another two experts in order to reach an agreement (the features and annotation were the same with Lin et al. (2014)).

## 3 Modelling and Predicting Two Variants

We carried out both a multivariate analysis and machine learning algorithm to explore the possible differences existing between Mainland and Taiwan Mandarin light verbs. Our analysis shows that for each light verb, there is at least one context where the two variants of Mandarin show differences in usage tendencies and thus can be differentiated, although the differences more often lie in the presence/absence of a tendency rather than complementary distribution.

### 3.1 Multivariate Analysis of Light Verb Variations

As introduced in Section 1, the five or some of the five light verbs sometimes can be interchangeably used in both Mainland and Taiwan Mandarin. This indicates that the interchangeable light verbs share some features. In other words, it is unlikely that a particular feature is preferred by only one light verb and thus differentiates the verb from the others. This is also proved in Lin et al. (2014). For instance, their study finds both Mainland and Taiwan 從事 *congshi* and 搞 *gao* significantly prefer nominal complements (POS.N). Therefore, to better explore the light verb differences in the two variants, we adopt a multivariate analysis for this study.

The multivariate analysis we used is polytomous logistic regression (Arppe 2008, cf. Han et al. 2013, Bresnan et al. 2007), and the tool we used is the Polytomous() function in the Polytoumous package in R (Arppe 2008). The polytomous logistic regression is an extension of standard logistic regression; it calculates the odds of the occurrence of a particular light verb when a particular feature is present, with all other features being equal (Arppe, 2008). In addition, it also allows for simultaneous estimation of the occurrence probability of all the five light verbs.

Before we discuss the light verb variations based on multivariate analysis, we will show that the polytomous multivariate model adopted is reliable for our study. Table 2 presents the probability estimates of Mainland and Taiwan light verbs calculated by the model. The results indicate that the overall performance of the model is good: the most frequently predicted light verb (in each column) corresponds to the light verb that actually occurs in the data (in each row) (see the numbers in bold).

In addition, the recall, precision, and F-measure of the estimates given in Table 3 show that each light verb in each variant can be successfully identified with a F-score better than chance (0.2), while the performance varies from light verb to light verb, which is thus consistent with the results in Lin et al. (2014). The only exception is 搞 *gao* in Mainland Mandarin, but the low F-score of 搞 *gao* (0.14) is consistent with the linguistic observation that this verb is rarely used as a light verb in Mainland Mandarin. More detailed information of the factors that can distinguish the five light verbs in each variant can also be found in Table 4. In the following of this section, we focus on the variations of each light verb in Mainland and Taiwan Mandarin.

| **Feature ID** | **Explanation** | **Values (example)** |
|---|---|---|
| 1. OTHERLV | Whether a light verb co-occurs with another light verbs | Yes (開始進行討論 ***kaishi*** *jinxing taolun* Start proceed discuss 'start to discuss')<br>No (進行討論 *jinxing taolun* proceed discuss 'to discuss') |
| 2. ASP | Whether a light verb is affixed with an aspectual marker (e.g., perfective 了 *le*, durative 著 *zhe*, experiential 過 *guo*) | ASP.le (進行了戰鬥 *jinxing-**le** zhandou* 'fighted')<br>ASP.zhe (進行著戰鬥 *jinxing-**zhe** zhandou* 'is fighting')<br>ASP.guo (進行過戰鬥 *jinxing-**guo** zhandou* 'fighted')<br>ASP.none (進行戰鬥 *jinxing zhandou* 'fight') |
| 3. EVECOMP | Event complement of a light verb is in subject position | Yes (比賽在學校進行 ***bisai*** *zai xuexiao jinxing* game at school proceed 'The game was held at the school')<br>No (在學校進行比賽 *zai xuexiao jinxing* ***bisai*** at school proceed game 'the game was held at the school') |
| 4. POS | The part-of-speech of the complement taken by a light verb | Noun (進行戰爭 *jinxing* ***zhanzheng*** proceed fight 'to fight')<br>Verb (進行戰鬥 *jinxing* ***zhandou*** proceed fight 'to fight') |
| 5. ARGSTR | The argument structure of the complement of a light verb, i.e. the number of arguments (subject and/or objects) that can be taken by the complement | One (進行戰鬥 *jinxing* ***zhandou*** proceed fight 'to fight')<br>Two (進行批評 *jinxing* ***piping*** proceed criticize 'to criticize')<br>Zero (進行戰爭 *jinxing* ***zhanzheng*** proceed fight 'to fight') |
| 6. VOCOMP | Whether the complement of a light verb is in the V(erb)-O(bject) form | Yes (進行投票 *jinxing* ***tou-piao*** proceed cast-ticket 'to vote')<br>No (進行戰鬥 *jinxing* ***zhan-dou*** proceed fight-fight 'to fight') |
| 7. DUREVT | Whether the event denoted by the complement of a light verb is durative | Yes (進行戰鬥 *jinxing* ***zhandou*** proceed fight-fight 'to fight')<br>No (加以拒絕 *jiayi* ***jujue*** inflict reject 'to reject') |
| 8. FOREVT | Whether the event denoted by the complement of a light verb is formal or official | Yes (進行國事訪問 *jinxing* ***guoshi fangwen*** proceed state visit 'to pay a state visit')<br>No (做小買賣 *zuo* ***xiao maimai*** do small business 'run a small business') |
| 9. PSYEVT | Whether the event denoted by the complement of a light verb is mental or psychological activity | Yes (加以反省 *jiayi* ***fanxing*** inflict retrospect 'to retrospect')<br>No (加以調查 *jiayi* ***diaocha*** inflict investigate 'to investigate') |
| 10. INTEREVT | Whether the event denoted by the complement of a light verb involves interaction among participants | Yes (進行討論 *jinxing* ***taolun*** proceed discuss 'to discuss')<br>No (加以批評 *jiayi* ***piping*** inflict criticize 'to criticize') |
| 11. ACCOMPEVT | Whether the event denoted by the complement of a light verb is an accomplishment | Yes (進行解決 *jinxing* ***jiejue*** proceed solve 'to solve')<br>No (進行戰鬥 *jinxing* ***zhandou*** proceed fight-fight 'to fight') |

Table 1: Features used to differentiate five Chinese light verbs.

| Predicted / Observed | *congshi* | | *gao* | | *jiayi* | | *jinxing* | | *zuo* | |
|---|---|---|---|---|---|---|---|---|---|---|
| | ML | TW | ML | TW | ML | TW | ML | TW | ML | TW |
| *congshi* | **131** | **64** | 1 | 87 | 62 | 39 | 1 | 10 | 5 | 0 |
| *gao* | 69 | 8 | **16** | **139** | 86 | 36 | 16 | 16 | 13 | 1 |
| *jiayi* | 1 | 0 | 1 | 0 | **192** | **190** | 6 | 6 | 0 | 4 |
| *jinxing* | 31 | 18 | 9 | 34 | 47 | 80 | **62** | **67** | 51 | 1 |
| *zuo* | 50 | 24 | 5 | 16 | 44 | 114 | 4 | 14 | **97** | **32** |

Table 2: Probability estimates of Mainland (ML) and Taiwan (TW) light verbs.

| | Recall | | Precision | | F-measure | |
|---|---|---|---|---|---|---|
| | ML | TW | ML | TW | ML | TW |
| *congshi* | 0.66 | 0.32 | 0.46 | 0.56 | 0.54 | 0.41 |
| *gao* | 0.08 | 0.70 | 0.5 | 0.5 | 0.14 | 0.58 |
| *jiayi* | 0.96 | 0.95 | 0.45 | 0.41 | 0.61 | 0.58 |
| *jinxing* | 0.31 | 0.34 | 0.70 | 0.59 | 0.43 | 0.43 |
| *zuo* | 0.49 | 0.16 | 0.58 | 0.84 | 0.53 | 0.27 |

Table 3: Recall, precision, and F-measure of the polytomous multivariate estimates.

| | *congshi* | | *gao* | | *jiayi* | | *jinxing* | | *zuo* | |
|---|---|---|---|---|---|---|---|---|---|---|
| | ML | TW | ML | TW | ML | TW | ML | TW | ML | TW |
| (Intercept) | (1/Inf) | (1/Inf) | *0.02271* | (1/Inf) | (1/Inf) | (1/Inf) | (1/Inf) | (1/Inf) | (1/Inf) | (1/Inf) |
| ACCOMPEVTyes | (1/Inf) | (0.3419) | *0.09863* | (1/Inf) | ***56.25*** | ***11.33*** | *0.1849* | (0.1607) | (1/Inf) | *0.2272* |
| ARGSTRtwo | *0.2652* | *0.1283* | ***2.895*** | (0.7613) | ***76.47*** | (Inf) | (1.481) | (0.7062) | *0.2177* | (1.217) |
| ARGSTRzero | (1.097) | (0.6219) | ***3.584*** | ***7.228*** | (1/Inf) | (4.396) | (1.179) | *0.5393* | *0.245* | *0.2068* |
| ASPle | (0.7487) | (1/Inf) | (0.1767) | (1/Inf) | (0.8257) | (0.3027) | (0.9196) | (Inf) | (1.853) | ***32.98*** |
| ASPno | (Inf) | (0.9273) | (1.499) | (0.6967) | (Inf) | (Inf) | (0.2307) | (Inf) | (0.2389) | (0.2385) |
| ASPzhe | (1.603) | | (1/Inf) | | (0.4571) | | (Inf) | | (1/Inf) | |
| DUREVTyes | (Inf) | (Inf) | (2.958) | (Inf) | (1/Inf) | (1/Inf) | (Inf) | (0.9575) | (Inf) | (Inf) |
| EVECOMPyes | (1/Inf) | (1/Inf) | (1.726) | (0.8491) | (1/Inf) | (1/Inf) | ***3.975*** | ***8.113*** | (1.772) | (0.5019) |
| FOREVTyes | (2.744) | *0.0867* | (1.227) | (Inf) | (Inf) | (Inf) | (0.7457) | (1.437) | *0.2679* | (1.467) |
| INTEREVTyes | *0.03255* | *0.1896* | (0.5281) | (1/Inf) | (0.5432) | (0.951) | ***18.67*** | ***10.47*** | *0.08902* | (0.398) |
| PSYEVTyes | (1/Inf) | (1/Inf) | (1/Inf) | (1/Inf) | ***19.87*** | (1.395) | (1/Inf) | (1/Inf) | (0.9619) | (3.323) |
| VOCOMPyes | (0.1346) | *0.18* | (3.043) | (2.35) | ***23.54*** | (Inf) | (1.086) | ***3.161*** | (0.5344) | (0.5956) |

Table 4: Multivariate analysis of light verb variations in Mainland and Taiwan Mandarin.

Table 4 summarizes the results estimated by the Polytomous multivaraite analysis. The numbers in the table are the odds for the features in favor of or against the occurrence of each light verb: odds larger than 1 indicate that the chance of the occurrence of a light verb is significantly increased by the feature, e.g., the chance of Mainland 加以 *jiayi* occurring is significantly increased by ARGSTRtwo (76.47: 1), followed by ACCOMPEVTyes (56.25: 1), VOCOMPyes (23.54: 1), PSYEVTyes (19.87: 1); odds smaller than 1 indicate that the chance of the occurrence of a light verb is significantly descreased by the feature, e.g., the chance of Mainland 進行 *jinxing* occurring is significantly decreased by ACCOMPEVTyse (0.1849: 1); in addition, "inf" and "1/inf" refer to odds larger than 10,000 and smaller than 1/10,000 respectively, and non-significant odds ($p$-value < 0.05) are given in parentheses, regardless of the odds value.

Table 4 finds that Mainland and Taiwan Mandarin indeed show some variations in each light verb. Furthermore, the variations of each light verb mainly lie in non-complementary distributional patterns. That is, as highlighted in dark grey colour in Table 4, the odds differences are more often between non-significance (odds in parentheses) and significance (odds larger or smaller than 1), rather than between significant preference (odds larger than 1) and significant dis-preference (odds smaller than 1). In other words, the difference of a light verb in the two variants is more **comparative**, rather than

**contrastive.** This explains why the variations are not easily found by traditional linguistic studies. The following summarizes the key variations of each light verb.

**從事 *congshi***

**從事** *congshi* in both Mainland and Taiwan Mandarin has no feature significantly in its favor and it is significantly disfavored by ARGSTRtwo (taking two-argument complements, e.g., 研究 *yanjiu* 'to research') and INTEREVTyes (taking complements denoting interactive activities, e.g., 商量 *shangliang* 'to discuss'). However, Taiwan 從事 *congshi* is differentiated from Mainland 從事 *congshi* in that the former is also disfavored by FOREVTyes (taking complements denoting formal events, e.g., 研究 *yanjiu* 'to research') and VOCOMPyes (taking complements in the form of V(erb)-O(bject), e.g., 投票 *toupiao* 'cast a vote'), whereas the latter is not. The finding that Taiwan 從事 *congshi* is less likely to take formal event as its complement is consistent with that in Huang et al. (2013).

**搞 *gao***

Both Mainland and Taiwan 搞 *gao* are significantly favored by *ARGSTRzero* (taking zero-argument complements, i.e. noun complement in this study). However, compared with Taiwan Mandarin, Mainland 搞 *gao* is more likely to take two-argument complements (ARGSTRtwo), but less likely to take complements denoting accomplishment events (ACCOMPEVTyes, e.g., 解決 *jiejue* 'to solve'), and it is also disfavored by the aggregate of default variable values (i.e. the intercept, 0.02: 1).

**加以 *jiayi***

Both Mainland and Taiwan 加以 *jiayi* are favored by the feature ACCOMPEVTyes (accomplishment complement such as 解決 *jiejue* 'to solve'), but the chance of occurrence of Mainland 加以 *jiayi* increases with the presence of two-argument complements (ARGSTRtwo), complements in VO form (VOCOMPyes), and complements denoting mental or phychological activities (PSYEVTyes, e.g., 反省 *fanxing* 'to introspect').

**進行 *jinxing***

Both Mainland and Taiwan 進行 *jinxing* have INTEREVTyes (taking complements denoting interactive activities) and EVECOMPyes (allowing event complements in subject position, e.g., 會議進行順利 *huiyi jinxing shunli* meeting procced smoothly 'The meeting proceeded smoothly') in their favor. However, 進行 *jinxing* in Mainland Mandarin is less likely to take accomplishment complements (ACCOMPEVTyes); whereas 進行 *jinxing* in Taiwan Mandarin is more disfavored by *ARGSTRzero*, but more likely to take complements in VO form, which is also consistent with the findings in Huang et al. (2013).

**做 *zuo***

The occurrence of 做 *zuo* in Mainland Mandarin is decreased by factors such as ARGSTRtwo, FOREVTyes, and INTEREVTyes, whereas the occurrence of 做 *zuo* in Taiwan Mandarin is decreased by ACCOMPTEVTyes, but significantly increased by ASP*le*. It is obvious to linguists that 做 *zuo* in both Mainland and Taiwan Mandarin are frequently found with the perfective marker 了 *le*, but our analysis reveals that the affixation 了 *le* to Taiwan **做** *zuo* is much more frequent than that in Mainland.

### 3.2 Clustering Analysis of Light Verb Variations

We adopted a vector space model (VSM) to represent the use of light verbs. The features in Table 1 could be expanded to 17 binary features. For example, ASP could be expanded into four binary features: ASP.le, ASP.zhe, ASP.guo, ASP.none. Each instance of a light verb in the corpus was represented by a vector with 17 dimensions. Each dimension stores the value of one of the 17 binary features determined by the context where the light verb is used.

| Cluster ID | | 0 | 1 | 2 | 3 | 4 | 5 | 6 | 7 | 8 | 9 |
|---|---|---|---|---|---|---|---|---|---|---|---|
| *congshi* | TW | 39 | 43 | 1 | 84 | 2 | 21 | 4 | 4 | 1 | 1 |
| | ML | 62 | 48 | 0 | 83 | 1 | 4 | 1 | 1 | 0 | 0 |
| *gao* | TW | 38 | 141 | 0 | 0 | 9 | 10 | 2 | 0 | 4 | 0 |
| | ML | 88 | 64 | 3 | 8 | 11 | 5 | 10 | 4 | 6 | 4 |
| *jiayi* | TW | 152 | 0 | 6 | 28 | 11 | 2 | 0 | 4 | 0 | 0 |
| | ML | 117 | 3 | 6 | 62 | 18 | 2 | 5 | 14 | 1 | 1 |
| *jinxing* | TW | 26 | 79 | 7 | 2 | 38 | 30 | 0 | 3 | 15 | 1 |
| | ML | 23 | 80 | 16 | 0 | 55 | 22 | 5 | 2 | 1 | 0 |
| *zuo* | TW | 20 | 3 | 0 | 2 | 23 | 130 | 20 | 2 | 1 | 6 |
| | ML | 23 | 44 | 3 | 16 | 38 | 45 | 20 | 11 | 8 | 3 |

Table 5: The distribution of data origin by the clustering result.

Then we adopt a clustering algorithm K-Means to identify the variations of light verbs in Taiwan and Mainland Mandarin. The assumption is that the instances of a light verb will form different clusters in the hyperspace according to the distances among them. Each cluster reflects a special use of a light verb. For example, there could be one cluster, where all the instances take non-accomplishment event argument, e.g., 加以分析/研究/評論 *jiayi fenxi/ yanjiu/ pinglun* inflict analyze/ research/ comment 'to analyze/ research/ comment', etc.

In this sense, if there are light verb variations between Mainland and Taiwan Mandarin, the light verbs will be distributed to two clusters, one with data mainly from Mainland Mandarin, whereas the other mainly from Taiwan Mandarin. Meanwhile, if a cluster contains much more data from one variant than the other, it indicates the usage of a light verb is mainly restricted to the variant with more data; or if a cluster contains data of similar amount from both Mainland and Taiwan Mandarin, it indicates that the two variants share common usages regarding the light verbs. Therefore, for each light verb, all 400 examples from both Mainland and Taiwan Mandarin are mixed together for the analysis.

As the K-Means algorithm requires an input of the number $N$ of the clusters, the selection of $N$ is then an issue we need to consider. Remembering that the clusters reflect the use of a light verb rather than data origin, the selection of N should be based on the consideration of how many different uses a light verb may have. As there are 17 expanded binary features, the whole space of the values of the vectors is $2^{17} = 128$K. However, the number of different uses for a light verb should not be too large. There is no problem if $N$ is set slightly larger than the real number of different uses of a light verb. For example, if there are 5 different uses for a light verb and we set N=6, then we can imagine that there may be two clusters that reflect the same use of the light verb. On the contrary, if $N$ is set too small, all different uses will be mixed together. Then, the clustering result may not be able to show any interesting result we expected. In our experiments, we set $N$=10 for all the five light verbs. Especially, we use the WEKA (Hall et al., 2009) implementation of the simple K-Means for our experiments. The result is shown in Table 5. The key variations of each light verb are summarized as follows.

**從事 *congshi***

Cluster 5 shows that Mainland 從事 *congshi* prefers to take complements denoting formal or official events in Mainland Mandarin. However, Taiwan 從事 *congshi* does not show such preference as it can take both formal and informal events. Clusters 6 and 9 show that Taiwan 從事 *congshi* can also take complements in VO form, e.g., 進行開票 *jinxing kaipiao* proceed ballot counting 'to proceed with ballot counting', but this is not preferred by Mainland 從事 *congshi.*

**搞 *gao***

Clusters 6 and 7 together show that the argument of Mainland 搞 *gao* can occur in the subject position in addition to the complement position, but such word order is rarely found in Taiwan data. Cluster 3 shows a possibility for Mainland 搞 *gao* to take arguments denoting events involving interactions of participants (e.g., 討論 *taolun* 'to discuss'). In addition, Cluster 9 shows the possibility that Mainland 搞 *gao* can take complements describing informal events, while the complements to Taiwan Mainland 搞 *gao* are more often formal events (especially political activities).

**加以 *jiayi***

Cluster 7 suggests Mainland 加以 *jiayi* show a preference over complements denoting mental or psychological events. However, although Clusters 1 and 6 show some difference between Mainland and Taiwan 加以 *jiayi*, our closer examination of the original data found that such differences actually do not reflect any variant-specific uses.

**進行 *jinxing***

Cluster 6 suggests that Mainland 進行 *jinxing* show a preference over the aspectual marker 了 *-le*, but such preference is not seen in Taiwan 進行 *jinxing*. Cluster 8 shows a preference by Taiwan 進行 *jinxing* that it could take VO compound (e.g., 投票 *toupiao* cast-ticket 'to vote') as complements, while this rarely happens in Mainland.

**做 *zuo***

Clusters 1 and 3 show that in Mainland Mandarin, it is common for 做 *zuo* to take the aspectual marker 了 *-le*, but such use of 做 *zuo* in Taiwan is not as common as in Mainland.

To sum up, the results from the machine learning method are consistent with that from the multivariate statistical analysis in Section 3.1. Bringing together, we find that while the light verbs in Mainland and Taiwan Mandarin show similarities (as the speakers of these two regions can communicate without difficulty), there are indeed also variations in the two variants.

## 4 Concluding Remarks

Our study is the one of the first comparable corpus driven computational modeling studies on newly emergent language variants. The automatic identification of Mainland and Taiwan syntactic variations has very significant linguistic and computational implications. Linguistically, we showed that our comparable corpus driven statistical approach can identify comparative differences which are challenging for human analysis. The fact that newly emergent variants differ from each other comparatively rather than contrastively may also have important linguistics implications. In addition, by successfully differentiating these two variants based on their uses of light verbs, the result also suggests that variations among such newly emergent variants may arise from categories that are semantically highly bleached and tend to be/or have been grammaticalized. Computationally, the ability of machine learning approaches to differentiate Mainland and Taiwan variants of Mandarin Chinese potentially contributes to overcoming the challenge of automatic identification of subtle language/dialect variations among other light verbs, other lexical categories, as well as other languages/dialects.

## Acknowledgements

The work is supported by a General Research Fund (GRF) sponsored by the Research Grants Council (Project no. 543512) and NTU Grant no. M4081117.100.500000.

## References

Arppe, Antti. 2008. Univariate, bivariate and multivariate methods in corpus-based lexicography - a study of synonymy. *Publications of the Department of General Linguistics*, University of Helsinki, volume 44.

Butt, Miriam and Wilhelm, Geuder. 2003. On the (semi) lexical status of light verbs. *Semi-lexical Categories*, Pages 323-370.

Bresnan, Joan, Anna Cueni, Tatiana Nikitina, and R. Harald Baayen 2007. Predicting the dative alternation. In: Cognitive Foundations of Interpretation. Boume, G., I. Kraemer, and J. Zwarts. Amsterdam: Royal Netherlands Academy of Science, pp. 69-94.

Cai, Wenlan. (1982). Issues on the complement of *jinxing* ( "進行" 帶賓問題). *Chinese Language Learning (漢語學習)* (3), 7-11.

Diao, Yanbin. 2004. *現代漢語虛義動詞研究 (Research on Delexical Verb in Modern Chinese)*. Dalian: Liaoning Normal University Press.

Hall, Mark, Eibe Frank, Geoffrey Holmes, Bernhard Pfahringer, Peter Reutemann and Ian H. Witten. 2009. The WEKA data mining software: An update. *SIGKDD Explorations*, 11(1):10-18.

Han, Weifeng, Antti Arppe, and John Newman. 2013. Topic marking in a Shanghainese corpus: from observation to prediction. *Corpus Linguistics and Linguistic Theory* (preprint).

Hong, Jia-fei, and Chu-Ren Huang. 2013. 以中文十億詞語料庫為基礎之兩岸詞彙對比研究 (Cross-strait lexical differences: A comparative study based on Chinese Gigaword Corpus). *Computational Linguistics and Chinese Language Processing*. 18(2):19-34.

Hong, Jia-fei, and Chu-Ren Huang. 2008. 語料庫為本的兩岸對應詞彙發掘. (A corpus-based approach to the discovery of cross-strait lexical contrasts). *Language and Linguistics*. 9 (2):221-238.

Huang, Chu-Ren. 2009. *Tagged Chinese Gigaword Version 2.0.* Philadelphia: Lexical Data Consortium, University of Pennsylvania. ISBN 1-58563-516-2

Huang, Chu-Ren and Jingxia Lin. 2013. The ordering of Mandarin Chinese light verbs. In *Proceedings of the 13th Chinese Lexical Semantics Workshop*. D. Ji and G. Xiao (Eds.): CLSW 2012, LNAI 7717, pages 728-735. Heidelberg: Springer.

Huang, Chu-Ren, Jingxia Lin, and Huarui Zhang. 2013. World Chineses based on comparable corpus: The case of grammatical variations of jinxing. *《澳门语言文化研究》*, pages 397-414.

Hwang, Jena D., Archna Bhatia, Clare Bonial, Aous Mansouri, Ashwini Vaidya, Nianwen Xue, Martha Palmer. 2010. PropBank annotation of multilingual light verb constructions. *Proceedings of the Fourth Linguistic Annotation Workshop, ACL 2010*, 82–90. Jespersen, Otto. 1965. *A Modern English Grammar on Historical Principles. Part VI, Morphology.* London: George Allen and Unwin Ltd.

Lin, Jingxia, Hongzhi Xu, Menghan Jiang and Chu-Ren Huang. 2014. Annotation and classification of light verbs and light verb variations in Mandarin Chinese. *COLING Workshop on Lexical and Grammatical Resources for Language Processing.* Dublin, August 24.

Nagy, István, Veronika Vincze, and Richárd Farkas. 2013. Full-coverage identification of English light verb constructions. *In Proceedings of the International Joint Conference on Natural Language Processing*, pages 329-337.

Qiu, Zhipu, 1990. 大陸和台灣差別詞典 *(Dictionary of Mainland and Taiwan Mandarin).* Nanjing University press.

Tu, Yuancheng and Dan Roth. 2011. Learning English light verb constructions: Contextual or statistical. In *Proceedings of the Workshop on Multiword Expressions: from Parsing and Generation to the Real World.* Association for Computational Linguistics.

Wang Tiekun and Li Xingjian, 1996. 兩岸詞彙比較研究管見 (Research on lexical differences between Mainland and Taiwan Mandarin), *World Chinese* ( *《華文世界》* ), volume 81.

Wei Li and Sheng Yuqi, 2000. 大陸及港澳台常用詞對比詞典. (Comparative Dictionary of Lexical use in Mainland, Hong Kong, Macau and Taiwan), Beijing Industry University Press.

Xu Danhui, 1995. 兩岸詞語差異之比較 (Lexical difference between Mainland and Taiwan Chinese). *1st symposium on Cross-Strait Lexical and Character differences* (第一屆兩岸漢語語彙文字學術研討會論文集).

Zeng Rongfen, 1995. 兩岸語言詞彙整理之我見 (Opinion on cross-Strait language differences)*1st* symposium *on Cross-Strait Lexical and Character differences* (第一屆兩岸漢語語彙文字學術研討會論文集).

Zhou, Gang. 1987. 形式動詞的次分類 (Subdivision of dummy verbs). *Chinese Language Learning (漢語學習),* volume 1, pages 11-14.

Zhu, Dexi. (1985). 現代書面漢語里的虛化動詞和名動詞 (Dummy verbs and NV in Modern Chinese). *Journal of Peking University (Humanities and Social Sciences)* (*北京大學學報(哲學社會科學版)),* volume 5, pages 1-6.

# Diachronic proximity vs. data sparsity in cross-lingual parser projection. A case study on Germanic

**Maria Sukhareva**
Goethe University Frankfurt
sukharev@em.uni-frankfurt.de

**Christian Chiarcos**
Goethe University Frankfurt
chiarcos@em.uni-frankfurt.de

## Abstract

For the study of historical language varieties, the sparsity of training data imposes immense problems on syntactic annotation and the development of NLP tools that automatize the process. In this paper, we explore strategies to compensate the lack of training data by including data from related varieties in a series of annotation projection experiments from English to four old Germanic languages: On dependency syntax projected from English to one or multiple language(s), we train a fragment-aware parser trained and apply it to the target language. For parser training, we consider small datasets from the target language as a baseline, and compare it with models trained on larger datasets from multiple varieties with different degrees of relatedness, thereby balancing sparsity and diachronic proximity.

Our experiments show

(a) that including related language data to training data in the target language can improve parsing performance,

(b) that a parser trained on data from two related languages (and none from the target language) can reach a performance that is statistically not significantly worse than that of a parser trained on the projections to the target language, and

(c) that both conclusions holds only among the three most closely related languages under consideration, but not necessarily the fourth.

The experiments motivate the compilation of a larger parallel corpus of historical Germanic varieties as a basis for subsequent studies.

## 1 Background and motivation

We describe an experiment on annotation projection (Yarowski and Ngai, 2001) between different Germanic languages, resp., their historical varieties, with the goal to assess to what extent sparsity of parallel data can be compensated by material from varieties related to the target variety, and studying the impact of diachronic proximity onto such applications.

Statistical NLP of historical language data involves general issues typical for low-resource languages (the lack of annotated corpora, data sparsity, etc.), but also very specific challenges such as lack of standardized orthography, unsystematized punctuation, and a considerable degree of morphological variation. At the same time, historical languages can be viewed as variants of their modern descendants rather than entirely independent languages, a situation comparable to low-resource languages for which a diachronically related major language exists. Technologies for the cross-lingual adaptation of NLP tools or training of NLP tools on multiple dialects or language stages are thus of practical relevance to not only historical linguistics, but also to modern low-resource languages.





*Proceedings of the First Workshop on Applying NLP Tools to Similar Languages, Varieties and Dialects*, pages 11–20, Dublin, Ireland, August 23 2014.

in this context, historical language allows to study the impact of the parameter of *diachronic relatedness*, as it can be adjusted relatively freely, e.g., by choosing dialects which common ancestor existed just a few generations before rather than languages separated for centuries. A focused study of the impact of diachronic relatedness on projected annotations requires sufficient amounts of parallel texts for major language stages, and comparable annotations as a gold standard for evaluation. In this regard, the Germanic languages provide us with a especially promising sandbox to develop such algorithms due to the abundance of annotated corpora and NLP tools of the modern Germanic languages, most noteably Modern English.

We employ annotation projection from EN to Middle English (ME), Old English (OE) and the less closely related Early Modern High German (DE) and Middle Icelandic (IS) for which we possess comparable annotations, and test the following hypotheses:

(H1) Adding data from related varieties **compensates the sparsity** of target language training data.

(H2) Data from related languages **compensates the lack** of target language training data.

(H3) The greater the **diachronic proximity**, the better the performance of (H1) and (H2).

We test these hypotheses in the following setup: (1) *Hyperlemmatization*: Different historical variants are normalized to a consistent standard, e.g., represented by a modern language (Bollmann et al., 2011). We emulate hyperlemmatization by English glosses automatically obtained through SMT. (2) *Projection*: We create training data for a fragment-aware dependency parser (Spreyer et al., 2010) using annotation projection from modern English. (3) *Combination and evaluation*: Parser modules are trained on different training data sets, and evaluated against existing gold annotations.

In our setting, we enforce data sparsity by using deliberately small training data sets. This is because we emulate the situation of less-documented languages that will be in the focus of subsequent experiments, namely, Old High German and Old Saxon, which are relatively poorly documented. We do hope, however, that scalable NLP solutions can be developed if we add background information from their descendants (Middle/Early Modern High German, Middle/Modern Low German), or closely related, and better documented varieties (Old English, Middle Dutch).

Hence, the goal of our experiment is not to develop state-of-the-art parsers, but to detect statistically significant differences in parsing performance. If these can be confirmed, this motivates creating a larger corpus of parallel texts in Germanic languages as a basis for subsequent studies and more advanced, projection-based technologies for older and under-resourced Germanic languages.

## 2 Languages and corpus data

We use parallel biblical texts in Old English (OE), Middle English (ME), Middle Icelandic (IS) and Early Modern High German (DE). This selection is determined by the availability of syntactically annotated corpora with closely related annotation schemes. As these schemes are derived from the Penn TreeBank (PTB) bracketing guidelines (Taylor et al., 2003a), we decided to use Modern English (EN) as a source for the projections.

**The Germanic languages** derive from Proto-Germanic as a common ancestor. OE and Old High German separated in the 5th c. The antecessor of IS separated from this branch about 500 years earlier. Among Germanic languages, great differences emerged, but most languages developed similarly towards a loss of morphology and a more rigid syntax, a tendency particularly prevalent in EN.

As compared to this, OE had a relatively free OV word order, with grammatical roles conveyed through morphological markers. The OE case marking system distinguished four cases, but eventually collapsed during ME, resulting in a strict strict VO word order in EN (Trips, 2002; van Kemenade and Los, 2009; Cummings, 2010).

Unlike EN, DE preserved four cases, and a relatively free word order (Ebert, 1976). A characteristic of German are separable verb prefixes, leading to $1 : n$ mappings in the statistical alignment with EN.

Figure 1: Workflow

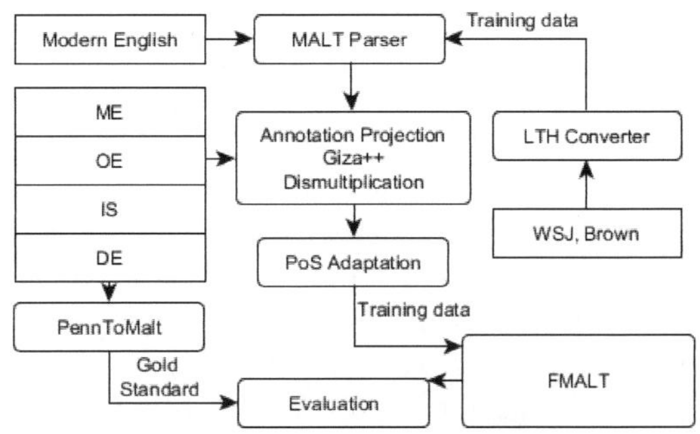


Unlike EN and DE, IS is a North Germanic language. It is assumed to be conservative, with relatively free word order with both OV and VO patterns and a rich morphology that leads to many $1 : n$ alignments with EN, e.g., for suffixed definite articles; we thus expect special challenges for annotation projection under conditions with limited training data.

Different from the old languages, EN developed a rigid word order and a largely reduced morphology. A direct adaptation of an existing English parser to (hyperlemmatized) OE, IS or DE is thus not promising. Therefore, we employ an approach based on annotation projection.

**The corpus data** we used consists of parsed bible fragments from manually annotated corpora, mostly the gospels of Matthew (Mt), Mark (Mr), John (J) and Luke (L), from which we drew a test set of 147 sentences and a training set of 437 sentences for every language.

**ME and OE** The Penn-Helsinki Parsed Corpus of Middle English (PPCME2)[1] and the York-Toronto-Helsinki Parsed Corpus of Old English Prose (Taylor et al., 2003b, YCOE) use a variant of the PTB annotation schema (Taylor et al., 2003a). YCOE contains the full West Saxon Gospel, but PPCME2 contains only a small fragment of a Wycliffite gospel of John, the ME data is thus complemented with parts of Genesis (G) and Numbers (N).

**IS** The Icelandic Parsed Historical Corpus (Rögnvaldsson et al., 2012, IcePaHC) is annotated following YCOE with slight modifications for specifics of IS. We use the gospel of John from Oddur Gottskálksson's New Testament, a direct translation from Luther.

**DE** The Parsed Corpus of Early New High German[2] contains three gospels from Luther's Septembertestament (1522). As an IcePaHC side-project, it adapts the IS annotation scheme.

**EN** For EN, we use the ESV Bible.[3] Due to a moderate number of archaisms, it is particularly well-suited for automated annotation.

## 3 Experimental setup

We study the projection of *dependency syntax*, as it is considered particularly suitable for free word-order languages like IS, OE and DE. The existing constituent annotations were thus converted with standard tools for PTB conversion. Figure 1 summarizes the experimental setup.

For **annotating EN**, we created dependency versions of WSJ and Brown sections of the PTB with the LTH Converter (Johansson and Nugues, 2007). We trained Malt 1.7.2 (Nivre, 2003), optimized its features with MaltOptimizer (Ballesteros and Nivre, 2012), and parsed the EN bible using the resulting feature model.

[1] http://www.ling.upenn.edu/hist-corpora/PPCME2-RELEASE-3/index.html
[2] http://enhgcorpus.wikispaces.com
[3] http://esv.org

The ME, OE, DE and IS datasets were **word aligned** with EN using GIZA++ (Och and Ney, 2003). $1 : n$ alignments were resolved to the most probable $1 : 1$ mapping. During **annotation projection**, we assume that the aligned words represent the respective heads for the remaining $n - 1$ words. These dependent words are assigned the dependency relation `FRAG` to the word that got the highest score in the translation table. This solution solves, among others, the problem of separable verb prefixes in DE, for example, DE *ruffen* with prefix *an* would be aligned to English word *call*: As $P(\text{"}call\text{"}|\text{"}an\text{"}) < P(\text{"}call\text{"}|\text{"}ruffen\text{"})$, the syntactic information of *"call"* will be projected to *"ruffen"* and *"an"* will be its dependent labeled with "FRAG". The projected dependency trees were checked on well-formedness, sentences with cycles were dismissed from the data set.

We formed **training sets** containing 437 sentences for ME, OE, DE, IS. Monolingual data sets were combined into bi-, tri- or quadrilingual training data sets with a simple concatenation, thereby creating less sparse, but more heterogeneous training data sets. For every language, **test data** was taken from J, 174 sentences per language.

We used the projected dependencies to train fMalt (Spreyer et al., 2010), a fragment-aware dependency parser, in order to maximize the gain of information from incomplete projections.

In our setting, fMalt used two features, POS and hyperlemmas.

**POS** The tagsets of the historical corpora originate in PTB, but show incompatible adaptations to the native morphosyntax. Tagset extensions on grammatical case in OE, IS and DE were removed and language-specific extensions for auxiliaries and modal verbs were leveled, in favor of a common, but underspecified tagset for all four languages. As these generalized tags preserve information not found in EN, they were fed into the parser.

**(hyper-)lemma** Lexicalization is utterly important for the dependency parsing (Kawahara and Uchimoto, 2007), but to generalize over specifics of historical language varieties, hyperlemmatization needs to be performed. Similar to Zeman and Resnik (2008), we use projected English words as hyperlemmas and feed them into the parser. Hyperlemmatization against a closely related languages is acceptable as we can expect that the syntactic properties of words are likely to be similar.

The projected annotations were then **evaluated** against dependency annotations created analoguously to the EN annotations from manual PTB-style constituency syntax. As LTH works exclusively on PTB data, the historical corpora were converted with its antecessor Penn2Malt[4] using user-defined head-rules (Yamada and Matsumoto, 2003).

## 4 Evaluation results

| | baseline | ΔUAS worst model | | | | ΔUAS best model | | | | ΔUAS |
|---|---|---|---|---|---|---|---|---|---|---|
| | UAS | +1 | | +2 | | +1 | | +2 | | +3 |
| ME | .60 | +DE | $+.00^{n.s.}$ | +DE+IS | $-.01^{n.s.}$ | +OE | $+.01^{n.s.}$ | +OE+IS | $+.01^{n.s.}$ | $-.00^{n.s.}$ |
| OE | .31 | +IS | $-.00^{n.s.}$ | +DE+IS | $-.02^{n.s.}$ | +DE | $+.02^{n.s.}$ | +ME+DE | $+.00^{n.s.}$ | $+.02^{n.s.}$ |
| DE | .41 | +OE | $+.02^{n.s.}$ | +OE+IS | $+.03^{*}$ | +ME | $+.04^{***}$ | +ME+IS | $+.03^{*}$ | $+.04^{**}$ |
| IS | .32 | +IS | $-.02^{n.s.}$ | +DE+OE | $-.02^{n.s.}$ | +ME | $+.00^{n.s.}$ | +ME+DE | $-.01^{n.s.}$ | $-.04^{**}$ |

(a) trained on **target and** related language(s)

| | baseline | ΔUAS worst model | | | | ΔUAS best model | | | | ΔUAS |
|---|---|---|---|---|---|---|---|---|---|---|
| | UAS | 1 | | 2 | | 1 | | 2 | | 3 |
| ME | .60 | OE | $-.09^{***}$ | DE-IS | $-.01^{n.s}$ | IS | $-.05^{***}$ | IS+OE | $-.02^{n.s.}$ | $-.02^{n.s.}$ |
| OE | .31 | DE | $-.03^{*}$ | ME-DE | $-.01^{n.s.}$ | ME | $-.02^{n.s.}$ | ME+IS | $-.01^{n.s.}$ | $-.00^{n.s.}$ |
| DE | .41 | OE | $-.01^{n.s.}$ | OE-IS | $+.02^{n.s.}$ | IS | $+.02^{n.s.}$ | IS+ME | $+.05^{***}$ | $+.04^{**}$ |
| IS | .32 | OE | $-.07^{***}$ | DE-OE | $-.02^{n.s.}$ | ME | $-.06^{***}$ | ME+DE | $-.02^{n.s.}$ | $-.04^{**}$ |

(b) trained on related language(s) **alone**

Table 1: Performance of best- and worst-performing parsing models (UAS diff. vs. baseline with $\chi^2$: $^{*}$ $p < .05$, $^{**}$ $p < .01$, $^{***}$ $p < .005$)

We evaluate the unlabeled attachment score (Collins et al., 1999, UAS), i.e., the proportion of tokens in a sentence (without punctuation) that are assigned the correct head, on test sets of 174 sentences in each language.

[4] http://stp.lingfil.uu.se/ nivre/research/Penn2Malt.html

As a **baseline** for the evaluation we take the performance of the parser trained solely on the target language data. As shown in Tab. 1 (second col.), the UAS scores mirror both the diachronic relatedness (ME>DE>IS), as well as the relative loss of morphology (ME>DE>IS/OE), indicating that diachronic relatedness may not be the only factor licensing the applicability of the annotation projection scenario (H3). It is also important, though, to keep in mind that the OE and IS translations of the Bible had considerable influence of Latin syntax, whereas DE and ME translations aimed for a language easy to understand.

Table 1a gives the best and worst results for the unlabeled attachment score for the parser trained on target and related language(s) **(H1)**. With the exception of DE, we observed no significant differences in UAS scores relative to the baseline. DE may benefit from ME because of its more flexible syntax (thus closer to ME [and OE] than to Modern English), and from IS because of Luther's direct influence on the IS bible. That ME did not mutually benefit from German may be due to the good quality of ME annotation projections (resulting from its proximity to EN). Parsers trained on trilingual and quadrilingual sets exhibited no improvement over the bilingual sets. Taken together, we found *no positive effect* of using additional training data from language stages diachronically separated for more than 500 years (e.g., OE/ME), but also, we did *not find* a negative effect among the West Germanic languages. If additional training material is carefully chosen among particularly closely related varieties, however, the DE effect can be replicated, and then, including related language data to training data in the target language can improve parsing performance.

While in our setting, training data from related languages may (but does not have to) improve a parser training if training data for the target language is available, it may very well be employed fruitfully *if no training data for the target language is available* **(H2)**: Table 1b shows that, unsurprisingly, parsers trained only on one related language had the lowest performance in the experiment, so using multiple train languages seems to compensate language-specific idiosyncrasies. The best-performing parsing models trained on *two* or more related languages achieved a performance not significantly worse (if not better) than models being trained on target language data. This effect extends to all languages except for IS and indicates that a *careful choice* of additional training data from related varieties may facilitate annotation projection. Equally important (and valid across all languages) is that *none* of the models trained on one language outperformed any of the model trained on two languages. Using training data from two related languages doesn't seem to hurt performance in our setting. Adding a third language did not yield systematic improvements, the scores for trilingual models are in the range of the bilingual models.

Again, DE is exceptionally good, benefitting from being a direct source of the IS translation as well as structurally comparable to ME. In both settings, the worst-performing language is IS, with a significant drop in annotation projection quality with Western Germanic material added, indicating that diachronic distance between Northern and Western Germanic languages limits the applicability of **(H2)**, thereby supporting **(H3)**.

Taken together, our results indicate

1. a significant positive effect for the Western Germanic languages (ME, OE, DE) for **(H2)**, and
2. a significant negative effect for Western and Northern Germanic languages (IS) for **(H2)**

As a tentative hypothesis, one may speculate that languages separated for 1000 years (OE-IS) or more are too remote from each other to provide helpful background information, but that languages separated within the last 750 years (ME-DE) or less are still sufficiently close. This novel assumption may provide a guideline for future efforts to project annotations among related languages, and is thus of immense practical relevance for developing future NLP tools for historical and less-resourced language varieties. Ultimately, one may formulate rules of best practice like the following:

- If no syntactic annotations for a target language are available, annotation projection among closely related languages may be a solution. Even with limited amounts of parallel data, diachronic distances of more than 500 years can be successfully bridged (EN/ME, baseline).

- If no syntactic annotations for a target language are available, a parser trained on hyperlemmatized corpora in two languages may yield a performance comparable to a parser trained on small amounts of target data. A parser trained on hyperlemmatized monolingual data may be significantly worse (H2).

- The sparsity of parallel text to conduct annotation projection and train a (hyperlemmatized) parser can only be compensated by adding parallel data from *one* related language if these are closely diachronically related (with a separation being less than, say, 500 years ago) *and* at a similar developmental stage (DE/ME, H1). Adding data from multiple, equally remote languages does not necessarily improve the results further.

At the current state, such recommendations would be premature, they require deeper investigation, but with the confirmation of **(H2)** and **(H3)**, we can now motivate larger-scale efforts to compile a massive parallel corpus of historical Germanic language varieties as a basis for subsequent studies. Initial steps towards this goal are described in the following section.

## 5 Towards a massive parallel corpus of historical Germanic languages

With the long-term goal to systematically assess the impact of the factor of diachronic proximity, we focus on annotation projection among the Germanic languages as test field. The Germanic languages represent a particularly well-resourced, well-documented and well-studied language family which development during the last 1800 years is not only well-explored, but also documented with great amounts of (parallel) data, ranging from the 4th century Gothic bible over a wealth of Bible translations since the middle ages to the modern age of communication with its abundance of textual resources for even marginal varieties. Motivated from our experiment, we thus began to compile a parallel corpus of historical and dialectal Germanic language varieties. Primary source data for a massive parallel corpus of historical varieties of any European language is mostly to be drawn from the Bible and related literature. The Bible is the single most translated book in the world and available in a vast majority of world languages. It is also often the case that there are several biblical translation existing for a language. Bible data also represents the majority of parallel data available for historical Germanic languages, and for the case of OS and OHG, gospel harmonies represent even the majority of data currently known. Beyond this, the corpus includes Bible excerpts and paraphrases from all Germanic languages and their major historical stages.

Tab. 2 gives an overview over the current status of the Parallel Bible Corpus. At the moment, 271 texts with about 38.4M tokens have been processed, converted from their original format and verse-aligned according to their original markup or with a lexicon-supported geometric sentence aligner (Tóth et al., 2008). In the table, 'text' means any document ranging from a small excerpt such as the Lord's Prayer (despite their marginal size valuable to develop algorithms for normalization/[hyper]lemmatization) over gospel harmonies and paraphrases to the entire bible that has been successfully aligned with Bible verses. The compiled corpus, excerpts and fragments for all Germanic languages marked up with IDs for verses, chapters and books. For data representation, we employed an XML version of the CES-scheme developed by Resnik et al. (1997). Having outgrown the scale of Resnik's earlier project by far, we are currently in transition to TEI P5.

As it is compiled from different sources, the corpus cannot be released under a free or an academic license. It contains material without explicit copyright statement, with proprietary content (e.g., from existing corpora), or available for personal use only. Instead, we plan to share the extraction and conversion scripts we used. For the experiments we aim to prepare, we focus on primary data, the texts in this collection are not annotated. Where annotations are available from other corpora or can be produced with existing tools, however, these annotated versions will be aligned with the Bibles and included in subsequent experiments.

| | after 1900 | 1800-1900 | 1600-1800 | 1400-1600 | 1100-1400 | before 1100 |
|---|---|---|---|---|---|---|
| | | | | | **West Germanic** | |
| English | 2 | 2 | 2 | 6 | 3 (+2) | 1 |
| Pidgin/Creol | 2 | | | | | |
| Scots | (6) | | | (1) | | |
| Frisian | 2 (+8) | (12) | | | | |
| Dutch | 4 | | 1 | 5 | | (1) |
| L. Franconian | (47) | (21) | | | | |
| Afrikaans | 3 | | | | | |
| German | 3 | 1 | (19) | 1 (+4) | 1 (+1) | 1 |
| dialects | 3 (+2) | | | | | |
| Yiddish | 1 | | | | | |
| Low German | 3 (+18) | (66) | | (2) | | 1 |
| Plautdietsch | 2 | | | | | |
| Danish | 1 | | | **North & East Germanic** | | |
| Swedish | 3 | | | (3) | (1) | |
| Bokmål | 2 | | | | | |
| Nynorsk | 2 | | | | | |
| Icelandic | | 1 | | 1 | | |
| Faroese | 1 | | | | | |
| Norn | | | (2) | | | |
| Gothic | | | | | | 1 |
| *tokens* | 21.8M | 3.2M | 2.7M | 9.2M | 1.2M | 0.2M |

Table 2: Verse-aligned texts in the Germanic parallel Bible corpus (parentheses indicate marginal fragments with less than 50,000 tokens)

## 6 Summary and outlook

This paper describes a motivational experiment on annotation projection, or more precisely, strategies to compensate data sparsity (the lack of parallel data) with material from related, but heterogeneous varieties to facilitate cross-language parser adaptation for low-resource historical languages. We used a fragment-aware dependency parser trained on annotation projections from ESV Bible to four historical languages.

Our results indicate a lexicalized fragment-aware parser trained on a small amount of annotation projections can yield good results on closely related languages. In a situation of the absence of training data for the target language (or, for example, in the situation where there is no parallel corpora for the target language), a hyperlemmatized parser trained on (projected) annotations from two or more related languages is likely to outperform a parser trained on a single related language.

We achieved statistically significant differences in parser performance trained on (a) target language data, and (b) target language and data from related varieties, resp. (c) data from related varieties only. These indicate that closely related languages (say, with a common ancestor about 750 years ago, such as DE and ME) have some potential to compensate sparsity of parallel data in the target variety, wheres this potential does not seem to exist for more remotely related languages (say, with a common ancestor more than 1000 years ago such as OE and IS).

The experimental results revealed that the parser performance can, indeed, be improved by means of including a related language to the training data, but we had a significant effect for only one language under consideration, indicating that the diachronic proximity of the languages considered was possibly too large, and thereby motivating subsequent experiments, and in particular, the creation of a larger parallel corpus of historical Germanic language varieties. We described initial steps in the compilation of this corpus.

Our experiment raises a number of open issues that are to be pursued in subsequent studies:

1. Our setup has a clear bias towards English (in the annotation schemes used and the source annotations), and parser performance was strongly affected by the syntactic difference between the target language and Modern English from which the syntactic dependencies were projected, indicating the relevance of diachronic relatedness as well as the developmental state of a related language. Subsequent experiments will hence address the inclusion of richer morphological features, projection from other languages and evaluation against syntactic annotations according to other schemes not derived from the Penn Treebank, as currently available, for example, for Old High German, Old Norse, and Gothic.

2. The *hyperlemmatization* in our approach was achieved through alignment/SMT, and a similar lexically-oriented approach has been suggested by (Zeman and Resnik, 2008). Alternative strategies more suitable for scenarios with limited amounts of training data may include the use of orthographical normalization techniques (Bollmann et al., 2011) or substring-based machine translation (Neubig et al., 2012) and are also subject to on-going research. We assume that SMT-based hyperlemmatization introduces more noise than these strategies, so that it is harder to achieve statistically significant results. Our findings are thus likely to remain valid regardless of the hyperlemmatization strategy. This hypothesis is, however, yet to be confirmed in subsequent studies.

3. Our experiment mostly deals with data translated from (or at least informed by) the Latin Vulgate. Our data may be biased by translation strategies which evolved over time, from very literal translations (actually, glossings) of Latin texts in the early middle ages to Reformation-time translations aiming to grasp the intended meaning rather than to preserve the original formulation. A focus on classical languages is, however, inherent to the parallel material in our domain. A representative investigation of annotation projection techniques thus requires the consideration of quasi-parallel data along with parallel data. This can be found in the great wealth of medieval religious literature, with Bible paraphrases, gospel harmonies, sermons and homilies as well as poetic and prose adaptations of biblical motives. The parallel corpus of Germanic languages thus needs to be extended accordingly.

4. One may wonder how the annotation projection approach performs in comparison to direct applications of modern language NLP tools to normalized historical data language (Scheible et al., 2011). While it is unlikely that such an approach could scale beyond closely related varieties, successful experiments on the annotation of normalized historical language have been reported, although mostly focused on token-level annotations (POS, lemma, morphology) of language stages which syntax does not greatly deviate from modern rules (Rayson et al., 2007; Pennacchiotti and Zanzotto, 2008; Kestemont et al., 2010; Bollmann, 2013). For the annotation of more remotely related varieties with more drastic differences in word order rigidity or morphology as considered here, however, projection techniques are more promising as they have been successfully applied to unrelated languages, as well, but still benefit from diachronic proximity, cf. Meyer (2011) for the projection-based morphological analysis of Modern and Old Russian.

The goal of our experiment was not to achieve state-of-the-art performance, but to show whether background material from related languages with different degrees of diachronic distance can help to compensate data sparsity, in this case with an experiment on annotation projection. This hypothesis could be confirmed and we found effects that – even on the minimal amounts of data considered for this study – indicated statistically significant improvements.

It is thus to be expected that even greater improvements can be achieved by considering more closely related pairs of languages, with greater amounts of data. The further exploration of this hypothesis is the driving force behind our efforts to compile a massive corpus of parallel and quasi-parallel texts for all major varieties of synchronic and historical Germanic languages. Algorithms successfully tested in this context can be expected to be applicable to other scenarios in which, e.g., well-researched modern languages may be employed to facilitate the creation of NLP tools for less-ressourced, related languages. Our efforts are thus not specific to historical languages.

As the diachronic development and the diversification of the Germanic languages is well-documented in this body of data, and the linguistic processes involved are well-researched, this data set represents an extraordinarily valuable resource for philological and comparitve studies as well as Natural Language Processing. In particular, we are interested in developing algorithms that explore and exploit the variable degree of diachronic relatedness found between the languages in our sample. At the same time, we cooperate with researchers from philology, historical and comparative linguistics, which research on intertextuality, diachronic lexicology, phonology, morphology and syntax we aim to support with NLP tools developed on the basis of this body of parallel text.

## References

Miguel Ballesteros and Joakim Nivre. 2012. Maltoptimizer: A system for maltparser optimization. In Nicoletta Calzolari (Conference Chair), Khalid Choukri, Thierry Declerck, Mehmet Uur Doan, Bente Maegaard, Joseph Mariani, Asuncion Moreno, Jan Odijk, and Stelios Piperidis, editors, *Proceedings of the Eight International Conference on Language Resources and Evaluation (LREC'12)*, Istanbul, Turkey, may. European Language Resources Association (ELRA).

Marcel Bollmann, Florian Petran, and Stefanie Dipper. 2011. Rule-based normalization of historical texts. In *Proceedings of the Workshop on Language Technologies for Digital Humanities and Cultural Heritage (LaTeCH-2011)*, pages 34–42, Hissar, Bulgaria, September.

Marcel Bollmann. 2013. POS tagging for historical texts with sparse training data. In *Proceedings of the 7th Linguistic Annotation Workshop and Interoperability with Discourse*, pages 11–18, Sofia, Bulgaria, August. Association for Computational Linguistics.

Michael Collins, Lance Ramshaw, Jan Hajič, and Christoph Tillmann. 1999. A statistical parser for czech. In *Proceedings of the 37th annual meeting of the Association for Computational Linguistics on Computational Linguistics*, pages 505–512. Association for Computational Linguistics.

Michael Cummings. 2010. *An Introduction to the Grammar of Old English: A Systemic Functional Approach*. Functional Linguistics. Equinox Publishing Limited.

Robert P. Ebert. 1976. *Infinitival complement constructions in Early New High German*. Linguistische Arbeiten. De Gruyter.

Richard Johansson and Pierre Nugues. 2007. Extended constituent-to-dependency conversion for English. In *Proceedings of NODALIDA 2007*, pages 105–112, Tartu, Estonia, May 25-26.

Daisuke Kawahara and Kiyotaka Uchimoto. 2007. Minimally lexicalized dependency parsing. In *Proceedings of the 45th Annual Meeting of the ACL on Interactive Poster and Demonstration Sessions*, pages 205–208. Association for Computational Linguistics.

Mike Kestemont, Walter Daelemans, and Guy De Pauw. 2010. Weigh your words: Memory-based lemma-retrieval for Middle Dutch literary texts. In *CLIN 2010. Computational linguistics in the Netherlands 20*, Utrecht, The Netherlands, May.

Roland Meyer. 2011. New wine in old wineskins? Tagging Old Russian via annotation projection from modern translations. *Russian linguistics*, 35(2):267–281.

Graham Neubig, Taro Watanabe, Shinsuke Mori, and Tatsuya Kawahara. 2012. Machine translation without words through substring alignment. In *Proceedings of the 50th Annual Meeting of the Association for Computational Linguistics (Volume 1: Long Papers)*, pages 165–174, Jeju Island, Korea, July. Association for Computational Linguistics.

Joakim Nivre. 2003. An efficient algorithm for projective dependency parsing. In *Proceedings of the 8th International Workshop on Parsing Technologies (IWPT)*.

Franz Josef Och and Hermann Ney. 2003. A systematic comparison of various statistical alignment models. *Computational linguistics*, 29(1):19–51.

Marco Pennacchiotti and Fabio Massimo Zanzotto. 2008. Natural language processing across time: An empirical investigation on italian. In *Advances in Natural Language Processing*, pages 371–382. Springer.

Paul Rayson, Dawn Archer, Alistair Baron, Jonathan Culpeper, and Nicholas Smith. 2007. Tagging the Bard: Evaluating the accuracy of a modern POS tagger on Early Modern English corpora. In *Proceedings of the 4th Corpus Linguistics Conference (CL-2007)*, Birmingham, UK.

Philip Resnik, Mari Broman Olsen, and Mona Diab. 1997. Creating a parallel corpus from the book of 2000 tongues. In *Proc. of the Text Encoding Initiative 10th Anniversary User Conference (TEI-10)*.

Eiríkur Rögnvaldsson, Anton Karl Ingason, Einar Freyr Sigurdhsson, and Joel Wallenberg. 2012. The Icelandic Parsed Historical Corpus (IcePaHC). In *LREC*, pages 1977–1984.

Silke Scheible, Richard J. Whitt, Martin Durrell, and Paul Bennett. 2011. Evaluating an 'off-the-shelf' POS-tagger on Early Modern German text. In *Proceedings of the 5th ACL-HLT Workshop on Language Technology for Cultural Heritage, Social Sciences, and Humanities (LaTeCH-2011)*, pages 19–23, Portland, OR, USA, June.

Kathrin Spreyer, Lilja Ovrelid, and Jonas Kuhn. 2010. Training parsers on partial trees: A cross-language comparison. In *Proc. of the 7th International Conference on Language Resources and Evaluation (LREC-2010)*, Valletta, Malta, May.

Ann Taylor, Mitchell Marcus, and Beatrice Santorini. 2003a. The Penn treebank: an overview. In *Treebanks*, pages 5–22. Springer.

Ann Taylor, Anthony Warner, Susan Pintzuk, and Frank Beths. 2003b. The york-toronto-helsinki parsed corpus of old english prose. *University of York.*

Krisztina Tóth, Richárd Farkas, and András Kocsor. 2008. Sentence alignment of hungarian-english parallel corpora using a hybrid algorithm. *Acta Cybern.*, 18(3):463–478, January.

C. Trips. 2002. *From OV to VO in Early Middle English.* Linguistics today. John Benjamins Pub.

A. van Kemenade and B. Los. 2009. *The Handbook of the History of English.* Blackwell Handbooks in Linguistics. John Wiley & Sons.

Hiroyasu Yamada and Yuji Matsumoto. 2003. Statistical dependency analysis with support vector machines. In *Proceedings of IWPT. Vol. 3. 2003.*

David Yarowski and Grace Ngai. 2001. Inducing multilingual POS taggers and NP bracketers via robust projection across aligned corpora. In *Proceedings of NAACL 2001*, pages 200–207.

Daniel Zeman and Philip Resnik. 2008. Cross-language parser adaptation between related languages. In *IJCNLP-08 Workshop on NLP for Less Privileged Languages*, pages 35–41, Hyderabad, India, Jan.

# Pos-tagging different varieties of Occitan with single-dialect resources

**Marianne Vergez-Couret**
CLLE-ERSS
Université de Toulouse
vergez@univ-tlse2.fr

**Assaf Urieli**
CLLE-ERSS
Université de Toulouse
assaf.urieli@univ-tlse2.fr
Joliciel Informatique
Foix, France
assaf@joli-ciel.com

### Abstract

In this study, we tackle the question of pos-tagging written Occitan, a lesser-resourced language with multiple dialects each containing several varieties. For pos-tagging, we use a supervised machine learning approach, requiring annotated training and evaluation corpora and optionally a lexicon, all of which were prepared as part of the study. Although we evaluate two dialects of Occitan, Lengadocian and Gascon, the training material and lexicon concern only Lengadocian. We concluded that reasonable results ($> 89\%$ accuracy) are possible with a very limited training corpus (2500 tokens), as long as it is compensated by intensive use of the lexicon. Results are much lower across dialects, and pointers are provided for improvement. Finally, we compare the relative contribution of more training material vs. a larger lexicon, and conclude that within our configuration, spending effort on lexicon construction yields higher returns.

## 1 Introduction

Pos-tagging is one of the first steps in many Natural Language Processing chains, and generally requires annotated corpora and lexicons to function properly. Substantial efforts are needed to create such resources, few of which exist in the required format for less-resourced languages like Occitan. Creating them is more challenging since less-resourced languages present spelling and dialectal variations and are not necessarily standardized. In this paper, we apply a tool that was initially developed for rich-resourced languages (French and English), the pos-tagger Talismane, to different varieties and dialects of literary Occitan. We evaluate whether adapting this tool with only little annotated data is worthwhile.

Various efforts have been made recently to adapt pos-taggers to lesser-resourced languages. Täckström et al. (2013) use a semi-supervised approach based on aligned bitext between a resource-rich and resource-poor language, and achieve substantial gains. In our case, without an aligned bitext resource, we were unable to attempt this approach. Garrette et al. (2013) perform an experiment giving annotators limited time (4 hours) to annotate either training corpora or lexicons (which they call token and type annotation) for 2 low-resourced languages. They conclude that lexicons provide higher initial gains. However, whereas their lexicons are constructed by automatically selecting the most frequent words from large unannotated corpora, our study can make use of existing wide-coverage lexical resources. Scherrer and Sagot (2013) use an approach where lexical cognates are identified between a resource-rich and resource-poor language, and their pos-tags are then used to help tagging the resource-poor language. Their approach is interesting for languages, unlike Occitan, with no lexical resources available. However, even cross-language approaches require a small manually-annotated corpus for accurate evaluation. It seems simpler to begin by using this corpus for both training and evaluation before attempting more complex approaches. A finer evaluation would then be required to determine whether data quality (a small purpose-built corpus) or quantity (a large cross-language corpus) are more important for the present task.

A pos-tagger for Occitan was also developped as an intermediate step for machine translation in Apertium (Armentano i Oller and Forcada, 2006; Sánchez-Martınez et al., 2007), where the most likely





*Proceedings of the First Workshop on Applying NLP Tools to Similar Languages, Varieties and Dialects*, pages 21–29, Dublin, Ireland, August 23 2014.

translation is used to select the correct pos-tags. However, since they only evaluate the resulting translation quality, and since Apertium is not available as a standalone pos-tagger, we were unable to perform comparisons.

Our article is organized as follows: in Section 2, we give an overview of the Occitan language and its dialects. In Section 3, we present the software used, Talismane, as well as the feature and rule sets applied. In Section 4, we discuss the various resources that were constructed for this study, including corpora and lexica. In Section 5 we give the experimental setup, and discuss the results in Section 6.

## 2 Occitan language

Occitan is a romance language spoken in southern France and in several valleys of Spain and Italy.

The number of speakers is hard to estimate: according to several studies it might reasonably be situated around 500,000 speakers. It is even harder to evaluate the number of people with an interest in Occitan. According to a socio-linguistic survey carried out in the Midi-Pyrénées Region in 2010, 4% of the population are native or fluent speakers, 14% are speakers with an average competence and 32% understand the language, with different degrees of competence, giving an estimated total of 1.5 million people for this region alone. The interest in Occitan is supported by a sizable network of non-profit associations. Among others, the primary and secondary immersive bilingual school system Calandreta, IEO (*Institut d'Estudis Occitans*) and CFPO (*Centre de Formacion Professionala Occitan*) provide opportunities for learning Occitan at any age. Occitan is also present in the French national education system in bilingual classes at the primary school level; as optional courses at the secondary school level; and as a major or optional classes in several universities.

### 2.1 Occitan dialects

Occitan is not standardized as a whole. It has several varieties organized into dialects. The most widely accepted classification proposed by Bec (1995) includes Auvernhat, Gascon, Lengadocian, Lemosin, Provençau and Vivaroaupenc.

In this article we focus on two Occitan dialects: Lengadocian, spoken in a zone delimited by the Rhône, the Garonne and the Mediterranean Sea; and Gascon, spoken in a zone delimited by the Pyrenees, the Garonne, and the Atlantic Ocean. Some examples of lexical variation from Lengadocian to Gascon include the transformation of a Latin $f$ into an $h$ (filh/hilh), dropping the intervocalic $n$ (luna/lua) and metathesis of the $r$ (cabra/craba) (Bec, 1995).

We assume that probabilities of pos-tag sequences will be fairly similar between Lengadocian and Gascon in most cases. However, several examples below show non-lexical differences between the two dialects that result in different pos-tag distributions.

1. Gascon has enunciative particles: "que" for affirmative sentences, "be" for exclamatory sentences, and "e" for interrogative sentences and subordinate clauses. There is no equivalent in Lengadocian.
   - Example: "I'm buying bread and apples". Gascon: *"**Que** crompi pans e pomas."* Lengadocian: *"Compri de pans e de pomas."*

2. There is no indefinite or partitive article in Gascon.
   - Example: "He's catching birds." Gascon: *"Que gaha ausèths."* Lengadocian: *"Trapa **d'**aucèls."*
   - Example: "I want some water." Gascon: *"Que vòli aiga."* Lengadocian: *"Vòli **d'**aiga."*

3. Object and reflective clitics occur more often after the verb in Gascon than in Lengadocian.
   - Example: "To come in and get served?" Gascon: *"Entrar e hèr-**se** servir ?"* Lengadocian: *"Dintrar e **se** far servir ?"*

4. Double-negatives in Gascon: the preceding "ne/no" is mandatory in Gascon, but not in Lengadocian.
   - Example: "He can't hear anything." Gascon: *"**N'**enten pas arren."* Lengadocian: *"Enten pas ren."*

### 2.2 Written Occitan

Written Occitan first appeared in medieval times, with all dialects represented in literature. This results in a lot of inter- and intra-dialectal variation within the texts. This geolinguistic variation corresponds to (i) variations in spelling reflecting variations in pronunciation (for instance *contes/condes*) and (ii) lexical variations (for instance *pomas de terra/mandòrra*). Numerous spelling conventions account for additional variation within Occitan text. The spelling used in medieval times is nowadays called the "troubadour spelling". This spelling gradually disappeared with the decline of literary production. Since the $19^{\text{th}}$ century, two major spelling conventions can be distinguished: the first was influenced by French spelling, and includes Mistral's spelling in Provence and the Gaston Febus' spelling in Bearn; the second, called "classical spelling" and inspired by the troubador spelling, appeared in the $20^{\text{th}}$ century. It is a unified spelling convention distributed across all of the Occitan territories (Sibille, 2007). Diachronic variation corresponds to changes in spelling conventions over time (for instance the evolution in the spelling of conjugated verbs: *avian* vs. *avìan*). Embracing all dialectal and spelling variations is one of the main objectives of the BaTelÒc project.

### 2.3 BaTelÒc Project

The BaTelÒc project (Bras and Thomas, 2011; Bras and Vergez-Couret, 2013) aims at creating a wide-coverage collection of written texts in Occitan, including literature (prose, drama and poetry) as well as other genres such as technical texts and newspapers. The texts aim to cover the modern and contemporary periods, as well as all dialectal and spelling varieties. More than one million words have already been gathered. The text base is also designed to provide online tools for interrogating texts, for example a concordancer to observe key forms in context. In the future, the aim is to enrich the text base with linguistic annotations, such as pos-tags. These would allow new querying possibilities, e.g. the disambiguation of homographs such as *poder* as a common noun ("power") and *poder* as a verb ("be able to"). In order to provide such annotations, Part-Of-Speech annotation tools are required. We therefore decided to use a probabilistic pos-tagger based on supervised machine learning methods: Talismane.

## 3 The Talismane pos-tagger

The present study trained the open source Talismane pos-tagger (Urieli, 2013) on an Occitan training corpus. Talismane has already been applied to English and French pos-tagging, attaining an accuracy $\approx 97\%$ (Urieli, 2014). It allows for the incorporation of a lexicon both as training features and as analysis rules. In terms of features, this comes down to saying, "if the word X is listed in the lexicon as a common noun, then it is more likely to be a common noun". This information is incorporated into the statistical model during training, along with other features listed below. Analysis rules override the statistical model's decisions during analysis, either imposing or prohibiting the choice of a certain category. For example, a rule might say, "the word X cannot be assigned the closed category *preposition* unless it is listed as a preposition in the lexicon".

To select the machine learning configuration of the Occitan pos-tagger, we performed a grid search of different classifier types and parameters, and settled on a linear SVM classifier with $\epsilon = 0.1$ and $C = 0.5$.

### 3.1 Features

We used the identical feature set for Occitan as the one used by Talismane for French and English. These include, for the token currently being analysed: $W$ the word form; $P$ each of the token's possible pos-tags according to the lexicon; $L$ each of the token's possible lemmas according to the lexicon; $U$ whether the current token is unknown in the lexicon; *1st* whether the token is the first in the sentence; *Last* whether the token is the last in the sentence; *Sfx* the last $n$ letters in the token; as well as various regular expression features testing whether the token starts with a capital letter, contains a dash, a space or a period, or contains only capital letters.

We also used the following additional features for the tokens before and after the current token (where the subscript indicates the position of the token with respect to the current token):

$W_{-1}, W_1, P_{-1}, P_1, L_{-1}, L_1, U_1$, where $P_{-1}$ looks at the pos-tag assigned to the previous token, and is thus the standard bigram feature. We also included various two-token and three-token combinations of all of the above basic features, e.g. $P_{-2}P_{-1}$ giving the standard trigram feature.

### 3.2 Rules

The following rules were defined around closed class pos-tags (i.e. non-productive functional categories) and open class pos-tags (i.e. productive lexical categories).

- Closed classes: for each closed class pos-tag (e.g. prepositions, conjunctions, pronouns, etc.), only allow the pos-tagger to assign this pos-tag if it exists in the lexicon. This prevents us, for example, from inventing new prepositions.
- Open classes: do not assign an open class pos-tag (e.g. common noun, adjective, etc.) to a token if it is only listed with closed classes in the lexicon. This prevents us, for example, from assigning a tag such as "common noun" to the token "*lo*" ("the").
- Rules which automatically assign the pos-tags `Card` and `Pct` respectively to numbers and punctuation. These were applied systematically in all experiments.

## 4 Resources

For Talismane to function properly, various resources are required: a training corpus from which the statistical model is learned, one or more evaluation corpora to evaluate performance, and optionally a lexicon for wide-coverage features and rules. These resources all rely on a tagset specifically designed for Occitan, shown in Table 1.

### 4.1 Lexicon and tagset

In the present study, we decided to construct a lexicon for one dialect only, the Lengadocian dialect, corresponding to our training corpus.

The lexicon was built from available digital resources: the Laus dictionary of Lengadocian (Laus, 2005), as well as certain closed-class entries and proper nouns from the Apertium lexicon. The Laus dictionary in particular covers different varieties of Lengadocian. For example, the entry for "night" includes three variants: *nuèch / nuèit / nuòch*. Inflected forms for verbs were gathered from *Lo congrès permanent de la lenga occitana*, which provides a complete verb-conjugation module[1]. A script was written to automatically generate inflected forms for adjectives, nouns and past participles from the base form entries. The number of entries for each pos-tag and total count are given in Table 1.

### 4.2 Training corpus

For training Talismane, a homogeneous corpus in the Lengadocian dialect was extracted from a single novel: *E la barta floriguèt* by Enric Molin, an Occitan author from the Rouergue region. Since the present study concentrates on differences between dialects and varieties, no attempt was made to construct a balanced training corpus. The corpus contains around 2500 tokens manually annotated with pos-tags, lemmas, and additional morpho-syntactic information (grammatical gender, number, person, tense and mood). The first 1000 tokens were annotated separately by three annotators, who then consolidated their annotations into a single gold standard, with an annotation guide. The remaining 1500 tokens were annotated by a single annotator, who consulted the others in cases of doubt.

In the present study, the annotated lemmas and additional morpho-syntactic information were not used.

### 4.3 Evaluation corpora

For evaluation, three different corpora were compiled: the first one, the *Rouergue* corpus, was extracted from: *Los crocants de Roergue* by Ferran Delèris, another author from the Rouergue region; the second one, the *Lot* corpus, was extracted from *Dels camins bartassièrs* by Marceu Esquieu, written in another

[1] `http://www.locongres.org/oc/aplicacions/verboc/conjugar`

| Tag | Description | Lexicon size |
|---|---|---|
| A | Adjective (general) | 29,638 |
| A$ | Adjective (possessive) | 85 |
| Adv | Adverb (general) | 751 |
| Adv$ | Adverb (negative, quantifier, exclamatory and interrogative) | 46 |
| Cc | Coordinating conjunction | 8 |
| Cs | Subordinating conjunction | 150 |
| Det | Article | 127 |
| Card | Cardinal number | 42 |
| Cli | Clitic | 72 |
| CliRef | Reflexive clitic | 17 |
| Inj | Interjection | 7 |
| Nc | Common noun | 25,817 |
| Np | Proper noun | 4,603 |
| Pct | Punctuation | 15 |
| Pe | Enunciative particle (Gascon only) | 0 |
| Pp | Present participle | 4,530 |
| Pr | Preposition | 521 |
| Prel | Relative pronoun | 37 |
| Pro | Pronoun | 81 |
| Ps | Past participle | 17,963 |
| PrepDet | Amalgamated preposition and article | 499 |
| Vc | Conjugated verb | 135,731 |
| Vi | Infinitive verb | 4,643 |
| Z | Consonant for phonetic liaison | 3 |
| **Total** | | **225,386** |

Table 1: Tagset

variety of Lengadocian; the third one, the *Gascon* corpus, was extracted from *Hont blanca* de Jan Loís Lavit, representing a variety of Gascon. The three corpora aim at representing different varieties of Occitan: firstly, two different dialects: Lengadocian and Gascon; secondly, two varieties of Lengadocian: Rouergue and Lot.

Table 2 shows a statistical comparison of the different corpora. As we can see, the percent of tokens unseen in the training corpus (excluding punctuation) ranges from 46% for the same dialectal variant (Rouergue) to 56% for a different dialect (Gascon). The difference is even more striking in terms of the Lengadocian lexicon: 17% unknown forms in the Rouergue corpus vs. 40% unknown forms in the Gascon corpus. Closed class coverage is particularly good for the two Lengadocian variants, with only 1.5% and 1% unknown forms, as opposed to 20% in the Gascon corpus.

## 5 Experiments

The resources we built were designed with several questions in mind:

- Which is the best strategy for each evaluation corpus?
- Is it always useful to apply closed-class rules?
- To what extent can a model built from a training corpus for a single dialectal variety be applied to other varieties and dialects?
- To what extent can a lexicon for one dialect be applied to another dialect?
- What methods can be used to improve analysis for a dialect different from the training/lexicon dialect?

| Corpus | Training | Rouergue | Lot | Gascon |
|---|---|---|---|---|
| Size | 2501 | 701 | 467 | 469 |
| Size (without punct.) | 2078 | 591 | 388 | 399 |
| % unknown in training corpus | | 46.36 | 48.97 | 56.39 |
| % unknown in lexicon | 0.10 | 16.58 | 19.85 | 40.10 |
| Open class tokens | 1111 | 324 | 201 | 203 |
| % unknown in training corpus | | 76.23 | 82.59 | 87.68 |
| % unknown in lexicon | 0.18 | 29.01 | 37.31 | 59.11 |
| Closed class tokens | 967 | 267 | 187 | 196 |
| % unknown in training corpus | | 10.11 | 12.83 | 23.98 |
| % unknown in lexicon | 0.00 | 1.50 | 1.07 | 20.41 |

Table 2: Training and evaluation corpora

A second range of experiments was designed to answer the following question: Given limited resources, is it better to annotate a larger training corpus, or compile a larger lexicon?

To this end, we divided the training corpus into two halves, `train1` and `train2`. We also created several sub-lexica: closed classes only (`closed`), closed classes + half of the open class entries (`half1`) closed classes + the other half of the open class entries (`half2`), the full lexicon (`full`) and an empty lexicon (`empty`). Finally, we tested with and without closed class rules. This gave us a total of 3 training corpus options $\times$ 5 lexicon options $\times$ 2 rule options = 30 evaluations per evaluation corpus.

We measured in each evaluation the total accuracy, the precision, recall and f-score for each pos-tag, and for all open pos-tags and all closed pos-tags combined. These were also measured separately for the set of tokens known and unknown in the lexicon.

## 6 Results

### 6.1 Overall results

Figure 1 shows results for the different lexicons and with/without closed-class rules (+rules on the figure). Not surprisingly, the best configuration for all evaluation corpora was the full training corpus, the full lexicon, and closed-class rules applied. This gives an accuracy of 87.02% for the Rouergue corpus, 89.08% for the Lot corpus, and 66.17% for the Gascon corpus. We can see that even a small training corpus provides reasonable results: almost 90% with only 2500 annotated tokens.

Within a given dialect, variation in style and genre seem more important than variation due to dialectal varieties: indeed, a training corpus in the Rouergue variety gave better results for an author in the Lot variety than for another author in the Rouergue variety. Another reason for handling dialects as a whole is that it would be very difficult and time consuming to construct a separate lexicon for each variety within a given dialect.

The much lower results for Gascon are expected, given the much lower training corpus coverage and lexicon coverage shown in Table 2, and the differences in pos-tag distribution presented in Section 2.1.

### 6.2 Closed class rules

The use of closed-class rules presented in Section 3.2 improved accuracy for all three corpora. The accuracy rose from 85.88% to 87.02% for the Rouergue corpus, from 88.01% to 89.08% in the Lot corpus, and 66.10% to 67.16% in the Gascon corpus. The last result is somewhat surprising, given the fact that 20% of the closed class tokens in the Gascon corpus are unknown in the lexicon.

### 6.3 Lexicons

The five lexicon setups described above allowed us to compare the contribution of different parts of the lexicon. Using a lexicon with only closed classes gives a fairly radical increase in all cases: together with rules, we gain 7.13% for Rouergue, 11.99% for Lot, and 4.9% for Gascon. When we add the full

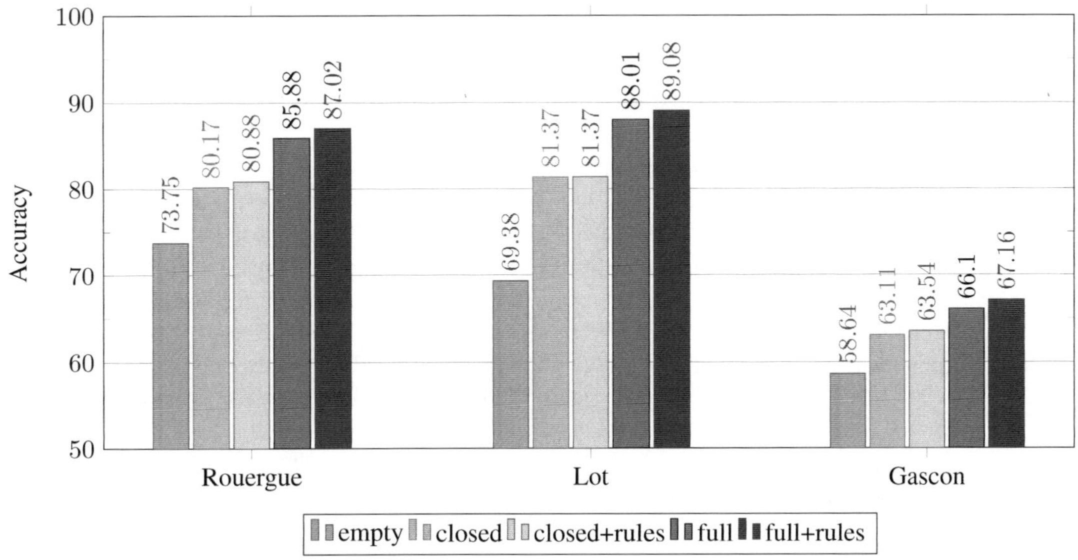


Figure 1: Pos-tagging lexicon/rules comparison: accuracy by corpus

lexicon with open and closed classes, we see an additional increase of 6.14% for Rouergue, 7.71% for Lot, and 3.62% for Gascon with respect to a closed-class lexicon only.

The open class gains are not directly correlated to the percentage of unknown words: the Lot corpus has far more unknown words than the Rouergue corpus, and yet gains more in terms of accuracy when the lexicon is added. Furthermore, the gains affect unknown words as well, probably through improvement in tagging of neighboring words and $n$-gram features: we see an average gain of 8.54% in accuracy for unknown words in Rouergue between the half1+rules/half2+rules and full+rules configurations, and 17.96% for unknown words in Lot.

### 6.4 Improving accuracy for other dialects

Given the relatively low score for Gascon, the question is, what can be done to improve this accuracy? In view of the training corpus in Lengadocian and the differences described in Section 2.1, it is clear that certain phenomena will be very difficult to detect, especially when Gascon lexical items are combined with uniquely Gascon pos-tag sequences. Additionally, one Gascon part-of-speech, the enunciative particle (annotated `Pe`), is entirely missing from Lengadocian. However, this pos-tag happens to be the most common one for the word *"que"*, and the only possibility for the word *"be"*.

We thus tested the addition of a new rule for Gascon only, stating that *"be"* is always annotated `Pe`, and *"que"* is annotated `Pe` whenever it's found at the start of a sentence, after a coordinating conjunction, or after a comma. For a total of 30 ennunciative particles, this rule gives us 17 true positives, 1 false positive, and 13 false negatives, for an f-score of 70.83%. It increases the total accuracy from 67.16% to 69.72%.

Beyond this rule (and possibly other similar rules), improving the accuracy necessarily requires more resources. Given the gains provided by small but complete closed-class lexica, a priority should thus be given to constructing a full-coverage closed-class lexicon for Gascon, and replacing the Lengadocian closed-class lexicon with this one during analysis. It is an open question whether it is better to use a higher-recall lexicon covering all dialects, or a higher-precision lexicon covering only Gascon. A similar question concerns training corpora, which are typically much more costly to construct than lexica, given that dictionaries in digital form are generally already available. Is it better to use a small training corpus per dialect, or to mix training corpora for all dialects into a larger training corpus? This of course depends on the degree of similarity between the dialects, and cannot be answered without empirical testing.

### 6.5 Build a training corpus or a lexicon?

To answer the question regarding the relative importance of annotating more training data or compiling larger lexica, we ran an experiment where the training corpus and open-class lexicon were each divided into two halves. We then compared the results provided by a single half of the training corpus and a single half of the lexicon (4 possible combinations) with results provided when including either the entire training corpus or the entire lexicon, but not both. Since the lexicon covers Lengadocian, we concentrate on the two Lengadocian corpora only, considering them as a single corpus.

The mean gain for doubling the training corpus from 1,250 tokens to 2,500 tokens is 1.46%, whereas the mean gain for doubling the open-class lexicon from 110K entries to 220K entries is 4.16%. It is thus much more productive to double the lexicon size, in our configuration. Note of course that there is no guarantee that this tendency would continue if we doubled the size of the training corpus and lexicon again. Also, while it is always possible (albeit costly) to annotate more text, there is a limit to the available lexical resources that can easily be compiled.

## 7 Conclusion and perspectives

In the present study, we show that supervised approaches, usually considered too costly for lesser-resourced languages, can achieve good results ($> 89\%$) with very little annotated material, as long as wide-coverage lexicon is available. We determined that given a limited amount of time, it is better to construct a larger lexicon than to annotate more training material. It would be interesting to repeat this experiment when we have gathered more training material and a wider-coverage lexicon, in order to view the tendencies in a graphical form.

One of the main objectives of the present study was to test a proof-of-concept for Occitan pos-tagging and identify guidelines for future efforts in this area. One of the first benefits of our work is that, in addition to the training and evaluation corpora and lexicon, we now have a functioning pos-tagger which can help efficiently construct more training and evaluation material, and an annotation guide to help correct this material.

Many recent studies have used semi-supervised cross-language pos-taggers, resulting in a larger quantity but lower quality of training data. It would be interesting to compare such an approach to our present supervised approach, as well as seeing whether the two can be combined (e.g. by giving more weight to the higher quality material during training).

The use of Talismane as a pos-tagger gives us a certain degree of robustness for handling language variants. Talismane is a hybrid toolkit: on the one hand, it provides robust supervised machine learning techniques, allowing us to ensure that as more data gets annotated, the results improve. On the other hand, it allows us to override the statistical models with symbolic rules, thus compensating for the low representativity of less common phenomena in the limited training material, as well as allowing us to take into account phenomena specific to the dialect or variety being analysed. The use of rules needs to be explored more deeply and extended to other phenomena than those explored in the present study.

In terms of the Gascon dialect, although the results are much better than random chance, they still leave much to be desired. Nevertheless, all of the phenomena observed for Lengadocian applied to Gascon as well, albeit to a lesser extent: the closed-class lexicon and related rules provided substantial gains (despite 20% unknown closed-class tokens in the lexicon), and additional gains were provided by the open-class lexicon. We tested with success a single rule for Gascon around the enunciative particle. Efforts would now be required to identify additional rules. However, the most promising perspective is the construction of a lexicon for Gascon, in particular giving full coverage for all closed classes. It is yet to be determined whether this lexicon should replace the Lengadocian lexicon during analysis, or complete it. A similar question applies to training corpora: if we annotate a Gascon training corpus, should it be combined with the Lengadocian corpus or should Gascon be trained separately.

Finally, there is another practical perspective from the present study: to use lists of unknown pos-tagged words as the initial input for the construction of wider-coverage lexica.

## References


Carme Armentano i Oller and Mikel L Forcada. 2006. Open-source machine translation between small languages: Catalan and aranese occitan. *Strategies for developing machine translation for minority languages*, page 51.

P. Bec. 1995. *La langue occitane*. Number 1059. Que sais-je ? Paris.

M. Bras and J. Thomas. 2011. Batelòc : cap a una basa informatisada de tèxtes occitans. In *L'Occitanie invitée de l'Euregio. Liège 1981 - Aix-la-Chapelle 2008 Bilan et perspectives*, Aix-la-Chapelle. Aache, Shaker.

M. Bras and M. Vergez-Couret. 2013. Batelòc : a text base for the occitan language. In *Proceedings of the International Conference on Endangered Languages in Europe*, Minde, Portugal.

Dan Garrette, Jason Mielens, and Jason Baldridge. 2013. Real-world semi-supervised learning of pos-taggers for low-resource languages. In *ACL 2013*, pages 583–592, Sofia, Bulgaria.

C. Laus. 2005. *Dictionnaire Français-Occitan*. IEO del Tarn.

Felipe Sánchez-Martınez, Carme Armentano-Oller, Juan Antonio Pérez-Ortiz, and Mikel L Forcada. 2007. Training part-of-speech taggers to build machine translation systems for less-resourced language pairs. In *Procesamiento del Lenguaje Natural (XXIII Congreso de la Sociedad Espanola de Procesamiento del Lenguaje Natural)*, volume 39, pages 257–264, September.

Yves Scherrer and Benoît Sagot. 2013. Lexicon induction and part-of-speech tagging of non-resourced languages without any bilingual resources. In *RANLP Workshop on Adaptation of language resources and tools for closely related languages and language variants*.

J. Sibille. 2007. L'occitan, qu'es aquò ? *Langues et Cité : bulletin de l'observation des pratiques linguistiques*, (10):2.

Oscar Täckström, Dipanjan Das, Slav Petrov, Ryan McDonald, and Joakim Nivre. 2013. Token and type constraints for cross-lingual part-of-speech tagging. *Transactions of the Association for Computational Linguistics*, 1:1–12.

Assaf Urieli. 2013. *Robust French syntax analysis: reconciling statistical methods and linguistic knowledge in the Talismane toolkit*. Ph.D. thesis, Université de Toulouse II le Mirail.

Assaf Urieli. 2014. Améliorer l'étiquetage de "que" par les descripteurs ciblés et les règles. In *Actes de la 21e conférence sur le Traitement Automatique des Langues Naturelles (TALN'2014)*, Marseille, France.

# Unsupervised adaptation of supervised part-of-speech taggers for closely related languages

**Yves Scherrer**
LATL-CUI
University of Geneva
Route de Drize 7, 1227 Carouge, Switzerland
yves.scherrer@unige.ch

**Abstract**

When developing NLP tools for low-resource languages, one is often confronted with the lack of annotated data. We propose to circumvent this bottleneck by training a supervised HMM tagger on a closely related language for which annotated data are available, and translating the words in the tagger parameter files into the low-resource language. The translation dictionaries are created with unsupervised lexicon induction techniques that rely only on raw textual data. We obtain a tagging accuracy of up to 89.08% using a Spanish tagger adapted to Catalan, which is 30.66% above the performance of an unadapted Spanish tagger, and 8.88% below the performance of a supervised tagger trained on annotated Catalan data. Furthermore, we evaluate our model on several Romance, Germanic and Slavic languages and obtain tagging accuracies of up to 92%.

## 1 Introduction

Recently, a lot of research has dealt with the task of creating part-of-speech taggers for languages which lack manually annotated training corpora. This is usually done through some type of annotation projection from a language for which a tagger or an annotated corpus exists (henceforth called RL for *resourced language*) towards another language that lacks such data (NRL for *non-resourced language*). One possibility is to use word-aligned parallel corpora and transfer the tags from the RL to the NRL along alignment links. Another possibility is to adapt the parameters of the RL tagger using bilingual dictionaries or manually built transformation rules.

In this paper, we argue that neither parallel corpora nor hand-written resources are required if the RL and the NRL are closely related. We propose a generic method for tagger adaptation that relies on three assumptions which generally hold for closely related language varieties. First, we assume that the two languages share a lot of cognates, i.e., word pairs that are formally similar and that are translations of each other. Second, we suppose that the word order of both languages is similar. Third, we assume that the set of POS tags is identical. Under these assumptions, we can avoid the requirements of parallel data and of manual annotation.

Following Feldman et al. (2006), the reasoning behind our method is that a Hidden Markov Model (HMM) tagger trained in a supervised way on RL data can be adapted to the NRL by translating the RL words in its parameter files to the NRL. This requires a bilingual dictionary between RL words and NRL words. In this paper, we create different HMM taggers using the bilingual dictionaries obtained with the unsupervised lexicon induction methods presented in our earlier work (Scherrer and Sagot, 2014).

The paper is organized as follows. In Section 2, we present related work on tagger adaptation and lexicon induction. In Section 3, we review Hidden Markov Models and their relevance for tagging and for our method of tagger adaptation. Section 4 presents a set of different taggers in some detail and evaluates them on Catalan, using Spanish as RL. In Section 5, we demonstrate the validity of the proposed approach by performing small-scale evaluations on a number of Romance, Germanic and Slavic languages: we transfer part-of-speech tags from Spanish to Aragonese, from Czech to Slovak and Sorbian, from Standard German to Dutch and Palatine German. We conclude in Section 6.





*Proceedings of the First Workshop on Applying NLP Tools to Similar Languages, Varieties and Dialects*, pages 30–38, Dublin, Ireland, August 23 2014.

## 2 Related work

The task of creating part-of-speech taggers (and other NLP tools) for new languages without resorting to manually annotated corpora has inspired a lot of recent research. The most popular line of work, initiated by Yarowsky et al. (2001), draws on parallel corpora. They tag the source side of a parallel corpus with an existing tagger, and then project the tags along the word alignment links onto the target side of the parallel corpus. A new tagger is then trained on the target side, using aggressive smoothing to reduce the noise caused by alignment errors.

In a similar setting, Das and Petrov (2011) use a more sophisticated graph-based projection algorithm with label propagation to obtain high-precision tags for the target words. Follow-up work by Li et al. (2012) uses tag dictionaries extracted from Wiktionary instead of parallel corpora, and Täckström et al. (2013) attempt to combine these two data sources: the Wiktionary data provides constraints on word *types*, whereas the parallel data is used to filter these constraints on the *token* level, depending on the context of a given word occurrence. Duong et al. (2013) show that the original approach of Das and Petrov (2011) can be simplified by focusing on high-confidence alignment links, thus achieving equivalent performance without resorting to graph-based projection. The research based on parallel corpora does not assume any particular etymological relationship between the two languages, but Duong et al. (2013) note that their approach works best when the source and target languages are closely related.

Other approaches explicity model the case of two closely related languages, such as Feldman et al. (2006). They train a tagger on the source language with standard tools and resources, and then adapt the parameter files of that tagger to the target language using a hand-written morphological analyzer and a list of cognate word pairs. Bernhard and Ligozat (2013) use a similar approach to adapt a German tagger to Alsatian; they show that manually annotating a small list of closed-class words leads to considerable gains in tagging accuracy. In a slightly different setting, Garrette and Baldridge (2013) show that taggers for low-resource languages can be built from scratch with only two hours of manual annotation work.

Even though recent work on closely related and low-resource languages presupposes manually annotated data to some extent, we believe that it is possible to create a tagger for such languages fully automatically. We adopt the general model proposed by Feldman et al. (2006), but use automatically induced bilingual dictionaries to translate the source language words in the tagger parameter files. The bilingual dictionaries are obtained with our unsupervised lexicon induction pipeline (Scherrer and Sagot, 2013; Scherrer and Sagot, 2014). This pipeline is inspired by early work by Koehn and Knight (2002), who propose various methods for inferring translation lexicons using monolingual data.

Our lexicon induction pipeline is composed of three main steps. First, a list of formally similar word pairs (cognate pairs) is extracted from monolingual corpora using the BI-SIM score (Kondrak and Dorr, 2004). Second, regularities occurring in these word pairs are learned by training and applying a character-level statistical machine translation (CSMT) system (Vilar et al., 2007; Tiedemann, 2009). Third, cross-lingual contextual similarity measures are used to induce additional word pairs. The main idea is to extract word n-grams from comparable corpora of both languages and induce word pairs that co-occur in the context of already known word pairs (Fung, 1998; Rapp, 1999; Fišer and Ljubešić, 2011). In our pipeline, the already known word pairs are those induced with CSMT.

In this paper, we extend our previous work (Scherrer and Sagot, 2014) in two aspects. First, we use a more powerful HMM tagging model instead of the simple unigram tagger that insufficiently accounts for the ambiguity in language. Second, we assess the impact of each lexicon induction step separately rather than merely evaluating the final result of the pipeline.

## 3 HMM tagging

Hidden Markov Models (HMMs) are a simple yet powerful formal device frequently used for part-of-speech tagging. A HMM describes a process that generates a joint sequence of tags and words by decomposing the problem into so-called transitions and emissions. Transitions represent the probabilities of a tag given the preceding tag(s), and emissions represent the probabilities of a word given the tag assigned to it (Jurafsky and Martin, 2009).

The main advantage of HMM taggers for our work lies in the independence assumption between transitions and emissions: crucially, the emission probability of a word only depends on its tag; it does not depend on previous words or on previous tags. Assuming, as stated in the introduction, that the word order is similar and the tag sets identical between the RL and the NRL, we argue that the transition probabilities estimated on RL data are also valid for NRL. Only the emission probabilities have to be adapted since RL words are formally different from NRL words.

Following earlier work (Feldman et al., 2006; Duong et al., 2013), we use the TnT tagger (Brants, 2000), an implementation of a trigram HMM tagger that includes smoothing and handling of unknown words. In contrast to other implementations that use inaccessible binary files, TnT stores the estimated parameters in easily modifiable plain text files.

### 3.1 Adapting emission counts

The goal of this work is to adapt an existing RL HMM tagger for a closely related NRL by replacing the RL words in the emission parameters by the corresponding NRL words. Let us explain this process with an example, using Spanish as RL and Catalan as NRL.

The TnT tagger creates an emission parameter file that contains, for each word, the tags and their frequencies observed in the training corpus. For example, a tagger trained on Spanish data may contain the following lines (word on the left, tag in the middle, frequency on the right):

(1)

| | | |
|---|---|---|
| intelectual | AQ | 11 |
| intelectual | NC | 3 |
| intelectuales | AQ | 3 |
| intelectuales | NC | 7 |

Furthermore, suppose that we have a dictionary that associates Catalan words (left) with Spanish words (center), where the weight (right) indicates the ambiguity level of the Catalan word, which is simply defined as the inverse of the number of its Spanish translations:

(2)

| | | |
|---|---|---|
| intel·lectual | intelectual | 0.5 |
| intel·lectual | intelectuales | 0.5 |
| intel·lectuals | intelectuales | 1 |

A new Catalan emission file is then created by taking, for each Catalan word, the union of the tags of its Spanish translations and by multiplying the tag weights with the dictionary weights. This yields the following entries:

(3)

| | | |
|---|---|---|
| intel·lectual | AQ | $(0.5 \cdot 11) + (0.5 \cdot 3) = 7$ |
| intel·lectual | NC | $(0.5 \cdot 3) + (0.5 \cdot 7) = 5$ |
| intel·lectuals | AQ | $1 \cdot 3 = 3$ |
| intel·lectuals | NC | $1 \cdot 7 = 7$ |

Or more formally: for each dictionary triple $\langle w_{RL}, w_{NRL}, f_d \rangle$ and each emission triple $\langle w_{RL}, t, f_e \rangle$ with matching $w_{RL}$, add the new emission triple $\langle w_{NRL}, t, f_d \cdot f_e \rangle$. Merge emission triples with identical $w_{NRL}$ and $t$ and sum their weights.

Finally, RL words occurring in the emission file that have not been translated to NRL (because no appropriate word pair existed in the dictionary) are copied without modification to the new emission file. In particular, this allows us to cover punctuation signs and numbers as well as named entities (which are mostly spelled identically in both languages).

## 4 Tagger adaptation for Catalan

In this section, we present seven taggers for Catalan. Three of them (Sections 4.2 to 4.4) are supervised taggers and serve as baseline taggers and as upper bounds. The four remaining taggers (Sections 4.6 to 4.9) are taggers created by adaptation from a Spanish tagger, using the method presented in Section 3.1;

they differ in the lexicons used to translate the emission counts. These four taggers represent the main contribution of this paper. We start by listing the data used in our experiments.

### 4.1 Data

Most taggers presented below are initially trained on a part-of-speech annotated corpus of Spanish. We use the Spanish part of the AnCora treebank (Taulé et al., 2008), which contains about 500 000 words.

The AnCora morphosyntactic annotation includes the main category (e.g. noun), the subcategory (e.g. proper noun), and several morphological categories (e.g., gender, number, person, tense, mode), yielding about 280 distinct labels. Since we are mainly interested in part-of-speech information, we simplified these labels by taking into account the two first characters of each label, corresponding to the main category and the subcategory. This simplified tagset contains 42 distinct labels, which is still considerably more than the 12 tags of Petrov et al. (2012) commonly used in comparable settings.

All taggers need to be evaluated on a Catalan gold standard that shares the same tagset as Spanish. For this purpose, we use the Catalan part of AnCora, which also contains about 500 000 words. We simplified the tags in the same way as above. The Catalan part of AnCora is also used to train the supervised models presented in Sections 4.3 and 4.4.

Finally, the lexicon induction algorithms require data on their own, which we present here for completeness. As in Scherrer and Sagot (2013), we use Wikipedia dumps consisting of 140M words for Catalan and 430M words for Spanish.[1]

### 4.2 Baseline: a Spanish tagger

Since Spanish and Catalan are closely related languages, one could presume that a lot of words are identical, and that a tagger trained on Spanish data would yield acceptable performance on Catalan test data without modifications. In order to test this hypothesis, we trained a TnT tagger on Spanish AnCora and tested it on Catalan AnCora. We obtained a tagging accuracy of 58.42% only, which suggests that this approach is clearly insufficient. (The results of all experiments are summed up in Table 1.) For comparison, Feldman et al. (2006) obtain 64.5% accuracy on the same languages with a smaller training corpus (100k instead of 500k words), but also with a smaller tagset (14 instead of 42).

We view this model as a baseline that we expect to beat with the adaptation methods.

### 4.3 Upper bound 1: a supervised Catalan tagger

The upper bound of the Catalan tagging experiments is represented by a tagger created under ideal data conditions: a tagger trained in a supervised way on an annotated Catalan corpus. We train a TnT tagger on Catalan AnCora and test it on the same corpus, using 10-fold cross-validation to avoid having the same sentences in the training and the test set. This yields an averaged accuracy value of 97.96%.

For comparison, Feldman et al. (2006) obtain 97.5% accuracy on their dataset. More recently, Petrov et al. (2012) report an accuracy of 98.5% by training on the CESS-ECE corpus, but do not mention the tagging algorithm used. In any case, our result obtained with TnT can be considered close to state-of-the-art performance on Catalan.

### 4.4 Upper bound 2: a tagger with Spanish transition counts and Catalan emission counts

We introduce a second upper bound that shares the assumption of structural similarity underlying the adaptation-based models. Concretely, we combine the transition probabilities from the baseline Spanish tagger (Section 4.2) with the emission probabilities of the supervised Catalan tagger (Section 4.3). The resulting tagger is evaluated again on Catalan AnCora using 10-fold cross-validation. We get an accuracy value of 97.66%, or just 0.3% absolute below the supervised tagger of Section 4.3.[2] This suggests that the transition probabilities are indeed very similar between the two languages, and that they can safely be kept constant in the adaptation-based models presented below.

[1] This is not exactly a realistic setting for the intended use for low-resource languages. However, Section 5 will illustrate the performance of the proposed models on smaller data sets. Note also that the lexicon induction methods do not require the two corpora to be of similar size.

[2] This difference is significant: $\chi^2(1; N = 1\,064\,002) = 109.9747799; p < 0.01$.

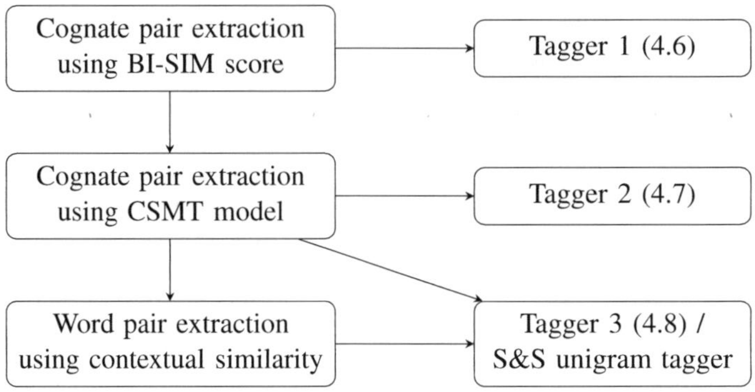


Figure 1: Flowchart of the lexicon induction pipeline and of the resulting taggers.

### 4.5 Lexicon induction methods for adaptation-based taggers

The adaptation-based taggers presented in Sections 4.6 to 4.8 differ in the bilingual dictionaries used to adapt the emission counts. These dictionaries have been created using the pipeline of Scherrer and Sagot (2014), which we summarize in this section (see Figure 1).

The pipeline starts with a cognate pair extraction step that uses the BI-SIM score to identify likely cognate pairs. The result of this step is used as training data for the second step, in which a CSMT model is trained to identify likely cognate pairs even more reliably. The result of the second step is in turn used as seed data for the third step, in which additional word pairs are extracted on the basis of contextual similarity. Scherrer and Sagot (2014) create a single unigram tagger (abreviated S&S in Figure 1) with the union of the word pairs obtained in the second and third steps (plus additional clues like word identity and suffix analysis, which are not required here).

The three steps are evaluated separately: Tagger 1 relies on the lexicon induced in the first step; Tagger 2 relies on the lexicon induced in the second step; Tagger 3 relies on the union of the lexicons induced in the second and third steps.

### 4.6 Tagger 1: cognate pairs induced with BI-SIM score

As first step of the lexicon induction pipeline, word lists are extracted from both Wikipedia corpora, and short words (words with less than 5 characters) as well as rare words (words accounting for the lowest 10% of the frequency distribution) are removed. Then, the BI-SIM score is computed between each Catalan word $w_{\text{ca}}$ and each Spanish word $w_{\text{es}}$. For each $w_{\text{ca}}$, we keep the $\langle w_{\text{ca}}, w_{\text{es}} \rangle$ pair(s) that maximize(s) the BI-SIM value, provided it is above the empirically chosen threshold of 0.8. When a $w_{\text{ca}}$ is associated with several $w_{\text{es}}$, we keep all of them. This creates a list of cognate pairs, albeit a rather noisy one since it does not take into account regular correspondences between languages, but merely counts letter bigram differences.

Tagger 1, the first adaptation-based tagger, is created by replacing the Spanish emission counts with their Catalan equivalents using the list of cognate pairs. Tagger 1 yields an accuracy of 68.32%, which is a full 10% higher than the baseline. This improvement is surprisingly high, as the cognate list is not only noisy, but also incomplete: only 17.91% of the words in the emission file could be translated with it.

### 4.7 Tagger 2: cognate pairs induced with CSMT

In this model, the Spanish emission counts are replaced using the list of cognate pairs obtained in the second step of the lexicon induction pipeline.

We train a CSMT system on the list of potential cognate pairs of the first step. We then apply this system to translate each Catalan word again into Spanish. We assume that the CSMT system learns useful generalizations about the relationship between Catalan and Spanish words, which the generic BI-SIM measure was not able to make. Moreover, the CSMT system is able to translate Catalan words even

| | Baseline | Tagger 1 | Tagger 2 | Tagger 3 | Tagger 4 | Upper bound 2 | Upper bound 1 |
|---|---|---|---|---|---|---|---|
| Tagging accuracy | 58.42% | 68.32% | 72.32% | 88.72% | 89.08% | 97.66% | 97.96% |
| Translated words | | 17.91% | 64.03% | 65.62% | | | |

Table 1: Results of the Catalan tagging experiments. The first line reports tagging accuracies of the different taggers. The second line shows – where applicable – how many words of the emission files could be translated.

if their Spanish translations have not been seen, on the basis of the character correspondences observed in other words.

This new dictionary allowed us to translate 64.03% of the words in the emission file. In consequence, the resulting tagger shows improved performance compared with Tagger 1: its accuracy lies at 72.32%, suggesting that the CSMT system yields a dictionary that is at the same time more precise and more complete than the one obtained with BI-SIM in the previous step.

### 4.8 Tagger 3: word pairs induced with CSMT and context similarity

In previous work (Scherrer and Sagot, 2014), we have argued that lexicon induction methods based on formal similarity alone are not sufficient, for the following reasons: (1) even in closely related languages, not all word pairs are cognates; (2) high-frequency words are often related through irregular phonetic correspondences; (3) pairs of short words may just be too hard to predict on the basis of formal criteria alone; (4) formal similarity methods are prone to inducing false friends, i.e., words that are formally similar but are not translations of each other. For these types of words, we have proposed a different approach that relies on contextual similarity.

We extract 3-gram and 4-gram contexts from both languages and form context pairs whenever the first and the last word pairs figure in the dictionary obtained with CSMT, allowing the word pair(s) in the center to be newly inferred. Several filters are added in order to remove noise.

In order to create Tagger 3, we merge the dictionary induced with CSMT and the dictionary induced with context similarity, giving preference to the latter. Again, the emission parameters of the baseline Spanish tagger are adapted using this dictionary. 65.62% of the words in the emission file could be translated, i.e. only 1.59% more than for Tagger 2. Nevertheless, the accuracy of Tagger 3 (88.72%) lies about 18% absolute above Tagger 2. This large gain in accuracy is due to the fact that context similarity mostly adds high-frequency words, which are few but crucial to obtain satisfactory tagging performance.

One goal of these experiments was to show whether the improved handling of ambiguity provided by HMMs in comparison with the unigram model used by Scherrer and Sagot (2013) is reflected in better overall tagging performance. This goal has been reached: the unigram model of Scherrer and Sagot (2013) shows a tagging accuracy of 85.1%, which is 3% absolute below Tagger 3, the most directly comparable HMM-based tagger.[3]

### 4.9 Tagger 4: re-estimate transition probabilities

In this last model, we challenge the initial assumption that the Spanish transition probabilities are "good enough" for tagging Catalan. Concretely, we use Tagger 3 to tag the entire Catalan Wikipedia corpus (the one also used for the lexicon induction tasks) and then train Tagger 4 in a supervised way on this data. The idea behind this additional step is that the transition (and emission) counts estimated on the large Catalan corpus are more reliable than those obtained by direct tagger adaptation.

Tagger 4 yields an accuracy value of 89.08%, outperforming Tagger 3 by only 0.36%.[4] This difference is consistent with the one observed between Upper Bound 1 and Upper Bound 2, suggesting once more

[3]The Catalan results reported in Scherrer and Sagot (2014) are based on a different test set, which is why we rather refer to the directly comparable Scherrer and Sagot (2013) results in this section.

[4]This difference is significant: $\chi^2(1; N = 1\,064\,002) = 35.84835013; p < 0.01$.

that transition counts only marginally influence the tagging performance if the former are estimated on a language that is structurally similar.

## 5 Multilingual experiments

In addition to the Spanish–Catalan experiment, we have induced taggers for several closely related languages from Romance, Germanic and Slavic language families and tested them on the multilingual data set used by Scherrer and Sagot (2014). Although the results of these additional experiments are less reliable than the Spanish–Catalan data due to the small test corpus sizes, they allow us to generalize our findings to other languages and language families. The experiments are set up as follows:

- The **Aragonese** taggers were adapted from a **Spanish** tagger trained on AnCora. They are tested on a Wikipedia excerpt of 100 sentences that was manually annotated with the simplified AnCora labels of Section 4.1. The Wikipedia corpora used for lexicon induction contained 5.4M words for Aragonese, and 431M words for Spanish.

- The **Dutch** and **Palatine German** taggers were adapted from a **Standard German** tagger trained on the TIGER treebank (900 000 tokens; 55 tags; Brants et al. (2002)). The gold standard corpora are Wikipedia excerpts of 100 sentences each, manually annotated with TIGER labels. The Wikipedia corpora used for lexicon induction contained 0.5M words for Dutch, 0.3M words for Palatine German, and 612M words for Standard German.

- The **Upper Sorbian**, **Slovak** and **Polish** taggers were adapted from a **Czech** Tagger trained on the Prague Dependency Treebank 2.5 (2M tokens; 57 simplified tags).[5] The gold standard corpora are Wikipedia excerpts of 30 sentences each, manually annotated with simplified PDT labels. The Wikipedia corpora used for lexicon induction contained 0.9M words for Upper Sorbian, 30M words for Slovak, 206M words for Polish, and 85M words for Czech.

The tagging accuracies are reported in the left part of Table 2. The accuracy values vary widely across languages, with baseline performances ranging from 24% to 81%. This variation essentially reflects the linguistic distance between the RL and the NRL: German and Dutch seem to be particularly distant, while Czech and Slovak are particularly closely related. In contrast, the overall tendency of the tagging models is the same for all languages: there are consistent gradual improvements from the baseline tagger to Tagger 3. These findings are in line with the Catalan experiments. The differences between Tagger 3 and Tagger 4 are not significant for any language, whereas the Catalan experiment showed a slight but significant improvement. Finally, Taggers 3 and 4 slightly outperform the unigram tagger of Scherrer and Sagot (2014) (S&S in Table 2) on most languages, although the difference is less marked than for Catalan.

The right half of Table 2 shows what percentage of the emission files could be translated at each step, analogously to the figures reported for Catalan in Table 1. The variation observed here mainly depends on the language proximity and on the size of the corpora used for lexicon induction.

Globally, the Germanic languages obtain the lowest accuracy scores. This is due to a combination of factors. First, as stated above, the baseline performance is already lower than in the other language families, which essentially results from a lower number of identical NRL–RL word pairs than in other language families. Second, the lexicon induction corpora are much smaller than for the other language families.[6] Third, Germanic languages tend to have longer words due to compounding, so that the BI-SIM threshold is more difficult to satisfy. The combination of the second and third factors lead to poor performance of the first lexicon induction step: less than 4% of the German words could be translated

[5]Similarly to AnCora, the morphosyntactic labels of the PDT consist of 15 positions that encode the main morphosyntactic category, the subcategory as well as various morphological categories. We simplify the tagset analogously to AnCora, keeping only the main category and the subcategory, which leads to 57 distinct labels.
The PDT is available at `http://ufal.mff.cuni.cz/pdt2.5/`.

[6]As in our earlier work, we used all of the Palatine German Wikipedia, whereas we reduced the Dutch Wikipedia corpus on purpose to better simulate the low-resource scenario.

| Language | | Tagging accuracy | | | | | Translated words | | |
|---|---|---|---|---|---|---|---|---|---|
| | Baseline | T1 | T2 | T3 | T4 | S&S | T1 | T2 | T3 |
| Aragonese | 72% | 74% | 74% | 87% | 87% | 85% | 16.11% | 42.65% | 43.23% |
| Dutch | 24% | 30% | 39% | 60% | 62% | 59% | 3.69% | 6.73% | 6.79% |
| Palatine German | 50% | 54% | 57% | 70% | 70% | 65% | 3.86% | 5.52% | 5.58% |
| Upper Sorbian | 70% | 72% | 77% | 84% | 84% | 84% | 5.70% | 11.60% | 11.69% |
| Slovak | 81% | 85% | 88% | 93% | 93% | 92% | 29.39% | 52.40% | 54.41% |
| Polish | 66% | 69% | 72% | 78% | 79% | 78% | 8.50% | 42.27% | 42.73% |

Table 2: Results of the multilingual tagging experiments. The left half of the table reports tagging accuracies and compares them with the results reported by Scherrer and Sagot (2014) (S&S column). The right half of the table shows how many words of the emission files could be translated.

when building Tagger 1. This obviously reduces the potential for accuracy gains in Tagger 1, but it also hampers the training of the CSMT system at the origin of Tagger 2. However, one should note that good tagging results can be achieved even with relatively low translation coverage, as shown by the Upper Sorbian experiment.

## 6 Conclusion

One goal of the experiments presented here was to validate the pipeline proposed earlier in Scherrer and Sagot (2014). By showing that there are gradual improvements from the baseline tagger to Tagger 3 on a large number of languages, we demonstrate that the overall approach of inducing word pairs in subsequent steps is sound, and that the order of these steps is reasonably chosen. Furthermore, we find that re-estimating the tagger parameters on a large monolingual corpus (Tagger 4) does not improve its performance substantially, as we have predicted in Section 4.4 on the basis of supervised Catalan taggers.

A second goal of these experiments was to show that the HMM taggers offer improved handling of ambiguity compared with the unigram tagger of Scherrer and Sagot (2014). We have indeed noted an accuracy gain of 3% on the Catalan data, and the multilingual data set shows similar (yet less marked) tendencies.

However, the Catalan experiments show that there still is a gap of about 10% absolute accuracy between the adaptation taggers and fully supervised taggers. We see two main reasons for this gap. First, the completely unsupervised lexicon induction algorithms obviously produce a number of erroneous word pairs, which may then result in erroneous tagging. Second, the lexicon induction algorithms currently do not allow a given NRL word to relate to two different RL words. As a result, the taggers are not able to model tagging ambiguities arising from translation ambiguities. Better ambiguity handling, for instance on the basis of token-level constraints as suggested by Täckström et al. (2013), could thus further improve tagging accuracy.

Finally, discriminative models using Maximum Entropy or Perceptron training have largely superseded HMMs for part-of-speech tagging in the last few years.[7] Such models take into account a larger set of features such as word suffixes, word structure (presence of punctuation signs, numerals, etc.) and external lexicon information. Further research will be needed to investigate how our adaptation methods can be applied to feature-based tagging models.


## Acknowledgements

The author would like to thank Benoît Sagot for his collaboration on earlier versions of this work. This work was partially funded by the Labex EFL (ANR/CGI), Strand 6, operation LR2.2.


[7]For an overview on recent English taggers, see for example `http://aclweb.org/aclwiki/index.php?title=POS_Tagging_(State_of_the_art)`.

## References


Delphine Bernhard and Anne-Laure Ligozat. 2013. Hassle-free POS-tagging for the Alsatian dialects. In Marcos Zampieri and Sascha Diwersy, editors, *Non-Standard Data Sources in Corpus Based-Research*, volume 5 of *ZSM Studien*, pages 85–92. Shaker.

Sabine Brants, Stefanie Dipper, Silvia Hansen, Wolfgang Lezius, and George Smith. 2002. The TIGER Treebank. In *Proceedings of the First Workshop on Treebanks and Linguistic Theories (TLT 2002)*, pages 24–41.

Thorsten Brants. 2000. TnT – a statistical part-of-speech tagger. In *Proceedings of ANLP 2000*, pages 224–231.

Dipanjan Das and Slav Petrov. 2011. Unsupervised part-of-speech tagging with bilingual graph-based projections. In *Proceedings of ACL-HLT 2011*, pages 600–609.

Long Duong, Paul Cook, Steven Bird, and Pavel Pecina. 2013. Simpler unsupervised POS tagging with bilingual projections. In *Proceedings of ACL 2013*, pages 634–639.

Anna Feldman, Jirka Hana, and Chris Brew. 2006. A cross-language approach to rapid creation of new morpho-syntactically annotated resources. In *Proceedings of LREC 2006*, pages 549–554.

Darja Fišer and Nikola Ljubešić. 2011. Bilingual lexicon extraction from comparable corpora for closely related languages. In *Proceedings of RANLP 2011*, pages 125–131.

Pascale Fung. 1998. A statistical view on bilingual lexicon extraction: from parallel corpora to non-parallel corpora. *Machine Translation and the Information Soup*, pages 1–17.

Dan Garrette and Jason Baldridge. 2013. Learning a part-of-speech tagger from two hours of annotation. In *Proceedings of NAACL-HLT 2013*, pages 138–147.

Daniel Jurafsky and James H. Martin. 2009. *Speech and language processing*. Pearson, 2nd edition.

Philipp Koehn and Kevin Knight. 2002. Learning a translation lexicon from monolingual corpora. In *Proceedings of the ACL 2002 Workshop on Unsupervised Lexical Acquisition (SIGLEX 2002)*, pages 9–16.

Grzegorz Kondrak and Bonnie Dorr. 2004. Identification of confusable drug names: A new approach and evaluation methodology. In *Proceedings of COLING 2004*, pages 952–958.

Shen Li, João Graça, and Ben Taskar. 2012. Wiki-ly supervised part-of-speech tagging. In *Proceedings of EMNLP-CoNLL 2012*, pages 1389–1398.

Slav Petrov, Dipanjan Das, and Ryan McDonald. 2012. A universal part-of-speech tagset. In *Proceedings of LREC 2012*, pages 2089–2096.

Reinhard Rapp. 1999. Automatic identification of word translations from unrelated English and German corpora. In *Proceedings of ACL 1999*, pages 519–526.

Yves Scherrer and Benoît Sagot. 2013. Lexicon induction and part-of-speech tagging of non-resourced languages without any bilingual resources. In *Proceedings of the RANLP 2013 Workshop on Adaptation of language resources and tools for closely related languages and language variants.*

Yves Scherrer and Benoît Sagot. 2014. A language-independent and fully unsupervised approach to lexicon induction and part-of-speech tagging for closely related languages. In *Proceedings of LREC 2014*, pages 502–508.

Oscar Täckström, Dipanjan Das, Slav Petrov, Ryan McDonald, and Joakim Nivre. 2013. Token and type constraints for cross-lingual part-of-speech tagging. *Transactions of the Association for Computational Linguistics*, 1:1–12.

Mariona Taulé, M. Antònia Martí, and Marta Recasens. 2008. Ancora: Multilevel annotated corpora for Catalan and Spanish. In *Proceedings of LREC 2008*, pages 96–101.

Jörg Tiedemann. 2009. Character-based PSMT for closely related languages. In *Proceedings of EAMT 2009*, pages 12–19.

David Vilar, Jan-Thorsten Peter, and Hermann Ney. 2007. Can we translate letters? In *Proceedings of WMT 2007*, pages 33–39.

David Yarowsky, Grace Ngai, and Richard Wicentowski. 2001. Inducing multilingual text analysis tools via robust projection across aligned corpora. In *Proceedings of HLT 2001*.

# Morphological Disambiguation and Text Normalization for Southern Quechua Varieties

**Annette Rios**
Institute of Computational Linguistics
University of Zurich
arios@ifi.uzh.ch

**Richard Castro Mamani**
Computer Science Department
Universidad Nacional de San Antonio Abad del Cuzco
rcastro@hinantin.com

## Abstract

We built a pipeline to normalize Quechua texts through morphological analysis and disambiguation. Word forms are analyzed by a set of cascaded finite state transducers which split the words and rewrite the morphemes to a normalized form. However, some of these morphemes, or rather morpheme combinations, are ambiguous, which may affect the normalization. For this reason, we disambiguate the morpheme sequences with conditional random fields. Once we know the individual morphemes of a word, we can generate the normalized word form from the disambiguated morphemes.[1]

## 1 Introduction

As part of our research project we have developed several tools and resources for Cuzco Quechua. This includes a hybrid machine translation system Spanish-Quechua. The core system is a classical rule-based transfer engine, that we aim to improve with the addition of statistical modules.

An issue that is generally difficult to deal with in a rule-based approach is the lexical choice of translation options: writing context rules for every possible translation of a given input word is not feasible. Another solution is to include a language model, trained on Quechua texts, that can handle the lexical disambiguation. The total number of available Quechua texts is relatively small, and to complicate matters even further, these texts are written in a wide range of different orthographies. Therefore, the first step in order to obtain a language model is the normalization of the different spellings into a standardized orthography. Not every morphological ambiguity needs to be disambiguated for the normalization alone, but we need fully disambiguated texts for other applications (e.g. parsing). Therefore, we chose to disambiguate not only the cases that are relevant for the normalization, but all types of morphological ambiguities.

## 2 Related Work

In general, almost every automatic processing of agglutinative languages relies on a correct morphological analysis. Extensive research on morphological disambiguation has been done on Turkish: Görgün et al. (2011) used the WEKA toolkit to train and test several classifiers. With over 50,000 disambiguated sentences for training, they achieved 95.6% accuracy with the J48 Tree algorithm.

Hakkani-Tür et al. (2002) trained an N-gram language model on Turkish roots and another model on so called inflectional groups (groups of morphemes), and used a combination of these two models to disambiguate the output of their finite state analyzer. With a training set of almost 700,000 tokens, they achieved 93.95% accuracy.

Sak et al. (2007) use the combined language models from Hakkani-Tür et al. (2002) to produce an n-best list of morphological parses for a given Turkish sentence. In a second step, they rank the candidates with the voted Perceptron algorithm, trained on 42,000 disambiguated tokens. With this additional step, they achieved an accuracy of 96.8%.



[1]The tool can be tested online at http://kitt.ifi.uzh.ch/kitt/quechua/normalizer.html.



*Proceedings of the First Workshop on Applying NLP Tools to Similar Languages, Varieties and Dialects*, pages 39–47,
Dublin, Ireland, August 23 2014.

While the morphological situation with Quechua is comparable to Turkish, the size of the available training data is not: we have less than 3000 manually disambiguated sentences ($\sim$38,000 tokens) that we can use for training. An approach such as the one described by Görgün et al. (2011), where the classifier learns to assign a class for each possible combination of morphemes (without the root), is therefore not feasible: the number of classes that can be learned from such a small training set will not suffice to classify unseen data. Similarly, a language model, even if trained on units smaller than words, as done by Hakkani-Tür et al. (2002), will not overcome the data sparseness in the training set.

For this reason, the approach presented in this paper attempts to break down the disambiguation process into several smaller steps: we move from the root to the last suffix, disambiguating only one morpheme class at a time. With this approach, we achieve an accuracy that is comparable to the results for Turkish.

## 3 Quechua

Quechua is a language family spoken in the Andes by 8-10 million people in Peru, Bolivia, Ecuador, Southern Colombia and the North-West of Argentina. Although Quechua is often referred to as a language and its local varieties as dialects, Quechua is a language family, comparable in depth to the Romance or Slavic languages (Adelaar and Muysken, 2004, 168). Mutual intelligibility, especially between speakers of distant 'dialects', is not always given.

In this project, we work with Cuzco Quechua (Southern Quechua), and in the following sections, the name Quechua is meant to refer explicitely to this variety. The number of available texts in this particular dialect is limited, therefore we have to include texts from other (similar) varieties of the Southern Quechua dialect group, such as Ayacucho and Bolivian Quechua.

### 3.1 Dialectal and Orthographic Variation within the Southern Quechua dialect group (QIIC)

Apart from lexical differences, there is one major dialectal divergence between the Cuzco/Bolivian dialects on one side, and the Ayacucho/Argentina varieties on the other side: Cuzco/Bolivian Quechua has, like Aymara, a three way distinction of stops (plain, glottalized and aspirated), whereas Ayacucho and Argentina Quechua have only plain stops. Furthermore, some suffixes appear in different forms, e.g. the progressive in Ayacucho is marked by *-chka*, in Cuzco by *-sha*, and in Bolivia by *-sa* or *-sya*. Other suffixes are restricted to a particular variety: some dialects that are in close contact with Aymara, such as the Quechua spoken in Puno, have borrowed a number of Aymara suffixes, e.g. *-thapi*, *-t'a*, *-naqa*, that are unknown in other dialects (Adelaar, 1987).

Additionally, there are some morphotactic differences concerning the combination of suffixes: for instance, a number of Quechua suffixes change their vowel in combination with certain suffixes, but the exact contexts that induce this vowel change differ to some extent across dialects. Furthermore, the order of suffixes in combinations can vary.

Apart from the dialectal differences, there is also a wide range of orthographic variation within the Southern Quechua dialect group. Several standards have been proposed, most notably the standardized orthography as defined by Cerrón-Palomino (1994). This standard has been adopted by the Bolivian government (Villarroel, 2000), with one small adaption: in Bolivia, the glottal fricative [h] is written as /j/ instead of /h/. In Peru, the situation is slightly more complicated: Although the Ministry of Education has defined an official standard orthography[2],there is still some disagreement regarding the correct spelling of Quechua words. Also, many Quechua texts are written in a more or less Spanish orthography, where for instance /wa/ is written as /hua/, and /ki/ is written as /qui/. Table 1 illustrates the orthography of the Academia Mayor de la Lengua Quechua in Cuzco (first row), a typical 'Spanish' spelling (second row) and an old, non-standardized Bolivian spelling (last row), as opposed to the unified standard orthography as defined by Cerrón-Palomino (1994). This is the orthography that we use for normalization.

[2]As declared in the *Resolución Ministerial N° 1218-85-ED de 1985*

| | |
|---|---|
| AMLQ | *mana qelqaq yachaq ñausa qelqa runasimipi kasqanku rayku...* |
| norm. | mana qillqaq yachaq ñawsa qillqa runasimipi kasqankurayku... |
| span. | *Cay teccsimuyuta, hanacc-pachatapas, Ccanmi tacyachinqui, Ccanmi ticrachinqui..* |
| norm. | Kay tiqsimuyuta, hanaq pachatapas, Qammi takyachinki, Qammi t'ikrachinki.. |
| boliv. | *Chaywampis paykuna onqosqa kashajtinku, noqaqa llakiy qhashqa p'achasta churakorqani.* |
| norm. | Chaywanpas paykuna unqusqa kachkaptinku, ñuqaqa llakiy qhachqa p'achakunata churakurqani. |

Abbreviations: AMLQ = Academia Mayor de la Lengua Quechua en Cusco, norm = normalized, span = Spanish orthography, boliv = (old) Bolivian orthography

Table 1: Different Orthographies with Corresponding Standardized Version

| | variations | standard |
|---|---|---|
| progressive | *-chka, -sha, -sa, -sya* | *-chka* |
| genitive (after vowel) | *-p/-q/-h/-j* | *-p* |
| evidential (after vowel) | *-m/-n* | *-m* |
| additive | *-pis/-pas* | *-pas* |
| euphonic | *-ni/ñi* | *-ni* |
| 1.&2. plural forms | *-chis/-chik/-chiq* | *-chik* |
| assistive | *-ysi/-schi/-scha* | *-ysi* |
| potential forms | *-swan/-chwan* | *-chwan* |

Table 2: Suffix Variation and Normalization

## 4 Morphological Analysis

Quechua is an agglutinative, suffixing language. There are over 130 Quechua suffixes, the exact number, as well as the form of the suffixes exhibit substantial variation across dialects. There are five functional classes of Quechua suffixes: nominalizing (noun→verb) and verbalizing (verb→noun), nominal (noun→noun) and verbal (verb→verb) suffixes and so-called independent or ambiguous suffixes, that can be attached to both verbal or nominal forms, without altering the part of speech. The position of these suffixes is at the end of the suffix sequence, their relative order is more or less fixed, though dialects show minor variations. The functions of the independent suffixes include data source, polar question marking and topic or contrast, amongst others (Adelaar and Muysken, 2004, 208).

Quechua roots are, apart from a small number of particles, either verbal or nominal. Adjectives do not constitute a word class on their own on a morphological level, as they behave exactly the same as nominal roots. There may be some syntactic restrictions on true adjectives (Adelaar and Muysken, 2004, 208), but these can be ignored for a morphological analysis. Many roots are indeed ambiguous and can be used either as noun or verb without any derivational suffixes:[3]

(1) *taki* *-y*
song/sing -1S.ps
'My song'

(2) *taki* *-ni.*
song/sing -1S
'I sing'

Furthermore, nominalizing (NS) and verbalizing (VS) suffixes are very productive and can occur more than once in a word.

We obtain the morphological analysis from a finite state analyzer that splits the word forms into morphemes, and also normalizes the surface form of the morphemes. Roots are mapped to their standardized form according to Cerrón-Palomino (1994), e.g. the word for brain, *ñutq'u* in the standard, may appear as *nushqun, ñusqhun, ñusq'un, ñusqun or ñutqun*, depending on the dialect. The normalizer rewrites all these variants to *ñutq'u*. The normalizer also rewrites the form of certain suffixes, see Table 2.

Some of these suffixes are ambiguous in their non-standardized forms, e.g. the direct evidential suffix, written as *-n*, could also be a third person singular marker (verbal or nominal). In order to generate the

[3]Abbreviations used in glosses: Acc: accusative, Add: additive, Dim: diminutive, DirE: direct evidential, Fact: factitive, Fut: future tense, IndE: indirect evidential, Inf: infinitive, Imp: imperative, Loc: locative, NS: nominalizing, P: plural, Perf: perfect, ps: possessive, Rflx: reflexive, S: singular, Top: topic, VS: verbalizing

| | Joven | Gregorio | Cancionero |
|---|---|---|---|
| normalizer | 97.86% | 73.00% | 42.56% |
| Spanish strict | 0.64% | 21.87% | 15.86% |
| normalizer relax | - | - | 34.88% |
| Spanish relax | - | 0.30% | 1.48% |
| guesser | 1.02% | 2.36% | 3.65% |
| total coverage | 99.52% | 97.64% | 98.43% |
| unknown words | 0.48% | 2.46% | 1.58% |

Table 3: Morphological Analysis Coverage

normalized form of a word with a suffix *-n*, we need to know whether this particular *-n* is a person marker or an evidential suffix. Only in the latter case, *-n* needs to be rewritten as *-m* during normalization.

We have two normalizers in our pipeline: the first one handles text in 'regular' orthographies that show some minor dialectal variations. The second normalizer allows for more 'extreme' orthographies: For instance, both [k] and [q] (velar and postvelar stops) are pronounced as fricatives in certain positions ([x] and [χ]). In many texts both are written as /j/ (or sometimes /h/) if pronounced as fricatives. This introduces new ambiguities, for instance, a root written as *sajsa* could be *saqsa* - 'certain variety of corn' or *saksa* - 'satisfied,full'. In order to avoid additional ambiguities resulting from an analysis with relaxed orthographic rules, the transducer with the additional orthographic rules handles only word forms that were not recognized by the standard normalizer.

As most Quechua texts contain Spanish words, we included two additional finite state transducers that recognize Quechua words with Spanish roots.[4]. The first one recognizes only word forms with correctly written Spanish roots, whereas the second transducer includes several rules that allow for an alternative spelling of the Spanish words (e.g. /c/ might be written as /k/ in a Quechua text). Furthermore, we implemented a guesser that attempts to split word forms into morphemes if the root is unknown. In order to prevent highly unlikely analyses, we restrict the guessing to roots of at least two syllables and with at least one Quechua suffix attached.

The five transducers are joined in a cascade: If the normalizer fails to analyze a word, the Spanish transducer is invoked. If this fails as well, the word is passed on to the second normalizer with relaxed orthography. If the word form has still no analysis, the second Spanish transducer with relaxed orthography attempts to find an analysis. Finally, if all transducers failed, the word is handed to the guesser. One of the texts used for evaluation, a story called *El joven que se subió al cielo* (Lira, 1990) contains relatively few words with Spanish roots, but in the other text, the biography of Quechua native speaker Gregorio Condori Mamani, almost every sentence contains at least one word with a Spanish root. In this case, the Spanish transducer makes a considerable difference: coverage increases by $\sim$22%, see Table 3. Furthermore, we tested the morphological analyzers on a third text, *Cancionero*, with an even more inconsistent spelling of Quechua words. The *Cancionero* contains religious (catholic) songs written in a 'Spanish' orthography, see the 'Spanish' example in Table 1. The restrictive Quechua and Spanish analyzers recognize only half of the word forms in this text, but the transducers with broader orthographic rules ('relax') increase the number of analyzed tokens to 96%, see Table 3.

## 5 Disambiguation

Given the fact that a Quechua word form can contain more than one morphological ambiguity, the disambiguation has to be done in several steps. The simplest approach is to disambiguate each word form from 'left to right':

- disambiguate the root (nominal vs. verbal)
- disambiguate nominalizing and verbalizing suffixes
- disambiguate verbal suffixes[5]

[4]The lexicon contains all the Spanish lemmas, except function words, from FreeLing (Padró and Stanilovsky, 2012)

[5]There are no ambiguous sequences within the nominal suffixes, therefore the third step involves only verbal suffixes.

```
suwa   suwa[NRoot][=ladrón]

papanchikta   papa[NRoot][=patata][--]nchik[NPers][+1.Pl.Incl.Poss][--]ta[Cas][+Acc]

tukunqa   tuku[NRoot][=lechuza][--]n[NPers][+3.Sg.Poss][--]qa[Amb][+Top]
tukunqa   tuku[VRoot][=acabar]][--]n[VPers][+3.Sg.Subj][--]qa[Amb][+Top]
tukunqa   tuku[VRoot][=acabar][--]nqa[VPers][+3.Sg.Subj.Fut]
```

Figure 1: Ambiguous Morphological Analysis for Example 3

| possible lemmas | case | possible root tags | possible morph tags |
|---|---|---|---|
| suwa | lc | NRoot | - |
| papa | lc | NRoot | +1.Pl.Incl.Poss, +Acc |
| tuku | lc | NRoot, VRoot | +3.Sg.Poss, +Top, +3.Sg.Subj, +3.Sg.Subj.Fut |

Table 4: Features for Disambiguation with Wapiti, Example 3

- disambiguate independent suffixes

We use Wapiti (Lavergne et al., 2010), a toolkit for sequence labelling that includes an implementation of conditional random fields, in order to train 4 crf models (one model for each step). We decided to use conditional random fields, as the task of morphology disambiguation is in many ways similar to PoS tagging. There is an inter-dependency between the labels: The decision which label a given instance should receive depends to certain extent on the labels of the previous *n* instances.

The training material consists of two Quechua texts that were analyzed with the xfst tools (see section 4) and then manually disambiguated: the biography of Quechua native speaker Gregorio Condori Mamani (Valderrama Fernandez and Escalante Gutierrez, 1977), that contains about 2500 sentences, and some stories from a collection (Lira, 1990), that amount to about 300 sentences.

### 5.1 Model 1: Disambiguation of Ambiguous Roots

Some Quechua roots can be used nominally or verbally without derivation, see Example 1 and 2. The disambiguation of roots can be regarded as PoS tagging with a very small tagset. Consider the following example (taken from a story in (Lira, 1990)):

(3) *..suwa papa -nchik -ta tuku -nqa..*
thief potato -1P.ps -Acc end -3S.Fut
'[..] the thief will take all our potatoes [..] (lit. 'the thief will end our potatoes')

The root *tuku-* 'to end' is ambiguous: *tuku-* can also be a nominal root with the meaning 'owl'. Furthermore, the sequence *-nqa* is ambiguous, apart from the 3rd singular future form, it could be a combination of *-n*, '3rd singular subject' or '3rd singular possessive', and *-qa*, 'topic', see Fig. 1 with the output of the xfst analyzer for this example. In a first step, the type of the root has to be determined, the ambiguity of *-nqa* is only relevant if the root is verbal and will be postponed for later. In order to disambiguate the root with Wapiti, every token needs to be converted into a set of features (an instance) extracted from the xfst output, see Table 4. The words *suwa* and *papanchikta* are not ambiguous and therefore have only one possible root tag, whereas *tukunqa* has two possible root tags: VRoot and NRoot. Model 1 will assign one of them as class label, considering the features and the context of the given token. Wapiti allows pre-labeled input data, therefore, we can already set the label of the unambiguous words *suwa* and *papanchikta*. Note that the instances do not contain the full word form; due to the small size of our training corpus, using full word forms leads to increased data sparseness and impairs the results.

### 5.2 Model 2: Disambiguation of Nominalizing and Verbalizing Suffixes

Even after the disambiguation of the root type, the final word form can still be either nominal or verbal, as certain nominalizing and verbalizing suffixes are homophonous with verbal or nominal morphemes.

Consider the following examples:

(4) *wasi -cha -y*
house -Fact(VS) -Inf(NS)/2.Imp
'to build a house' or 'build a house!'

*wasi -cha -y*
house -Dim -1S.ps
'my small house, cottage'

(5) *rikhu -sqa -yki*
see -Perf(NS) -2S.ps
'the one you saw, your seeing'

*rikhu -sqayki*
see -1S>2S.Fut
'I will see you'

The suffix *-cha* attached to a nominal root can be either a diminutive or a factitive suffix ('make'): With the diminutive, the resulting word form is still a noun, whereas the factitive suffix produces a verb. In total, model 2 handles eight different cases of ambiguous verbalizing/nominalizing vs. verbal/nominal suffixes. The features in models 2-4 are essentially the same as those in model 1 (see Table 4), but of course the root type is no longer ambiguous, consequently there is only one root tag. With models 2-4, we classify only words that exhibit a verbalizing/nominalizing vs. nominal/verbal ambiguity, whereas words that are unambiguous for the particular model receive a dummy label ('none').

### 5.3 Model 3: Disambiguation of Verbal Morphology

In the next step, we disambiguate six possible ambiguities in verb forms. One of the ambiguities in question is the sequence *-nqa* from example 3: After applying model 1, we know that the root *tuku* in *tukunqa* is verbal, but *-nqa* can still be either the 3rd singular future form or a combination of 3rd singular present and topic marker, see example 6. Other ambiguities of this type involve *-sun*, which can be either the imperative or future form of the first plural inclusive, as well as the sequence *-sqaykiku*, which can be either the indirect past or future form of the first plural exclusive acting on a 2nd singular person.

(6) *tuku -nqa*
end -3S.Fut
'he will end'

*tuku -n -qa*
end -3S -Top
'he ends'

(7) *llamk'a -sun*
work -1Pl.incl.Fut
'we will work'

*llamk'a -sun*
work -1Pl.incl.Imp
'let's work'

(8) *qhawa -sqaykiku*
look -1Pl.excl.>2S
'we (excl.) watch you'

*qhawa -sqa -ykiku*
look -IPst -1Pl.excl
'we (excl.) watched [they say]'

### 5.4 Model 4: Disambiguation of Independent Suffixes

Model 4 disambiguates ambiguities that concern independent suffixes. None of these potential ambiguities occur in all dialects and orthographies, but all of them concern the normalization and are therefore important. There are 3 types of ambiguities that relate to independent suffixes:

The most common case involves the suffix *-n*, when the word form is nominal and *-n* follows a vowel: in this case, *-n* can be the 3rd singular possessive, or it can be the allomorph of the evidential suffix *-mi*. The latter is written as *-m* in the standard orthography, as well as in texts written in Ayacucho Quechua, but occurs as *-n* in many texts written in Cuzco and Bolivian Quechua, see Example 9. A further ambiguity that occurs only in Cuzco and Bolivian Quechua concerns the sequence *-pis*: *-pis* can be the additive suffix (in Ayacucho Quechua always *-pas*) or a combination of the locative suffix *-pi* and the evidential suffix *-s*, see Example 10. The third ambiguity of this type concerns Spanish words that end in *-s*: In this case, *-s* can be an evidential suffix, but it can also be the Spanish plural[6], see Example 11.

[6] In certain Bolivian dialects *-s* is also used on native roots as plural suffix, see the Bolivian word *p'achasta* (normalized *p'achakunata*) in Table 1.

| | | | gregorio | joven |
|---|---|---|---|---|
| model 1 | root tag | Wapiti | **95.35** | **85.71** |
| | | baseline | 65.12 | 72.62 |
| model 2 | NS/VS | Wapiti | **97.44** | **87.88** |
| | | baseline | 80.49 | 17.47 |
| model 3 | verbal s. | Wapiti | 85.71 | 66.67 |
| | | baseline | **88.89** | **75.00** |
| model 4 | independent s. | Wapiti | **85.37** | **86.11** |
| | | baseline | 64.10 | 50.00 |

Table 5: Evaluation: Precision of the Morphological Disambiguation Steps

(9) *wasi -n*
house -DirE
'house'
*wasi -n*
house -3S.ps
'his house'

(10) *chay -pis*
this -Add
'also this'
*chay -pi -s*
this -Loc -IndE
'there [they say]'

(11) *derechu -s*
right -IndE
'right [they say]'
*derechus*
rights
'rights'

## 6 Evaluation

We used the same test sets as for the evaluation of the morphological analysis in section 4: The last 72 sentences from the autobiography of Gregorio Condori Mamani (Valderrama Fernandez and Escalante Gutierrez, 1977), and the Andean story *El joven que se subió al cielo* from (Lira, 1990) with about 250 sentences. Both test texts were excluded from the training set.

Table 5 illustrates the percentage of correctly disambiguated words with the particular ambiguity for each step. Note that there were only a handful test cases for model 3 (verbal suffixes) in both texts, therefore, the results for this step might not be accurate. Furthermore, the number of instances extracted from the training material for model 3 is smaller than for the other models, as these types of ambiguities are relatively rare. For the normalization, errors in model 3 do not affect the outcome, as these ambiguities have no effect on the surface forms in the standard orthography. Considering for instance example 6, *-nqa* will be *-nqa* in the standard, irrespective of whether the analysis is *-n -qa* or *-nqa*.

Table 6 contains the evaluation of the whole texts. Although the percentage of tokens with a wrong morphological analysis is almost the same in both texts, the total number of correctly analyzed words is lower in the biography. This is due to the fact that this text contains many words with Spanish roots, sometimes with 'quechuized' spelling. Many of these words were not recognized by the xfst analyzer and were therefore not normalized.

The baseline for both Table 5 and 6 was calculated based on the frequencies of the forms in the training material: The baseline shows the results that we obtain if we disambiguate the test texts choosing always the most frequent class in every decision. The biggest difference as opposed to the Wapiti models is that with this approach, we do not consider any context information. As you can see in Table 5, Wapiti outperforms the baseline in every step except for model 3, where the training instances are too sparse. There is a considerable difference in the baseline for the two test texts (see Table 6): on the biography, the baseline is much higher. This is due to the fact that the largest part of the training material is part of the same book, therefore the probability distribution of the individual classes in this test text correlates better with the frequencies calculated from the training material. While the conditional random fields improve the disambiguation on the test set similar to training material only slightly compared to the baseline (+2%), the effect they have on the results for a test set from a different text is considerable: >10%. Table 6 also contains the results obtained with the RFTagger (Schmid and Laws, 2008) and Morfette (Grzegorz et al., 2008) for comparison. The main difference between our approach and the morphological taggers is that the latter analyze and label the complete word form at once, whereas with our approach, we disambiguate and normalize each word in several steps, proceeding from left to right. The tagset used by the morphological taggers is thus much more fine-grained, as each tag contains the

| | *El joven que subió al cielo* | | *Gregorio Condori Mamani* | |
|---|---|---|---|---|
| total sentences: | 258 | | 72 | |
| total token | 1865 | | 1015 | |
| punctuation marks: | 567 | | 171 | |
| xfst failures: | 9 | 0.48% | 25 | 2.46% |
| total word forms | 1298 | | 844 | |
| correct analysis: | 1252 | **96.46%** | 789 | **93.48%** |
| wrong analysis: | 33 | 2.54% | 17 | 2.01% |
| guessed, no analysis in gold: | 4 | 0.31% | 6 | 0.71% |
| ambiguous words: | 282 | 21.73% | 127 | 15.05% |
| still ambiguous: | 0 | | 7 | 5.51% |
| correct of ambig.: | 249 | 88.30% | 103 | 81.10% |
| wrong of ambig.: | 33 | 11.70% | 17 | 13.39% |
| morphological tagging (tag whole word form): | | | | |
| RFTagger (bigrams): | | 65.49% | | 72.21% |
| Morfette: | | 65.1% | | 78.32% |
| baseline (most frequent morphemes): | | 85.98% | | 91% |

Table 6: Evaluation: Disambiguated Texts

morphology of the whole word. The results show clearly that our training corpus is too small to achieve satisfactory results with morphological tagging. As mentioned before, not all ambiguities are relevant for the normalization. In fact, many morphological ambiguities are not relevant for the conversion to the standard orthography, therefore, the number of correctly normalized forms is higher than the proportion of correctly disambiguated words from Table 6. In the text *El joven que subió al cielo*, the percentage of correctly normalized words amounts to 99.61%, whereas for the biography of Gregorio Condori Mamani, we achieve only 98.93%.

## 7 Conclusions

As standardized spelling is an indispensable prerequisite for any statistical processing, we built a pipeline to normalize Quechua texts through morphological analysis and disambiguation. The morphological analysis includes 5 cascaded transducers, two with Quechua root lexica and two with Spanish root lexica, as Spanish loan words occur very frequently in Quechua texts. In every pair of transducers, the first one follows a relatively strict orthography, whereas the second one has a set of phonological rules that allow for more variation in the spelling of word forms. Furthermore, the cascade includes a guesser that attempts to split word forms into morphemes if all the other transducers failed to do so. The transducers rewrite the individual morphemes according to the Unified Southern Quechua orthography (Cerrón-Palomino, 1994), but many words involve morphological ambiguities that might affect the normalized form. In order to choose the correct analysis, we conduct a morphological disambiguation with conditional random fields. We disambiguate the Quechua words in 4 steps, with four models trained to classify the different types of ambiguities. Finally, we generate the normalized word forms from the now disambiguated sequence of morphemes. Our initial results are comparable to morphological disambiguation on Turkish texts, despite the fact that we have a much smaller training corpus ($\sim$ 2800 sentences, compared to over 50,000 (Görgün and Yildiz, 2011) and 45,000 sentences (Sak et al., 2007)). A possible explanation is that Turkish morphology is more complex: Turkish has more productive suffixes than Quechua, and there are relatively complex morpho-phonological rules that determine word formation, such as two dimensional vowel harmony and context-sensitive realizations of consonants (Oflazer, 1994). Quechua on the other hand, is a very regular agglutinative language.

Certain parts of the disambiguation pipeline suffer from data sparseness, in fact, at least one possible ambiguous sequence never occurred in our training corpus and can therefore not be disambiguated, see section 5.4. As the annotation of our treebanks proceeds, we will have more manually disambiguated text, since the syntax trees are built on morphemes, not on whole words. With more training material, the accuracy of the disambiguation and normalization process should increase.

## References


Willem F. H. Adelaar and Pieter Muysken. 2004. *The Languages of the Andes*. Cambridge Language Surveys. Cambridge University Press, Cambridge, UK.

Willem F. H. Adelaar. 1987. Aymarismos en el quechua de Puno. *Indiana*, 11:223–231.

Rodolfo Cerrón-Palomino. 1994. *Quechua sureño, diccionario unificado quechua-castellano, castellano-quechua*. Biblioteca Nacional del Perú, Lima.

Onur Görgün and Olcay Taner Yildiz. 2011. A Novel Approach to Morphological Disambiguation for Turkish. In Erol Gelenbe, Ricardo Lent, and Georgia Sakellari, editors, *Computer and Information Sciences II - 26th International Symposium on Computer and Information Sciences*, pages 77–83, London, UK. Springer.

Chrupala Grzegorz, Georgiana Dinu, and Josef van Genabith. 2008. Learning Morphology with Morfette. In Khalid Choukri Bente Maegaard Joseph Mariani Jan Odijk Stelios Piperidis Daniel Tapias Nicoletta Calzolari (Conference Chair), editor, *Proceedings of the Sixth International Conference on Language Resources and Evaluation (LREC'08)*, Marrakech, Morocco. European Language Resources Association (ELRA).

Dilek Z. Hakkani-Tür, Kemal Oflazer, and Gökhan Tür. 2002. Statistical Morphological Disambiguation for Agglutinative Languages. *Computer and the Humanities*, 36:381–410.

Thomas Lavergne, Olivier Cappé, and François Yvon. 2010. Practical Very Large Scale CRFs. In *Proceedings the 48th Annual Meeting of the Association for Computational Linguistics (ACL)*, pages 504–513, Uppsala, Sweden. Association for Computational Linguistics.

Jorge Lira. 1990. *Cuentos del Alto Urubamba*. Centro de Estudios Regionales Andinos "Bartolomé de las Casas", Cuzco, Peru.

Kemal Oflazer. 1994. Two-level Description of Turkish Morphology. *Literary and Linguistic Computing*, 9(2).

Lluís Padró and Evgeny Stanilovsky. 2012. FreeLing 3.0: Towards Wider Multilinguality. In *Proceedings of the Language Resources and Evaluation Conference (LREC 2012)*, Istanbul, Turkey, May. ELRA.

Haşim Sak, Tunga Güngör, and Murat Saraçlar. 2007. Morphological disambiguation of Turkish text with perceptron algorithm. In A. Gelbukh, editor, *Proceedings of the International Conference on Intelligent Text Processing and Computational Linguistics*, pages 107–118, Mexico City, Mexico. Springer.

Helmut Schmid and Florian Laws. 2008. Estimation of conditional probabilities with decision trees and an application to fine-grained POS tagging. In *Proceedings of the 22nd International Conference on Computational Linguistics*, volume 1 of *COLING '08*, pages 777–784. Association for Computational Linguistics.

Ricardo Valderrama Fernandez and Carmen Escalante Gutierrez. 1977. *Gregorio Condori Mamani - Autobiografía*. Biblioteca de la Tradición Oral Andina. Centro de Estudios Rurales Andinos 'Bartolomé de las Casas', Cuzco, Peru.

Alfredo Quiroz Villarroel. 2000. *Gramática Quechua*. Ministerio de Educación, Cultura y Deportes, Fondo de las Naciones Unidas para la Infancia (UNICEF), Bolivia.

# The *Varitext* platform and the *Corpus des variétés nationales du français* (CoVaNa-FR) as resources for the study of French from a pluricentric perspective

**Sascha Diwersy**
Institute of Romance Languages /
Centre de Recherche Interdisciplinaire sur la France et la Francophonie (CIFRA)
University of Cologne
sascha.diwersy@uni-koeln.de

**Abstract**

This paper reports on the francophone corpus archive *Corpus des variétés nationales du français* (CoVaNa-FR) and the lexico-statistical platform *Varitext*. It outlines the design and data format of the samples as well as presenting various usage scenarios related to the applications featured by the platform's toolbox.

## 1 Introduction

This contribution presents the francophone corpus archive *Corpus des variétés nationales du français* (CoVaNa-FR) and its hosting platform *Varitext*.

The paper is structured as follows. Section 2 will outline the rationale behind the corpus archive, its composition and its data format. In section 3, we will then introduce the toolbox implemented by the Varitext platform, by illustrating some of its functionalities and giving brief sketches of corresponding usage scenarios. Section 4 provides a brief summary and discusses possible directions for the future development of the resources presented in this paper.

## 2 The CoVaNa-FR corpus archive

### 2.1 Rationale and composition of the CoVaNa-FR

The creation of the *Corpus des variétés nationales du français* (CoVaNa-FR) is motivated by the aim of offering a large-scale resource to researchers working on the French language from a pluricentric perspective. It is thus primarily designed to provide methodological support for investigations in the French tradition of 'lexicologie différentielle' ('variationist differential lexicography') focusing on elements of endonormative differentiation, i.e. the emergence of regionally specific norms compared to a supposed metropolitan standard variety of French (for studies on various francophone regions, see Rézeau 2007, Thibault 2008; for studies especially focusing on Subsaharan Africa and the Maghreb, cf. Queffélec 1997, Lafage 2002, Naffati and Queffélec 2004, Nzesse 2009, to mention just a few examples of a sizable body of literature). Alongside the lexico-statistical toolbox implemented by the *Varitext* platform (cf. Section 3 below), the design of the CoVaNa-FR goes beyond the rather conventional lexicographic rationale of the lexicological framework just mentioned and can be seen as a contribution to meeting the desideratum, voiced by Stein (2003:14f), of carrying out large-scale investigations on Francophone varieties using contemporary corpus linguistic methods. In this regard, the CoVaNa-FR differs from existing French corpora such as *Frantext* (cf. ATILF-CNRS), *Québétext* (cf. Trésor de la langue française au Québec) and *Suistext* (cf. Trésor des Vocabulaires francophones Neuchâtel) in offering broad regional coverage (bundling samples from Africa, Europe and North America), a wider range of query functionalities and free access (large parts of *Frantext* not being accessible free of charge and *Suistext* only being available locally at its hosting institution, cf. Thibault 2007:480). Apart from corpus linguistic uses, the CoVaNa-FR could also be a valuable resource for research on the automatic classification of language varieties, which has recently aroused considerable interest in the field of NLP (for relevant contributions see, amongst others, Ranaivo-Malancon 2006, Ljubešić et al. 2007, Tiedemann and Ljubešić 2012,





*Proceedings of the First Workshop on Applying NLP Tools to Similar Languages, Varieties and Dialects*, pages 48–57, Dublin, Ireland, August 23 2014.

Trieschnigg et al. 2012, Zampieri and Gebre 2012, Tan et al. 2014). It should be noted, though, that in accordance with copyright restrictions, the CoVaNa-FR is not directly available for download and can only be consulted via the GUI of the password-protected *Varitext* platform.

Due to its focus on endonormative differentiation, the CoVaNa-FR is less balanced with respect to genre than similar corpora for other languages such as the *International Corpus of English* (ICE, cf. Greenbaum 1996), the *Corpus of Contemporary American English* (COCA, cf. Davies 2009), the *Corpus de Referencia del Español Actual* (CREA, cf. Real Academia Española), the *Corpus del Español* (cf. Davies 2002) or the *Corpus do Português* (cf. Davies 2014).[1] The initial version of the CoVaNa-FR, accessible on the *Varitext* platform, is made up of journalistic texts published by national newspapers in different Francophone countries in Africa, Europe and North America. The choice of national newspapers as primary sources is based on the assumption made by Glessgen (2007:97) that these are particularly representative of contemporary standard varieties ("les grands journaux [...] reflètent assez bien les variétés standard actuelles"). Work is also underway on the extension of the CoVaNa-FR, such that future versions will include a subcorpus of fiction and academic texts. In its present state, the CoVaNa-FR is divided into 11 samples collected across a span of at least two years and categorized by regional parameters as listed in Table 1.

| Sample code | Country | Sources | Number of word tokens[2] |
|---|---|---|---|
| DZA | Algeria | El Watan, La Tribune d'Alger | 45,600,000 |
| CAM | Cameroon | Cameroon Tribune, La Nouvelle Expression, Mutations | 46,500,000 |
| CAN | Canada (Québec) | Le Devoir, Le Soleil | 53,500,000 |
| COD | Congo (D.R.C.) | Le Potentiel | 27,300,000 |
| FRA | France | Le Figaro, Le Monde | 53,300,000 |
| CIV | Ivory Coast | Fraternité Matin, Notre Voie | 18,800,000 |
| MLI | Mali | Aurore, L'Essor, L'Indépendant | 25,100,000 |
| MAR | Morocco | Aujourd'hui le Maroc, Le Matin du Sahara | 43,600,000 |
| SEN | Senegal | Le Soleil, Wal Fadjri | 27,100,000 |
| CHE | Switzerland | Le Temps, La Tribune de Genève | 28,000,000 |
| TUN | Tunisia | La Presse, Le Quotidien, Le Temps | 50,900,000 |
| Total | | | 419,700,000 |

Tab. 1: Composition of the CoVaNa-FR (on-line version accessible via the *Varitext* platform).

The compilation of the overall corpus archive outlined in Table 1 has been carried out according to the requirement that each country be represented by a sample comprising at least two newspapers with articles from the same (or similar) two years. It should be noted, though, that some samples do not fully meet these guidelines, as is the case with the corpora representing Algeria and Canada (containing two newspapers from single and different years) or the sample representing the Democratic Republic of Congo (containing three years of only one newspaper).

## 2.2 Processing format of the CoVaNa-FR

All documents in the CoVaNa-FR corpus are formatted in eXtensible Markup Language (XML) with the structural units (i) subcorpus, (ii) text, (iii) paragraph, and (iv) sentence. The texts are annotated with (i) part-of-speech (PoS) tags, (ii) lemmas and (iii) dependency-parses using the commercially licensed Connexor annotation tool (Tapanainen and Järvinen 1997). The corpus files are in standard CWB input format (cf. Evert and Hardie 2011:5f) with XML tags and each token record (one surface form + associated TAB-delimited token-level annotations) appearing on separate lines.

The set of XML tagged structural units is specified by the DTD given in Figure 1. Note that the top level <corpus>...</corpus> element defines one country related sample and that each subcorpus corresponds to a one year newspaper volume. The element attributes which are provided inside the query

[1]See the projects' web sites at `http://ice-corpora.net/ICE/INDEX.HTM`, `http://corpus.byu.edu/coca/`, `http://corpus.rae.es/creanet.html`, `http://www.corpusdelespanol.org` and `http://www.corpusdoportugues.org` respectively.

[2]Numbers are rounded down to the nearest 100,000.

platform as metadata categories for corpus partitioning or the description of concordance extracts are highlighted in boldface.

```
<!DOCTYPE varcorpus [
<!-- country related sample -->
<!ELEMENT corpus (subcorpus)+>
<!-- one year newspaper volume -->
<!ELEMENT subcorpus (text)+>
<!-- newspaper article -->
<!ELEMENT text (p)+>
<!-- paragraph -->
<!ELEMENT p (s)+>
<!-- sentence -->
<!ELEMENT s (#PCDATA)>
<!ATTLIST corpus                    id CDATA #REQUIRED
                                    name CDATA #REQUIRED
                                    code CDATA #REQUIRED
                                    geocode CDATA #REQUIRED
                                    geoname CDATA #REQUIRED
>
<!ATTLIST subcorpus                 id CDATA #REQUIRED
                                    name CDATA #REQUIRED
                                    code CDATA #REQUIRED
                                    source CDATA #REQUIRED
                                    year CDATA #REQUIRED
>
<!ATTLIST text                      id CDATA #REQUIRED
                                    title CDATA #REQUIRED
                                    author CDATA #REQUIRED
                                    date CDATA #REQUIRED
                                    section CDATA #REQUIRED
>
<!ATTLIST p                         id CDATA #REQUIRED
                                    type CDATA #IMPLIED
>
<!ATTLIST s                         id CDATA #REQUIRED>

]>
```

Fig. 1: DTD specifying the structural elements of the country-related samples in the CoVaNa-FR corpus archive.

As for the token rows, their core structure is basically defined according to the so-called CoNLL format, introduced on the occasion of the correspondent 2007 shared task on dependency parsing (cf. Nivre et al. 2007:916). For rather technical reasons, this structure has been extended by a number of fields whose purpose is to optimize the processing of queries exploring the dependency relations annotated in the corpus. The fields in question are marked by an asterisk in the following table, which outlines the overall structure of the token records:

| Field name | Description |
|---|---|
| id | sentence internal numerical token identifier (counter starting at 1 for each sentence) |
| word | surface form or punctuation sign |
| lemma | lemma corresponding to the surface form |
| cpos | coarse grained part of speech (PoS) |
| pos | fine grained PoS + morphological features |
| headid | token identifier of the syntactic head |
| headoffset * | distance between syntactic head and token |
| deprel | syntactic function of the token in the dependency relation to its head |
| headword * | surface form of the syntactic head |
| headlemma * | lemma of the syntactic head |
| headcpos * | coarse grained PoS of the syntactic head |
| headpos * | fine grained PoS + morphological features of the syntactic head |
| pmarkword * | surface form of the function word (adposition or conjunction) dependent on the token[3] |
| pmarklemma * | lemma of the function word dependent on the token |
| pmarkcpos * | PoS of the function word dependent on the token |

Tab. 2: Structure of the token records contained by the corpus files.

The 11 country specific samples making up the present online version of the CoVaNa-FR (see Table 1 above) have been encoded by means of the IMS Open Corpus Workbench (CWB, cf. Evert and Hardie 2011; see also the project's web site `http://cwb.sourceforge.net/`), the total size of the corresponding index files summing up to 58,4 GB of disk space. The components of CWB are integrated as main query processing tools in the *Varitext* platform, which will be described in more detail in the following section.

## 3 The *Varitext* platform

### 3.1 Design and GUI

*Varitext* is a web-based platform (cf. `http://syrah.uni-koeln.de/varitext/` and `http://extranet-ldi.univ-paris13.fr/varitext/`) providing free-of-charge access to the CoVaNa-FR corpus archive presented in section 2. As is indicated by its name, it is open to host corpora for other languages compiled according to the same rationale of large-scale variationist research in a pluricentric perspective. Work has already been completed on the prototype of a hispanophone corpus archive, which will be released via *Varitext* in the near future. There are also plans to compile similar resources for Portuguese, Russian and Arabic.

The toolbox implemented by the *Varitext* platform is built upon three major software components: CWB for query processing, the UCS toolkit version 0.6 (cf. Evert 2005, the software being available at `http://www.collocations.de/software.html`) for cooccurrence analysis and R (R Core Team 2014) for statistical computing and plotting.

The platform's user interface allows fairly complex queries in terms of subsampling and the formulation of search expressions. Using the menu options relating to the available metadata categories (such as country code, newspaper volume or thematic section), it is possible to create subcorpora and partitions with different degrees of granularity, as is shown by Fig. 2:

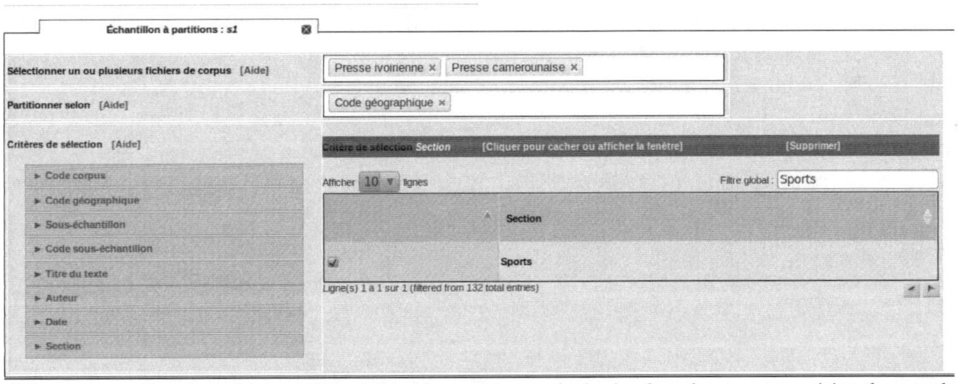


Fig. 2: Using menu options to build a partition defined by country on the basis of a subcorpus comprising the samples representing Cameroon and the Ivory Coast and filtered by the thematic section 'Sports'

As for the formulation of query expressions, the interface integrates a sub-menu to set up search constraints flexibly by combining several token properties (such as lemma, PoS or syntactic function; see the data model outlined in table 2 above) and / or assembling sequences of various length (see Figure 3).

[3]The annotation model of Connexor treats adpositions and conjunctions as markers dependent on content words (verbs, nouns, adjectives, adverbs).

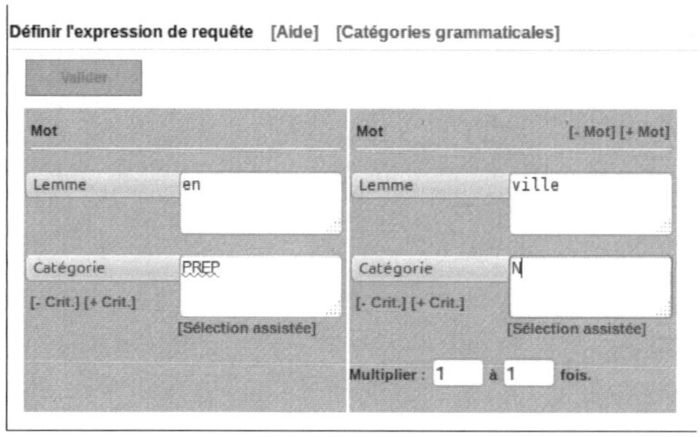


Fig. 3: Using the platform's interface to build up a query expression matching the sequence *en ville* ("in town")

In its present state, the *Varitext* platform features as its standard applications a KWIC concordancer and a set of tools for frequency computing, key word analysis and collocation processing, the latter of which will be outlined in some detail below. Future releases of the platform will also include advanced functionalities of statistical computing and plotting that are currently under development and testing and which will be briefly sketched at the end of this section.

## 3.2 Usage Scenario: Sample Specific Frequencies and Lexical Differences

### 3.2.1 *chaussure* vs. *soulier*

One of the platform's standard applications besides KWIC concordancing is the computation of sample specific frequencies and key word analysis. In a corpus-based perspective, these methods can be used for instance as diagnostics to test the results of 'differential' lexicology. Similar to Thibault's (2007) study on some lexical specificities of Canadian (Quebec), Swiss and metropolitan standard French, it would be possible to analyze geographical lexical variants in terms of their frequency distribution. An example also mentioned by Thibault (2007:468-475) is provided by the nouns *chaussure* and *soulier* ("shoe"), with *soulier* being regarded as regional variant especially of Canadian French (cf. the reference dictionary *Le Petit Robert* (Rey-Debove and Rey 2006) s.v. SOULIER). A key word analysis based on the samples representing Canada/Quebec (geographical code: CAN), France (FRA) and Switzerland (CHE) yields the log-likelihood ratio (LL) scores given by the following bar plots in Fig. 4 (for the use of the log likelihood ratio in key word analysis see Rayson 2003). The computation has been carried out on a 2x2 basis, with one sample as the main corpus and the combination of the remaining two as the reference corpus.

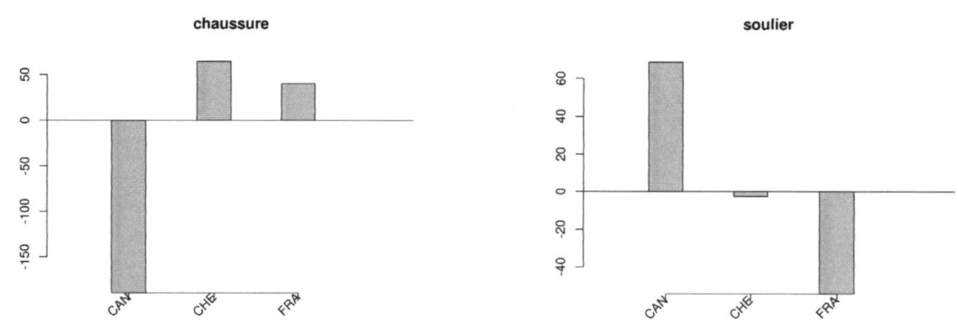


Fig. 4: LL scores for the nouns *chaussure* and *soulier* in the samples representing Canada/Quebec, Switzerland and France

These figures indicate that there are clear-cut distributional divergences, with the two nouns being respectively under- and overrepresented in the samples related to Quebec and France. This seems to suggest that *soulier* is still part of the French standard as it evolves in Quebec, or at least in its national newspapers, which qualifies to some extent the findings of Thibault (2007:474), according to which Quebec newspaper language is moving towards greater conformity with French metropolitan usage in the case of *chaussure* and *soulier*. It should be noted that Thibault only considers the relative frequencies of the two items within each national sample. Applying this approach to our corpus data would provide no more than a confirmation of Thibault's findings. In light of the aforementioned key word analysis, though, there is sufficient evidence to conclude that, in Quebec French, the relationship between the two variants is rather more complex and should be subjected to a more detailed analysis in terms of collocational distribution. One promising approach in this respect would be Hoey's (2005) lexical priming theory.

### 3.2.2 Quebec Specific Lexical Items

At this point, it is worth noting that, although major national newspapers might reflect trends of standard varieties quite faithfully (see our reference to Glessgen 2007 in section 2), the data obtained from these sources should be handled with some caution (cf. also Thibault 2007:474). This is of particular importance if we adopt a corpus-driven approach, which involves identifying the most characteristic features in a sample by means of statistical techniques such as key word analysis.

This may be illustrated with the results of a key word analysis contrasting the Quebec subcorpus as a whole with the sample representing France.

| Lemma | Frequency CAN | Frequency FRA | Rel. Freq.[4] CAN | Rel. Freq. FRA | LL score | Rank |
|---|---|---|---|---|---|---|
| Québec | 93269 | 828 | 1740.4 | 15.53 | 120592.82 | 1 |
| Montréal | 44257 | 472 | 825.83 | 8.85 | 56578.51 | 2 |
| Canada | 43612 | 1808 | 813.8 | 33.9 | 47579.89 | 3 |
| ⋮ | ⋮ | ⋮ | ⋮ | ⋮ | ⋮ | ⋮ |
| chum | 1191 | 4 | 22.22 | 0.08 | 1597.32 | 243 |
| ⋮ | ⋮ | ⋮ | ⋮ | ⋮ | ⋮ | ⋮ |
| magasiner | 183 | 1 | 3.41 | 0.02 | 241.78 | 1987 |
| ⋮ | ⋮ | ⋮ | ⋮ | ⋮ | ⋮ | ⋮ |
| placoter | 18 | 0 | 0.34 | 0 | 24.87 | 10744 |
| ⋮ | ⋮ | ⋮ | ⋮ | ⋮ | ⋮ | ⋮ |
| paqueter | 13 | 0 | 0.24 | 0 | 17.96 | 13473 |
| ⋮ | ⋮ | ⋮ | ⋮ | ⋮ | ⋮ | ⋮ |

Tab. 3: Words specific to the Quebec sub-corpus in contrast with the sample representing France.

The data given in Table 3 show that the most specific items are proper nouns closely related to socio-cultural context, whereas words which clearly qualify as Quebecisms, such as *chum* ("friend, pal"), *magasiner* ("to go shopping"), *placoter* ("to chat"; cf. Poirier 1995:32) or *paqueter* ("to pack"; cf. Poirier ibid) only come at lower ranks, their log-likelihood scores being nonetheless highly significant.

## 3.3 Usage Scenario: Lexical Cooccurrences and Collocational Variation

The second main application provided by the platform's toolbox is collocation analysis. We will illustrate this functionality by considering the example of the causative support verb *occasionner* ("to occasion sth") and the semantic associations instantiated by its most significant collocates within each of the

[4]Figures are given in terms of token per million.

samples making up the CoVaNa-Fr corpus archive.

The following cross table which is based on the lexicogram (defined as list of collocates specified by association scores; see Tournier 1987) computed for *occasionner* displays some of the nouns in direct object position significantly collocating with this verb in terms of the log-likelihood ratio (the use of the latter as an association measure for collocation analysis having been proposed, amongst others, by Dunning 1993).

| Collocate | CAN[5] | CHE | CIV | CMR | COD | DZA | FRA | MAR | MLI | SEN | TUN |
|---|---|---|---|---|---|---|---|---|---|---|---|
| accident | - | - | - | 67.8 | - | 65.4 | - | - | 61.2 | - | - |
| accroissement | - | - | - | - | 68.5 | - | - | - | - | - | - |
| augmentation | - | - | - | - | 52.4 | - | - | - | - | - | - |
| baisse | - | - | - | - | 41.7 | - | - | - | 59.5 | - | - |
| coût | 90.3 | - | - | - | - | - | - | - | - | - | - |
| dégât | - | 87.6 | - | 91.8 | 268.5 | 1059.3 | 62.3 | 255.7 | 157.6 | 208.5 | 143.9 |
| perte | 298.8 | 109.4 | 267.8 | 178.0 | 208.8 | 381.4 | 64.9 | 134.1 | 492.9 | 170.5 | 129.7 |
| problème | 62.37 | - | - | - | - | 23.1 | - | - | - | - | 33.1 |

Tab. 4: Significant direct object noun collocates of *occasionner* across all the samples contained by the CoVaNa-FR.

It is easy to see that the combinatorial profile of *occasionner* is essentially characterized by negative semantic prosody throughout all the samples under investigation (for the concept of semantic prosody, see Stubbs 1995 and Xiao and McEnery 2006). At the same time, however, it exhibits some degree of regional variation; in the case of the sub-corpus representing the Congo (COD), for example, there is an additional semantic feature in evidence which may be described as INTENSITY (cf. the collocates *accroissement* ["increase, growth"], *augmentation* ["increase, rise"] and *baisse* ["decrease, fall"]).
A similar statement can be made with regard to the significant noun collocates of *causer* ("to cause"), although in this case it is the Quebec sample which adds more neutral marked elements (*surprise* ["sur-prise"]) to the overall picture. We illustrate this by a means of a plot generated by a correspondence analysis (CA, see Lebart et al. 1998:47ff) performed on the sample specific lexicograms comprising the direct object nouns significantly associated[6] with the verb in question (further examples of using CA to explore the CoVaNa-FR are given by Diwersy and Loiseau forthcoming):

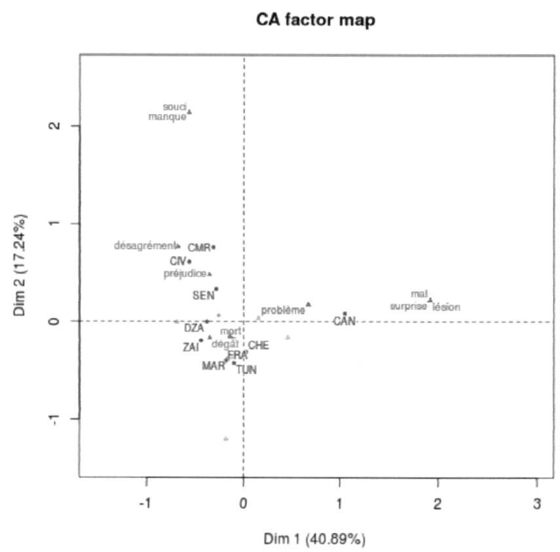


Fig. 5: Plot generated by a CA performed on the country specific lexicograms of *causer*.

[5]Sample name as translated to their corresponding ISO 3166-1 alpha-3 country codes (see the UN Statistic Division's page at `http://unstats.un.org/unsd/methods/m49/m49alpha.htm`).

[6]The collocates used for further processing have been selected according to a frequency threshold of 20 and an LL score threshold of 10.83.

The CA plot[7] given in Fig. 5 highlights in its main (horizontal) dimension the contrast between the Quebec subcorpus and the remaining samples, this contrast being paralleled by the contrast between the noun *surprise* and other items such as *souci* ("worry") and *dégât* ("damage").[8]
Correspondence analysis is a useful technique in providing a condensed view of divergences relating to samples and lexical items. It will be included in the next release of the Varitext platform.

## 4 Conclusion

As the examples in the preceding section have shown, there is considerable scope for using corpus-related techniques (beyond concordancing) to investigate geographical variation from a pluricentric perspective, but researchers must exercise caution when working on the diverse sets of data which can be obtained using the resources outlined in this paper. A major case in point is the composition of the corpus archive and its current restriction to journalistic texts, which may bring about phenomena related to the socio-cultural context rather than the linguistic one (although, from the point of view of media discourse analysis and communication studies, these thematic „side effects" could be of quite some interest).
It should be obvious, then, that our present activities focus on diversifying the corpus resources, especially with regard to other written genres. At the same time, we are engaged in extending the overall text archive to include corpora for different languages, the rationale being to apply the methodological framework implemented by the Varitext platform to linguistic areas other than Francophonia.
This framework is itself undergoing considerable modifications which will lead to the integration of advanced statistical functionalities. At present, our main interest is to enhance the platform's toolbox by implementing several exploratory multivariate techniques, which will be tested in experimental settings that, however, go beyond the narrow focus of this paper.
That said, the development of the corpus archive and of the platform is still in its infancy, and is set to evolve further in various ways and directions. At least, this is what should happen if the community makes good use of it.


## Acknowledgements

The author wishes to thank the reviewers for their valuable comments which helped to clarify the main points of the paper.


## References


ATILF-CNRS. *Base textuelle* FRANTEXT. ATILF-CNRS Nancy & Université de Lorraine. http://www.frantext.fr/.

Mark Davies. 2002. Un corpus anotado de 100.000.000 palabras del español histórico y moderno. *SEPLN 2002* (Sociedad Española para el Procesamiento del Lenguaje Natural), 21–27.

Mark Davies. 2009. The 385+ Million Word Corpus of Contemporary American English (1990-2008+): Design, Architecture, and Linguistic Insights. *International Journal of Corpus Linguistics*, 14: 159–190.

Mark Davies. 2014. Creating and Using the Corpus do Português and the Frequency Dictionary of Portuguese. Tony Berber Sardinha and Telma de Lurdes São Bento Ferreira (eds.): *Working with Portuguese Corpora*. London: Bloomsbury Publishing, 89–110.

Sascha Diwersy and Sylvain Loiseau. Forthcoming. La différenciation du français dans l'espace francophone: l'apport des statistiques lexicales. Kirsten A. Jeppesen Kragh, Jan Lindschouw and Lene Schøsler (eds.): *Les variations diasystématiques dans les langues romanes et leurs interdépendances*. Société de Linguistique Romane.

Ted Dunning. 1993. Accurate methods for the statistics of surprise and coincidence. *Computational Linguistics*, 19(1): 61–74.


[7]The given CA plot has been generated by means of the R package FactoMineR (cf. Husson et al. 2013).

[8]To be more precise, the main dimension (read from right to left) puts into contrast nouns opposed by the features (1) 'neutral' vs. 'negative' (affect) polarity (*surprise* vs. *souci*), (2) 'physical' vs. 'material' damage (*lésion* ["injury, lesion"] vs. *dégât* / *préjudice* ["damage"]) and (3) 'non-lethal' vs. 'lethal' impact (*lésion* vs. *mort* ["death"]).

Stefan Evert. 2005. Empirical research on association measures: The UCS toolkit. *Software demonstration at the Phraseology 2005 Conference*, Louvain-la-Neuve, Belgium. [abstract available at http://purl.org/stefan.evert/PUB/Evert2005phraseology.pdf]

Stefan Evert and Andrew Hardie. 2011. Twenty-first century corpus workbench: Updating a query architecture for the new millennium. *Proceedings of the Corpus Linguistics 2011 Conference*, Birmingham, UK. [pdf version available for download at http://www.birmingham.ac.uk/documents/college-artslaw/corpus/conference-archives/2011/Paper-153.pdf]

Martin-Dietrich Glessgen. 2007. *Linguistique romane, domaine et méthode – Domaines et méthodes en linguistique française et romane*. Paris: Armand Colin.

Sidney Greenbaum (ed.). 1996. *Comparing English Worldwide: The International Corpus of English*. Oxford: Clarendon Press.

Michael Hoey. 2005. *Lexical Priming: A New Theory of Words and Language*. London: Routledge.

François Husson, Julie Josse, Sebastien Lê and Jeremy Mazet. 2013. *FactoMineR: Multivariate Exploratory Data Analysis and Data Mining with R*. http://CRAN.R-project.org/package=FactoMineR.

Suzanne Lafage. 2002. *Le lexique français de Côté-d'Ivoire (Appropriation et créativité)*. Nice: CNRS.

Ludovic Lebart, André Salem and Lisette Berry. 1998. *Exploring Textual Data*. Dordrecht: Springer.

Nikola Ljubešić, Nives Mikelić and Damir Boras. 2007. Language Identification: How to Distinguish Similar Languages? *Proceedings of the 29th International Conference on Information Technology Interfaces*, Zagreb, Croatia.

Habiba Naffati and Ambroise Queffélec. 2004. *Le français en Tunisie*. Nice: CNRS.

Joakim Nivre, Johan Hall, Sandra Kübler, Ryan Mcdonald, Jens Nilsson, Sebastian Riedel, Deniz Yuret. 2007. The CoNLL 2007 Shared Task on Dependency Parsing. *Proceedings of the CoNLL Shared Task Session of EMNLP-CoNLL 2007*, Prague, Czech Republic, 915–932.

Ladislas Nzesse. 2009. *Le français au Cameroun: d'une crise sociopolitique à la vitalité de la langue française (1990-2008)*. Nice: CNRS.

Claude Poirier. 1995. Les variantes topolectales du lexique français: propositions de classement à partir d'exemples québécois. Michel Francard and Danièle Latin (eds.): *Le régionalisme lexical*. Louvain-la-Neuve: De Boeck, 13–56.

Ambroise Queffélec. 1997. *Le français en Centrafrique: lexique et société*. Vanves: Editions Classiques d'Expression Française (EDICEF).

Bali Ranaivo-Malancon. 2006. Automatic identification of close languages - case study: Malay and Indonesian. *ECTI Transactions on Computer and Information Technology* (2): 126–134.

Paul Rayson. 2003. *Matrix: A statistical method and software tool for linguistic analysis through corpus comparison*. Ph.D. thesis, Lancaster University. [pdf version available for download at http://ucrel.lancs.ac.uk/people/paul/publications/phd2003.pdf]

R Core Team. 2014. *R: A language and environment for statistical computing*. R Foundation for Statistical Computing, Vienna, Austria. [http://www.R-project.org/]

Real Academia Española. *Corpus de referencia del español actual*. http://www.rae.es.

Josette Rey-Debove and Alain Rey (eds.). 2006. *Le Nouveau Petit Robert: Dictionnaire alphabétique et analogique de la langue française*. Paris: Dictionnaires Le Robert.

Pierre Rézeau (ed.). 2007. *Richesse du français et géographie linguistique*, volume 1. Louvain-la-Neuve: de Boeck.

Achim Stein. 2003. Lexikalische Kookkurrenz im afrikanischen Französisch. *Zeitschrift für französische Sprach- und Literaturwissenschaft*, 113: 1–17.

Michael Stubbs. 1995. Collocations and semantic profiles: On the cause of the trouble with quantitative studies. *Functions of Language*, 2(1): 23–55.

Liling Tan, Marcos Zampieri, Nikola Ljubešić and Jörg Tiedemann. 2014. Merging Comparable Data Sources for the Discrimination of Similar Languages: The DSL Corpus Collection. *Proceedings of the 7th Workshop on Building and Using Comparable Corpora: Building Resources for Machine Translation Research*, Reykjavik, Iceland.

Pasi Tapanainen and Timo Järvinen. 1997. A non-projective dependency parser. *Proceedings of the 5th Conference on Applied Natural Language Processing*, Washington, DC, 64–74.

André Thibault. 2007. Banques de données textuelles, régionalismes de fréquence et régionalismes négatifs. *ACILPR XXIV*, volume 1, 467–480.

André Thibault (ed.). 2008. *Richesse du français et géographie linguistique*, volume 2. Louvain-la-Neuve: de Boeck.

Jörg Tiedemann and Nikola Ljubešić. 2012. Efficient discrimination between closely related languages. *Proceedings of COLING 2012*, Mumbai, India, 2619–2634.

Trésor de la langue française au Québec. *Base textuelle* QUÉBÉTEXT. Université Laval, Département de Langues, linguistique et traduction. `http://www.tlfq.ulaval.ca/quebetext/`

Trésor des Vocabulaires francophones Neuchâtel. *Base textuelle* SUISTEXT. Université de Neuchâtel, Centre de dialectologie et d'étude du français régional.

Dolf Trieschnigg, Djoerd Hiemstra, Mariët Theune, Franciska de Jong and Theo Meder. 2012. An exploration of language identification techniques for the Dutch Folktale Database. *Proceedings of LREC 2012*, Istanbul, Turkey.

Maurice Tournier. 1987. Cooccurrences autour de travail (1971-1976). *Mots*, 14: 89–123.

Richard Xiao and Tony McEnery. 2006. Collocation, semantic prosody, and near synonymy: A cross-linguistic perspective. *Applied linguistics*, 27(1): 103–129.

Marcos Zampieri and Binyam Gebrekidan Gebre. 2012. Automatic Identification of Language Varieties: The Case of Portuguese. *Proceedings of KONVENS 2012*, Vienna, Austria, 233–237.

# A Report on the DSL Shared Task 2014

**Marcos Zampieri[1], Liling Tan[2], Nikola Ljubešić[3], Jörg Tiedemann[4]**
Saarland University, Germany[1,2]
University of Zagreb, Croatia[3]
Uppsala University, Sweden[4]
marcos.zampieri@uni-saarland.de, liling.tan@uni-saarland.de
jorg.tiedemann@lingfil.uu.se, nljubesi@ffzg.hr

**Abstract**

This paper summarizes the methods, results and findings of the Discriminating between Similar Languages (DSL) shared task 2014. The shared task provided data from 13 different languages and varieties divided into 6 groups. Participants were required to train their systems to discriminate between languages on a training and development set containing 20,000 sentences from each language (closed submission) and/or any other dataset (open submission). One month later, a test set containing 1,000 unidentified instances per language was released for evaluation. The DSL shared task received 22 inscriptions and 8 final submissions. The best system obtained 95.7% average accuracy.

## 1 Introduction

Discriminating between similar languages is one of the bottlenecks of state-of-the-art language identification systems. Although in recent years systems have been trained to discriminate between more languages[1], they still struggle to discriminate between similar languages such as Croatian and Serbian or Malay and Indonesian.

From an NLP point of view, the difficulty systems face when discriminating between closely related languages is similar to the problem of discriminating between standard national language varieties (e.g. American English and British English or Brazilian Portuguese and European Portuguese), henceforth varieties. Recent studies show that language varieties can be discriminated automatically using words or characters as features (Zampieri and Gebre, 2012; Lui and Cook, 2013) . However, due to performance limitations, state-of-the-art general-purpose language identification systems do not distinguish texts from different national varieties, modelling pluricentric languages as unique classes.

To evaluate how state-of-the-art systems perform in identifying similar languages and varieties, we decided to organize the Discriminating between Similar Languages (DSL)[2] shared task. This shared task was organized within the scope of the workshop on Applying NLP Tools to Similar Languages, Varieties and Dialects (VarDial) in the 2014 edition of COLING.

The motivation behind the DSL shared task is two-fold. Firstly, we have observed an increase of interest in the topic. This is reflected by a number of papers that have been published about this task in recent years starting with Ranaivo-Malançon (2006) for Malay and Indonesian and Ljubešić et al. (2007) for South Slavic languages. In the DSL shared task we tried to include (depending on the availability of data) languages that have been studied in previous experiments, such as Croatian, English, Indonesian, Malay, Portuguese and Spanish.

The second aspect that motivated us to organize this shared task is that, to our knowledge, no shared task focusing on the discrimination of similar languages has been organized previously. The most similar shared tasks to DSL are the DEFT 2010 shared task (Grouin et al., 2010), in which systems were required to classify French journalistic texts with respect to their geographical location as well as the



[1]Brown (2013) reports results on a system trained to recognize more than 1,100 languages

[2]http://corporavm.uni-koeln.de/vardial/sharedtask.html



*Proceedings of the First Workshop on Applying NLP Tools to Similar Languages, Varieties and Dialects*, pages 58–67, Dublin, Ireland, August 23 2014.

decade in which they were published. Other related shared tasks include the ALTW 2010 multilingual language identification shared task, a general-purpose language identification task containing data from 74 languages (Baldwin and Lui, 2010) and finally the Native Language Identification (NLI) shared task (Tetreault et al., 2013) where participants were provided English essays written by foreign students of 11 different mother tongues (Blanchard et al., 2013). Participants had to train their systems to identify the native language of the writer of each text.

## 2 Related Work

Among the first studies to investigate the question of discriminating between similar languages is the study published by Ranaivo-Malançon (2006). The author presents a semi-supervised model to distinguish between Indonesian and Malay, two closely related languages from the Austronesian family represented in the DSL shared task. The study uses the frequency and rank of character trigrams derived from the most frequent words in each language, lists of exclusive words, and the format of numbers (Malay uses decimal points whereas Indonesian uses commas). The author compares the performance of this method with the performance obtained by *TextCat* (Cavnar and Trenkle, 1994).

Ljubešić et al. (2007) proposed a computational model for the identification of Croatian texts in comparison to Slovene and Serbian, reporting 99% recall and precision in three processing stages. The approach includes a 'black list', which increases the performance of the algorithm. Tiedemann and Ljubešić (2012) improved this method and applied it to Bosnian, Croatian and Serbian texts. The study reports significantly higher performance compared to general purpose language identification methods.

The methods applied to discriminate between texts from different language varieties and dialects are similar to those applied to similar languages[3]. One of the methods proposed to identify language varieties is by Huang and Lee (2008). This study presented a bag-of-words approach to classify Chinese texts from the mainland and Taiwan with results of up to 92% accuracy.

Another study that focused on language varieties is the one published by Zampieri and Gebre (2012). In this study, the authors proposed a log-likelihood estimation method along with Laplace smoothing to identify two varieties of Portuguese (Brazilian and European). Their approach was trained and tested in a binary setting using journalistic texts with accuracy results above 99.5% for character n-grams. The algorithm was later adapted to classify Spanish texts using not only the classical word and character n-grams but also POS distribution (Zampieri et al., 2013).

The aforementioned study by Lui and Cook (2013) investigates computational methods to discriminate between texts from three different English varieties (Canadian, Australian and British) across different domains. The authors state that the results obtained suggest that each variety contains characteristics that are consistent across multiple domains, which enables algorithms to distinguish them regardless of the data source.

Zaidan and Callison-Burch (2013) propose computational methods for the identification of Arabic language varieties[4] using character and word n-grams. The authors built their own dataset using crowdsourcing and investigated annotators' behaviour, agreement and performance when manually tagging instances with the correct label (variety).

## 3 Methods

In the following subsections we will describe the methodology adopted for the DSL shared task. Due to the lack of comparable resources, the first decision we had to take was to create a dataset that could be used in the shared task and also redistributed to be used in other experiments. We opted for the creation of a corpus collection based on existing datasets as discussed in 3.1 (Tan et al., 2014).

Groups interested in participating in the DSL shared task had to register themselves in the shared task website to receive the training and test data. Each group could participate in one or two types of

[3]In the DSL shared task and in this paper we did not distinguish between language varieties and similar languages. More on this discussion can be found in Clyne (1992) and Chamber and Trudgill (1998).

[4]Zaidan and Callison-Burch (2013) use the terms 'varieties' and 'dialects' interchangeably whereas Lui and Cook (2013) use the term 'national dialect' to refer to what previous work describes as 'national variety'.

submission as follows:

- **Closed Submission:** Using only the DSL corpus collection for training.
- **Open Submission:** Using any other dataset including or not the DSL collection for training.

In the open submission we did not make any distinction between systems using the DSL corpus collection and those that did not. This is different from the types of submissions for the NLI shared task 2013. The NLI shared task offered proposed two types of open submissions: open submission 1 - any dataset including the aforementioned TOEFL11 dataset (Blanchard et al., 2013) and open submission 2 - any dataset excluding TOEFL11.

For each of these submission types, participants were allowed to submit up to three runs, resulting in a maximum of six runs in total (three closed submissions and three open submissions).

### 3.1 Data

As previously mentioned, we decided to compile our own dataset for the shared task. The dataset was entitled DSL corpus collection and its compilation was motivated by the absence of a resource that allowed us to evaluate systems on discriminating similar languages. The methods behind the compilation of this collection and the preliminary baseline experiments are described in Tan et al. (2014).

The DSL corpus collection consists of 18,000 randomly sampled training sentences, 2,000 development sentences and 1,000 test sentences for each language (or variety) containing at least 20 tokens[5] each. The languages are presented in table 1 with their ISO 639-1 language codes[6]. For language varieties the country code is appended to the ISO code (e.g. *en-GB* refers to the British variety of English).

| Group | Language/Variety | Code |
|---|---|---|
| A | Bosnian | *bs* |
| | Croatian | *hr* |
| | Serbian | *sr* |
| B | Indonesian | *id* |
| | Malay | *my* |
| C | Czech | *cz* |
| | Slovak | *sk* |
| D | Brazilian Portuguese | *pt-BR* |
| | European Portuguese | *pt-PT* |
| E | Argentine Spanish | *es-AR* |
| | Castilian Spanish | *es-ES* |
| F | British English | *en-GB* |
| | American English | *en-US* |

Table 1: Language Groups - DSL 2014 Shared Task

For this collection, randomly sampled sentences from journalistic corpora (and corpora collections) were selected for each of the 13 classes. Journalistic corpora were preferred because they represent standard language, which is an important factor to be considered when working with language varieties. Other data sources (e.g. Wikipedia) do not make any distinction between language varieties and they are therefore not suitable for the purpose of the shared task. A number of studies mentioned in the related work section use journalistic texts for similar reasons (Huang and Lee, 2008; Grouin et al., 2010; Zampieri and Gebre, 2012)

Given what has been said in this section, we consider the collection to be a suitable comparable corpora from this task, which was compiled to avoid bias in classification towards source, register and topics. The

[5]We considered a token as orthographic units delimited by white spaces.

[6]http://www.loc.gov/standards/iso639-2/php/English_list.php

DSL corpus collection was distributed in tab delimited format; the first column contains a sentence in the language/variety, the second column states its group and the last column refers to its language code.[7]

### 3.1.1 Problems with Group F

There are no major problems to report regarding the organization of the shared task nor with the compilation of the DSL corpus collection apart from some issues in the Group F data. The organizers and a couple of teams participating in the shared task observed very poor performance when distinguishing instances from group F (British English - American British). For example, the baseline experiments described in Tan et al. (2014) report a very low 0.59 F-measure for Group F (the lowest score) and 0.84 for Group E (the second lowest score). Some of the teams asked human annotators to try to distinguish the sentences manually and they concluded that some instances were probably misclassified.

We decided to look more carefully at the data and noticed that the instances were originally tagged based on the websites (newspapers) that they were retrieved from and not the country of the original publication. There are, however, many cases of cross citation and republication of texts that the original data sources did not take into account (e.g. British texts that were later republished by an American website). As the DSL is a corpus collection and manually checking all 20,000 training and development instances per language was not feasible, we assumed that the original sources[8] from which the texts were retrieved provided the correct country of origin. The assumption was correct for all language groups but English.

To illustrate the issues above we present next some misclassified examples. Two particular cases raised by the UMich team are the following:

(1) I think they can afford to give North another innings and some time in Shield cricket and take another middle order batsman. (en-US)

(2) ATHENS, Ohio (AP) Albuquerque will continue its four-game series in Nashville Thursday night when it takes on the Sounds behind starter Les Walrond (3-4, 4.50) against Gary Glover, who is making his first Triple-A start after coming down from Milwaukee. (en-GB)

Example number one was tagged as American English because it was retrieved from the online edition of The New York Times but it was in fact first published in Australia. The second example is a text published by Associated Press describing an event that took place in Ohio, United States, but it was tagged as British English because it was retrieved by the UK Yahoo! sports section.

Our solution was to exclude the language group F from the final scores and perform a manual check in all its 1,000 test instances[9], thus giving the chance to participants to train their algorithms on other data sources (open submission).

## 3.2 Schedule

The DSL shared task spanned from March 20$^{th}$ when the training set was released, to June 6$^{th}$ when participants could submit a paper (up to 10 pages) describing their system. We provided one month between the release of the training and the test set. The schedule of the DSL shared task 2014 can be seen below.

| Event | Date |
|---|---|
| Training Set Release | March 20$^{th}$, 2014 |
| Test Set Release | April 21$^{st}$, 2014 |
| Submissions Due | April 23$^{rd}$, 2014 |
| Results Announced | April 30$^{th}$, 2014 |
| Paper Submission | June 6$^{th}$, 2014 |

Table 2: DSL 2014 Shared Task Schedule

[7] To obtain the data please visit: `https://bitbucket.org/alvations/dslsharedtask2014`

[8] See Tan et al. (2014) for a complete description of the data sources of the DSL corpus collection.

[9] Our manual check suggests that about 25% of the instances in the English dataset was likely to have been misclassified.

## 4 Results

This section summarises the results obtained by all participants of the shared task who submitted final results.[10] The DSL shared task included 22 enrolled teams from different countries (e.g. Australia, Estonia, Holland, Germany, United Kingdom and United States). From the 22 enrolled teams, eight of them submitted their final results. Most of the groups opted to exclusively use the DSL corpus collection and therefore participated solely in the closed submission track. Two of them compiled comparable datasets and also participated in the open submission.

Given that the dataset contained misclassified instances, group F (English) was not taken into account to compute the final shared task scores. In the next subsections we report results in terms of macro-average F-measure and accuracy.

### 4.1 Closed Submission

Table 3 presents the best F-measure and Accuracy results obtained by the eight teams that submitted their results for the closed submission track ordered by accuracy.

| Team | Macro-avg F-score | Overall Accuracy |
|---|---|---|
| NRC-CNRC | 0.957 | 0.957 |
| RAE | 0.947 | 0.947 |
| UMich | 0.932 | 0.932 |
| UniMelb-NLP | 0.918 | 0.918 |
| QMUL | 0.925 | 0.906 |
| LIRA | 0.721 | 0.766 |
| UDE | 0.657 | 0.681 |
| CLCG | 0.405 | 0.453 |

Table 3: Open Submission - Results

In the closed submissions, we observed a group of five teams whose systems (best runs) obtained results over 90% accuracy. This is comparable to what is described in the state-of-the-art literature for discriminating similar languages and language varieties (Tiedemann and Ljubešić, 2012; Lui and Cook, 2013). These five teams submitted system descriptions that allowed us to look in more detail at successful approaches for this task. System descriptions will be discussed in section 5.

Three of the eight teams obtained substantially lower scores, from 45.33% to 76.64% accuracy. These three groups unfortunately did not submit system description papers. From our point of view, this would create an interesting opportunity to look more carefully at the weaknesses of approaches that did not obtain good results in this task.

### 4.2 Open Submission

Only two systems submitted results for the open submission track and their F-measure and Accuracy results are presented in table 3.

| Team | Macro-avg F-score | Overall Accuracy |
|---|---|---|
| UniMelb-NLP | 0.878 | 0.880 |
| UMich | 0.858 | 0.859 |

Table 4: Closed Submission - Results

The UniMelb-NLP (Lui et al., 2014) group used data from different corpora such as the BNC, EUROPARL and Open Subtitles whereas UMich (King et al., 2014) compiled journalistic corpora from different sizes for each language ranging from 695,597 tokens for Malay to 20,288,294 tokens for British English.

[10] Visit `https://bitbucket.org/alvations/dslsharedtask2014/downloads/dsl-results.html` for more detail on the shared task results or at the aforementioned DSL shared task website.

Comparing the results of the closed to the open submissions, we observed that the UniMelb-NLP submission was outperformed by UMich system by about 1.5% accuracy in the closed submission, but in the open submission they scored 2.1% better than UMich. This difference can be explained by investigating these two factors: 1) the quality and amount of the collected training data; 2) the robustness of the method to obtain correct predictions across different datasets and domains as previously discussed by Lui and Cook (2013) for English varieties.

### 4.3 Accuracy per Language Group

In this subsection we look more carefully at the performance of systems in discriminating each class within groups A to E. Table 5 presents the accuracy scores obtained per language group for each team sorted alphabetically. The best score per group is displayed in bold.

| | CLCG | LIRA | NRC-CNRC | QMUL | RAE | UDE | UMich | UniMelb-NLP |
|---|---|---|---|---|---|---|---|---|
| A | 0.338 | 0.333 | **0.936** | 0.879 | 0.919 | 0.785 | 0.919 | 0.915 |
| B | 0.503 | 0.982 | **0.996** | 0.935 | 0.994 | 0.892 | 0.992 | 0.972 |
| C | 0.500 | **1.000** | **1.000** | 0.962 | **1.000** | 0.493 | 0.999 | **1.000** |
| D | 0.496 | 0.892 | **0.956** | 0.905 | 0.948 | 0.493 | 0.926 | 0.896 |
| E | 0.503 | 0.843 | **0.910** | 0.865 | 0.888 | 0.694 | 0.876 | 0.807 |

Table 5: Language Groups A to E - Accuracy Results

The top 5 systems plus the LIRA team obtained very good results for groups B (Malay and Indonesian) and C (Czech and Slovak). Four out of eight systems obtained perfect performance when discriminating Czech and Slovak texts. Perfect performance was not achieved by any of the systems when distinguishing Malay from Indonesian texts, but even so, results were fairly high and the best result was 99.6% accuracy obtained by the NRC-CNRC group. The perfect results obtained by four groups when distinguishing texts from group C suggest that Czech and Slovak texts are not as similar as we assumed before the shared task, and that they therefore possess strong systemic and/or orthographic differences that allow well-trained classifiers to perform perfectly. Figure 1 presents the accuracy results of the top 5 groups.

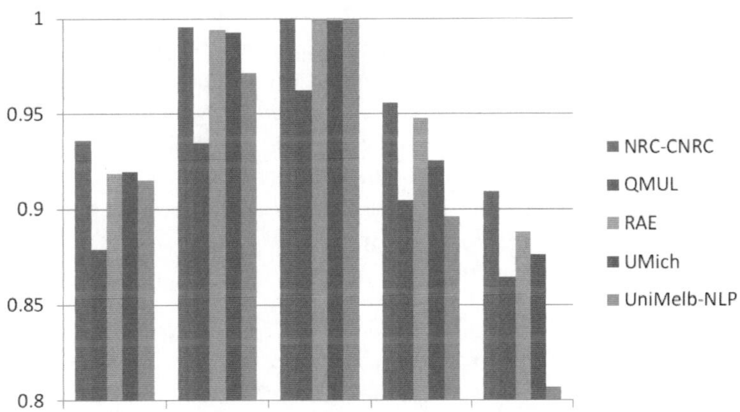


Figure 1: Language Groups A to E Accuracy - Top 5 Systems

Distinguishing between languages from group A (Bosnian, Croatian and Serbian), the only group containing 3 languages, proved to be a challenging task as discussed in previous research (Ljubešić et al., 2007; Tiedemann and Ljubešić, 2012). The best result was again obtained by the NRC-CNRC group with 93.5% accuracy. The groups containing texts written in different language varieties, namely D (Portuguese) and E (Spanish) were the most difficult to discriminate, particularly the Spanish varieties. These results also corroborate the findings of previous studies (Zampieri et al., 2013).

The QMUL system that was the 5th best system in the closed submission track did not outperform any of the other top 5 systems in groups A, B or C. However, the system did better when distinguishing texts from the two most difficult language groups (D and E), outperforming the UniMelb-NLP submission on two occasions. The simplicity of the approach proposed by the QMUL, which the author describes as 'a simple baseline' (Purver, 2014) may be an explanation for the regular performance across different language groups.

### 4.4 Results Group F

To document the problems in the group F (British and American English) dataset we included the results of both the open and closed submissions for this language group in table 6. As previously mentioned, submitting group F results was optional and we did not include these results in the final shared task results. Six out of eight systems decided to submit their predictions as closed submissions and the two groups participating in the open submission track also submitted their group F results.

| Team | F-score | Accuracy | Type |
|---|---|---|---|
| UMich | 0.639 | 0.639 | Open |
| UniMelb- NLP | 0.581 | 0.583 | Open |
| NRC-CNRC | 0.522 | 0.524 | Closed |
| LIRA | 0.450 | 0.493 | Closed |
| RAE | 0.451 | 0.481 | Closed |
| UMich | 0.463 | 0.464 | Closed |
| UDE | 0.451 | 0.451 | Closed |
| UniMelb-NLP | 0.435 | 0.435 | Closed |

Table 6: Group F - Accuracy Results

The results confirm the problems in the DSL dataset discussed in section 3.1.1. After a careful manual check of the 1,000 test instances, open submissions scores were still substantially lower than the other groups: 69.9% and 58.3% accuracy. Closed submissions proved to be impossible and only one of the six systems scored slightly above the 50% baseline.

It should be investigated more carefully in future research whether the poor results for group F reflect only the problems in the dataset or also the actual difficulty in discriminating between these two varieties of English. Moderate differences in orthography (e.g. *neighbour* (UK) and *neighbor* (US)) as well as lexical choices (e.g. *rubbish* (UK) and *garbage* (US) or *trousers* (UK) and *pants* (US)) are present in texts from these two varieties and these can be informative features for algorithms to discriminate between them. Discriminating between other English varieties already proved to be a challenging yet feasible task in previous research (Lui and Cook, 2013).

## 5 System Descriptions

All eight systems that submitted their final results to the shared task were invited to submit papers describing their systems and the top 5 systems in the closed track submitted their papers, namely: NRC-CNRC, RAE, UMich, UniMelb-NLP and QMUL.

The best scores were obtained by the NRC-CNRC (Goutte et al., 2014) team which proposed a two-step approach to predict first the language group than the language of each instance. The language group was predicted in a 6-way classification using a probabilistic model similar to a Naive Bayes classifier, and later the method applied SVM classifiers to discriminate within each group: binary for groups B-F and one versus all for group A, which contains three classes (Bosnian, Croatian and Serbian).

An interesting contribution proposed by the RAE team (Porta and Sancho, 2014) are the so-called 'white lists' inspired by the 'blacklist' classifier (Tiedemann and Ljubešić, 2012). These lists are word lists exclusive to a language or variety, similar to one of the features that Ranaivo-Malançon (2006) proposed to discriminate between Malay and Indonesian.

Two groups used Information Gain (IG) to select the best features for classification, namely UMich (King et al., 2014) and UniMelb-NLP (Lui et al., 2014). These teams were also the only ones to submit open submissions. The UniMelb-NLP team tried different classification methods and features (including delexicalized models) in each run. The best results were obtained by their own method, the off-the-shelf general-purpose language identification software *langid.py* (Lui and Baldwin, 2012). This method has been widely used for general-purpose language identification and its performance is regarded superior to similar general-purpose methods such as *TextCat*. In the shared task, the system was modelled hierarchically firstly identifying the language group that a sentence belongs to and subsequently the specific language, achieving performance comparable to the state-of-the-art, but still slightly below the other three systems.

The QMUL team (Purver, 2014) proposed a linear SVM classifier using words and characters as features. The author investigated the influence of the cost parameter $c$ (from 1.0 to 100.0), in the classifiers' performance. The cost parameter $c$ is responsible for the trade-off between maximum margin and classification errors. According to the system description the optimal parameter for this task lies between 30.0 and 50.0. Purver (2014) also notes that the linear SVM classifier performs well with word uni-gram language models in comparison to methods using character n-grams. This observation corroborates the findings of previous experiments that rely on words as important features to distinguish similar languages and varieties (Huang and Lee, 2008; Zampieri, 2013)

The features and algorithms presented so far, as well as the system paper descriptions, are summarised in table7.[11]

| Team | Algorithm | Features | System Paper |
|---|---|---|---|
| NRC-CNRC | Prob. Class. and Linear SVM | Words 1-2, Char. 2-6 | (Goutte et al., 2014) |
| RAE | MaxEnt | Words 1-2, Char. 1-5, 'Whitelist' | (Porta and Sancho, 2014) |
| UMich | Naive Bayes | Words 1-2, Char. 2-6 (IG Feat. Selection) | (King et al., 2014) |
| UniMelb-NLP | *langid.py* | Words, Char., POS (IG Feat. Selection) | (Lui et al., 2014) |
| QMUL | Linear SVM | Words 1, Char. 1-3 | (Purver, 2014) |

Table 7: Top 5 Systems - Features and Algorithms at a Glance

## 6 Conclusion

Shared tasks are an interesting way of comparing algorithms, computational methods and features using the same dataset. Given what has been presented in this paper, we believe that the DSL shared task filled an important gap in language identification and will allow other researchers to look in more detail at the problem of discriminating similar languages. Accurate methods for discriminating similar languages can help to improve performance not only in language identification but also in a number of NLP tasks and applications such as part-of-speech-tagging, spell checking and machine translation.

The best system obtained 95.71% accuracy and F-measure for a set of 11 languages and varieties divided into 5 groups (A to E), using only the DSL corpus collection. Systems that performed best modelled their algorithms to perform two-step predictions: first the language group, then the actual class and used characters and words as features. As we regard the corpus to be a balanced sample of the news domain, the results obtained confirm the assumption that similar languages and varieties possess systemic characteristics that can be modelled by algorithms in order to distinguish languages from other similar languages or varieties using lexical or orthographical features.

Another lesson learned from this shared task is regarding the compilation of group F (English) data. Researchers, including us, often rely on previously annotated meta-data which sometimes may contain inaccurate information and errors. Corpus collection for this purpose should be thoroughly checked (manually if possible). The issues with the group F might have discouraged some of the participants to continue in the shared task (particularly those who were interested only in the discrimination of English varieties).

[11] UniMelb-NLP experimented different methods in their 6 runs. In this report we commented on the algorithm that achieved the best performance.

### 6.1 Future Perspectives

The shared task was a very fruitful and positive experience for the organizers. We would like to organize a second edition of the shared task containing, for example, new language groups for which we could not find suitable corpora before the 2014 edition. This includes, most notably, the cases of Dutch and Flemish or the varieties of French and German which could not be included in the DSL shared task due to the lack of available data.

The DSL corpus collection is freely available and can be used as a gold standard for language identification or to train algorithms for other NLP tasks involving similar languages. We would like to use the dataset to investigate, for example, lexical variation between similar languages and varieties as proposed by Piersman et al. (2010) and Soares da Silva (2010) or syntactic variation using annotated data as discussed in Anstein (2013).

At present, we are investigating the influence of the length of texts in the discrimination of similar languages. It is a well known fact that the longer texts are, the more likely they are to contain features that allow algorithms to identify their language. However, this variable was not explored within the scope of the DSL shared task and we are using the DSL dataset and the results for this purpose. Another direction that our work may take is the linguistic analysis of the most informative features in classification as was done recently by Diwersy et al. (2014).

## Acknowledgements

The authors would like to thank all participants of the DSL shared task for their comments and suggestions throughout the organization of this shared task. We would also like to thank Joel Tetreault and Binyam Gebrekidan Gebre for their valuable feedback on this report.

## References

Stefanie Anstein. 2013. *Computational approaches to the comparison of regional variety corpora : prototyping a semi-automatic system for German.* Ph.D. thesis, University of Stuttgart.

Timothy Baldwin and Marco Lui. 2010. Multilingual language identification: ALTW 2010 shared task data. In *Proceedings of Australasian Language Technology Association Workshop*, pages 4–7.

Daniel Blanchard, Joel Tetreault, Derrick Higgins, Aoife Cahill, and Martin Chodorow. 2013. TOEFL11: A Corpus of Non-Native English. Technical report, Educational Testing Service.

Ralf Brown. 2013. Selecting and weighting n-grams to identify 1100 languages. In *Proceedings of the 16th International Conference on Text Speech and Dialogue (TSD2013), Lecture Notes in Artificial Intelligence (LNAI 8082)*, pages 519–526, Pilsen, Czech Republic. Springer.

William Cavnar and John Trenkle. 1994. N-gram-based text catogorization. *3rd Symposium on Document Analysis and Information Retrieval (SDAIR-94).*

Jack Chambers and Peter Trudgill. 1998. *Dialectology (2nd Edition).* Cambridge University Press.

Michael Clyne. 1992. *Pluricentric Languages: Different Norms in Different Nations.* CRC Press.

Sascha Diwersy, Stefan Evert, and Stella Neumann. 2014. A semi-supervised multivariate approach to the study of language variation. *Linguistic Variation in Text and Speech, within and across Languages.*

Cyril Goutte, Serge Léger, and Marine Carpuat. 2014. The NRC system for discriminating similar languages. In *Proceedings of the 1st Workshop on Applying NLP Tools to Similar Languages, Varieties and Dialects (VarDial)*, Dublin, Ireland.

Cyril Grouin, Dominic Forest, Lyne Da Sylva, Patrick Paroubek, and Pierre Zweigenbaum. 2010. Présentation et résultats du défi fouille de texte DEFT2010 où et quand un article de presse a-t-il été écrit? *Actes du sixième DÉfi Fouille de Textes.*

Chu-ren Huang and Lung-hao Lee. 2008. Contrastive approach towards text source classification based on top-bag-of-word similarity. In *Proceedings of PACLIC 2008*, pages 404–410.

Ben King, Dragomir Radev, and Steven Abney. 2014. Experiments in sentence language identification with groups of similar languages. In *Proceedings of the 1st Workshop on Applying NLP Tools to Similar Languages, Varieties and Dialects (VarDial)*, Dublin, Ireland.

Nikola Ljubešić, Nives Mikelic, and Damir Boras. 2007. Language identification: How to distinguish similar languages? In *Proceedings of the 29th International Conference on Information Technology Interfaces.*

Marco Lui and Timothy Baldwin. 2012. langid.py: An off-the-shelf language identification tool. In *Proceedings of the 50th Meeting of the ACL.*

Marco Lui and Paul Cook. 2013. Classifying English documents by national dialect. In *Proceedings of Australasian Language Tchnology Workshop*, pages 5–15.

Marco Lui, Ned Letcher, Oliver Adams, Long Duong, Paul Cook, and Timothy Baldwin. 2014. Exploring methods and resources for discriminating similar languages. In *Proceedings of the 1st Workshop on Applying NLP Tools to Similar Languages, Varieties and Dialects (VarDial)*, Dublin, Ireland.

Yves Piersman, Dirk Geeraerts, and Dirk Speelman. 2010. The automatic identification of lexical variation between language varieties. *Natural Language Engineering*, 16:469–491.

Jordi Porta and José-Luis Sancho. 2014. Using maximum entropy models to discriminate between similar languages and varieties. In *Proceedings of the 1st Workshop on Applying NLP Tools to Similar Languages, Varieties and Dialects (VarDial)*, Dublin, Ireland.

Matthew Purver. 2014. A simple baseline for discriminating similar language. In *Proceedings of the 1st Workshop on Applying NLP Tools to Similar Languages, Varieties and Dialects (VarDial)*, Dublin, Ireland.

Bali Ranaivo-Malançon. 2006. Automatic identification of close languages - case study: Malay and Indonesian. *ECTI Transactions on Computer and Information Technology*, 2:126–134.

Augusto Soares da Silva. 2010. Measuring and parameterizing lexical convergence and divergence between European and Brazilian Portuguese: endo/exogeneousness and foreign and normative influence. *Advances in Cognitive Sociolinguistics.*

Liling Tan, Marcos Zampieri, Nikola Ljubešić, and Jörg Tiedemann. 2014. Merging comparable data sources for the discrimination of similar languages: The DSL corpus collection. In *Proceedings of The Workshop on Building and Using Comparable Corpora (BUCC)*, Reykjavik, Iceland.

Joel Tetreault, Daniel Blanchard, and Aoife Cahill. 2013. A report on the first native language identification shared task. In *Proceedings of the Eighth Workshop on Innovative Use of NLP for Building Educational Applications*, Atlanta, GA, USA, June. Association for Computational Linguistics.

Jörg Tiedemann and Nikola Ljubešić. 2012. Efficient discrimination between closely related languages. In *Proceedings of COLING 2012*, pages 2619–2634, Mumbai, India.

Omar F Zaidan and Chris Callison-Burch. 2013. Arabic dialect identification. *Computational Linguistics.*

Marcos Zampieri and Binyam Gebrekidan Gebre. 2012. Automatic identification of language varieties: The case of Portuguese. In *Proceedings of KONVENS2012*, pages 233–237, Vienna, Austria.

Marcos Zampieri, Binyam Gebrekidan Gebre, and Sascha Diwersy. 2013. N-gram language models and POS distribution for the identification of Spanish varieties. In *Proceedings of TALN2013*, pages 580–587, Sable d'Olonne, France.

Marcos Zampieri. 2013. Using bag-of-words to distinguish similar languages: How efficient are they? In *Proceedings of the 14th IEEE International Symposium on Computational Intelligence and Informatics (CINTI2013)*, pages 37–41, Budapest, Hungary.

# Employing Phonetic Speech Recognition for Language and Dialect Specific Search


**Corey Miller**
UMD CASL
7005 52nd Avenue
College Park, MD
20740
cmiller6@umd.edu

**Rachel Strong**
UMD CASL
7005 52nd Avenue
College Park, MD
20740
rstrong1@umd.edu

**Evan Jones**
UMD CASL
7005 52nd Avenue
College Park, MD
20740
jone1072@umd.edu

**Mark Vinson**
UMD CASL
7005 52nd Avenue
College Park, MD
20740
mvinson@umd.edu



## Abstract

We discuss the notion of language and dialect-specific search in the context of audio indexing. A system is described where users can find dialect or language-specific pronunciations of Afghan placenames in Dari and Pashto. We explore the efficacy of a phonetic speech recognition system employed in this task.


## 1 Introduction

The Audio Gazetteer hotspotting tool was developed by MITRE (2012) and employs the Nexidia phonetic speech recognition engine (Gavalda and Schlueter, 2010) in several languages, including Dari (the Afghan variety of Persian) and Pashto, the two main languages of Afghanistan. These languages are both members of the Iranian language family and share a number of phonetic characteristics (Miller et al., 2013). This tool enables a user to load audio clips and to search them for words contained within them using one of three methods: the Dari or Pashto alphabets, a Romanization scheme, or phonetics in SAMPA (Wells, 1997). Such a search will yield each starting timepoint in an audio file where the system has identified the term being searched, along with a number between 0 and 100 indicating the level of confidence the system has in its determination. While terms of any kind can be searched, the system provides additional mapping capabilities for placenames.

Audio hotspotting, also known as keyword spotting or audio indexing, is a form of information retrieval employing speech recognition that is used for quickly identifying passages of interest within audio files. It can be used to identify calls of interest in call centers, or to explore reports of natural disasters or political crises in the media. There are two main approaches to audio hotspotting; one involves speech-to-text (STT), also known as large vocabulary continuous speech recognition (LVCSR), and the other employs phonetic speech recognition.

STT ingests speech and outputs orthographic text. To do this, it requires language-specific acoustic and language models mediated by a pronunciation model or dictionary that maps words to phonetic forms. The output text transcript can then be mined for terms of interest. Raytheon's BBN Broadcast Monitoring System is an example of such a system (Raytheon, 2012). One liability of this approach is the need to establish the vocabulary, upon which the language and pronunciation models depend, up-front. That means that one cannot easily search for terms that have not been programmed into the system beforehand. This is an especially challenging impediment when confronting natural disasters and political crises in regions with towns and personalities whose names are "out of vocabulary" (OOV).

Phonetic speech recognition uses language-specific acoustic models directly; allowing users to query phonetic strings, possibly with the aid of a pronunciation model allowing orthographic search. The ability to query phonetic strings removes the OOV problem; any string that can be composed of the phonemes of a particular language can be searched. While this technology is useful for keyword spotting, it cannot be used to generate a meaningful orthographic transcript of speech, due to its lack of a language model.






*Proceedings of the First Workshop on Applying NLP Tools to Similar Languages, Varieties and Dialects*, pages 68–75, Dublin, Ireland, August 23 2014.

Our purpose is to explore the feasibility of using phonetic speech recognition technology to explore subtle dialect and language differences, with the ultimate aim of enabling language or dialect specific search. In such a scenario, a user is not simply interested in finding a particular term of interest, he is also interested in the sociolinguistic characteristics of the speaker of that term of interest.

Various researchers have performed promising experiments using STT to explore phonetic variation. These experiments utilize STT in forced alignment mode; that is, given a pre-existing orthographic transcript, they ask the recognizer to focus on deciding which pronunciation among a finite set supplied by the researcher maps best onto particular audio exemplars. Fox (2006) used this technique to examine several realizations of syllable-final /s/[1] in Spanish including [s], [h] and deletion, while Wester et al. (2001) explored variable deletion of /n/, /r/ and /t/ in Dutch, as well as schwa-insertion and deletion. Both demonstrated promising agreement between the STT-based approaches and human coding.

In contrast, the phonetic speech recognizer employed here requires neither an orthographic transcript, nor a predetermined set of phonetic variants from which to choose. For that reason, we felt it offered a flexible platform from which to explore phonetic variation, and thus enabled employing knowledge of that variation to perform dialect and language-specific search for Dari and Pashto.

## 2 Data collection and transcription

We developed an interview protocol consisting of three components: a sociolinguistic background interview, a map task and a word list. This interview was designed to elicit Afghan placename data from Afghans residing in the United States whose native language was either Dari or Pashto. Speakers bilingual in Dari and Pashto were interviewed in both languages sequentially. Seven Dari and three Pashto interviews, comprising approximately six hours in total, were digitally recorded and later downsampled to 16 MHz with 16-bit precision.

The purpose of the sociolinguistic background interview was to establish the language and dialect profile of each speaker. Where possible, it was conducted in the speaker's native language, and established the location and duration of each place where he or she resided. In addition, the interview established the location and language of instruction of each school attended, as well as the language and dialect used with family members and friends. The interview inquired about all the languages and dialects both spoken and understood by the speakers.

The purpose of the map task was to gather subjects' pronunciations of placenames in Afghanistan in a casual style. A large colored map of Afghanistan, using native lettering, was placed before the subjects and they were asked to explain in Dari or Pashto how to get to and from various points.

The final part of the interview involved reading a word list in Dari or Pashto containing the names of over 200 placenames, including provinces, provincial capitals, other large towns, administrative divisions, regions, mountain ranges, passes, bodies of water, airports and deserts. In Pashto interviews, each placename was read both by itself for the direct case and in frames designed to elicit the oblique and ablative cases. As a result of the three-part interview, we obtained several tokens of many placenames, along a scale of more casual style in the sociolinguistic and map tasks to more formal in the word list.

The placenames in each audio file were transcribed using Praat (Boersma, 2001). Up to five of the following transcription tiers were used:

- English: one spelling for each placename was used as an index for each utterance of a given place, regardless of any particularities in individual utterances.
- Native: Pashto or Dari spelling.
- Phonetic: fairly broad transcription in the International Phonetic Alphabet (IPA).
- Language: Dari or Pashto. In general, a given task was in one language at a time. However, when working with bilingual subjects, they would occasionally explicitly remark on the pronunciation of the placename in the other language, so it was necessary to indicate the language for each placename.
- Case: for Pashto, indication of whether the particular utterance was in the direct, oblique or ablative case.

[1] Square brackets [] are used for allophones or sequences when no particular phonemic claims are being made; slashes // are used for phonemes.

The purpose of the phonetic transcription was to represent a human phonetic judgment that could be compared to the hypotheses of the phonetic speech recognition engine. In its documentation, Nexidia provides separate phoneme inventories in SAMPA for Dari and Pashto[2]. Sometimes Nexidia does not provide a symbol to express certain distinctions. For example, a schwa [ə] is provided for Pashto, but not Dari. Schwa is a phoneme in Pashto; however, in Dari it is a possible allophone of some short vowels. In order to facilitate experimentation with the system, in the course of phonetic transcription of a given language, we limited ourselves to the speech recognizer's phoneme inventory for that language.

## 3 Placename pronunciation variation

The field of toponym resolution attempts to identify which particular place, or geocode, a given placename refers to: for example, in some contexts "London" may refer to a place in England; in others, to a place in Canada. Research in this field has primarily focused on clues in surrounding text or audio to disambiguate such placenames (Leidner, 2007; Buscaldi, 2010). To our knowledge, pronunciation variation in placenames has not yet been exploited to assist in disambiguation.

Pronunciation of placenames is well known to vary; indeed one example of this is the phenomenon known as "local pronunciation" (Forster, 1981). Some common examples from the English-speaking world include Cairo [kero], Illinois vs. Cairo [kajro], Egypt, and Houston [hawstən] Street in New York City vs. Houston [hjustən], Texas. The notion of local pronunciation is even more salient in a bilingual society; for example, French-speaking inhabitants of Montreal call their city [mɔ̃real], while English-speaking residents say [mʌntriɒl], not to mention Americans, who might say [mɑntriɔl].

In Afghanistan, Pashto and Dari are the principal languages among many other languages spoken (Farhadi, 1955; MacKenzie, 1959). Pashto and Dari-speaking communities are both located throughout the country, so it is very common for placenames to have Pashto and Dari variants, as well as variants for particular dialects of each language.

Table 1 illustrates some variation within Dari pronunciation of placenames that we encountered. This variation is not limited to placenames; in fact, each of the phonetic phenomena has been reported by Farhadi (1955), and one variant of each word may be deemed formal and the other colloquial.

| Phenomenon | Place | Formal | Colloquial |
|---|---|---|---|
| /h/ dropping and compensatory lengthening | Herat هرات | [hɛrɑt] | [erɑt] |
| /ʔ/ dropping and compensatory lengthening | Qalah-ye Now قلعه نو | [qalaʔɛnaw] | [qalɑɛnaw] |
| /a/ → [aj] / _n | Panjsher پنجشير | [panʃer] | [pajnʃɛr] |

Table 1: Pronunciation variation within Dari

Table 2 illustrates placename pronunciation variation within Pashto. The southwest dialect of Pashto, including Kandahar, pronounces the Pashto letter ښ as /ʂ/, while the northeast dialect, including Peshawar, Pakistan and neighboring regions of Afghanistan, pronounces it as /x/ (Miller, 2014).

| Phenomenon | Place | Southwest | Northeast |
|---|---|---|---|
| /ʂ/ ~ /x/ | Lashkar Gah لښکر گاه | [laʂkargɑ] | [laxkargɑ] |
| /ʂ/ ~ /x/ | Maydan Shar ميدان ښار | [majdɑnʂɑr] | [majdɑnxɑr] |

Table 2: Pronunciation variation within Pashto

Table 3 illustrates variation in Pashto based on case. Pashto has three cases, which may cause the pronunciation of placenames to vary. The direct case is used by default, the oblique case is used when

[2] Nexidia Dari Guide 1.1, Nexidia Pashto Guide 1.0

the placename is the object of certain prepositions and when the placename is the subject of transitive sentences in the past tense, and the ablative (also known as oblique II) is used in certain prepositional constructions meaning "from" (Penzl, 1955). Not all placenames exhibit variation based on case. Interestingly, the words that do feature a distinct oblique case take a plural ending. One interview subject suggested that in that case, the word may be interpreted as a group of people or tribe.

| Place | Direct | Oblique | Ablative |
|---|---|---|---|
| Kabul کابل | [kabʊl] | [kabʊl] | [kabʊlə] |
| Bamyan بامیان | [bɑmjɑn] | [bɑmjɑno] | [bɑmjɑnə] |
| Wardak وردک | [wardag] | [wardago] | [wardagə] |

Table 3: Case variation within Pashto

Table 4 illustrates pronunciation variation between Dari and Pashto for particular places, reflecting language differences reported in Miran (1969), Penzl (1955), and elsewhere. When the native spelling used is common between the two languages, it is placed in the "Place" column; when it differs, it is placed in the "Dari" and "Pashto" columns.

| Phenomenon | Place | Dari | Pashto |
|---|---|---|---|
| Dari /ɛ/ ~ Pashto /ɪ/ | Helmand هلمند | [hɛlmand] | [hɪlmand] |
| Pashto final devoicing | Faryab فاریاب | [fɒrjɒb] | [fɑrjɑp] |
| Dari /ɒ/ ~ Pashto /ɑ/ | Kapisa کاپیسا | [kɒpisɒ] | [kɑpisɑ] |
| Dari /r/ ~ Pashto /ɽ/ | Kunar | [konar] کنر | [kunaɽ] کنړ |
| Dari /q/ ~ Pashto /k/ | Qalah-ye Now قلعه نو | [qalaʔɛnaw] | [kalaenaw] |

Table 4: Variation between Dari and Pashto

As can be seen in Table 4, the vowel systems of Dari and Pashto differ somewhat. Dari generally employs a more rounded long *a*, which we can abstractly label /ā/, compared to Pashto. That is, Dari often uses /ɒ/ in contrast to Pashto /ɑ/. The SAMPA provided by Nexidia for each language only contains one /ā/ per language, so it is not possible to assess the system's efficacy at recognizing the rounded or unrounded variant by searching within one language; however, a method involving crosslingual search will be discussed below. In addition, future research will aim to measure the acoustic properties of the two varieties of /ā/.

With regard to consonants, Pashto has a retroflex /ɽ/, while Dari does not. In Kunar, the Pashto /ɽ/ corresponds to Dari /r/. Note, however, that when speaking Pashto as a second language, Dari speakers replace Pashto /ɽ/ with /l/ more often than /r/ (Miran, 1969). Dari preserves the Arabic voiceless uvular stop /q/, in contrast to Pashto, which generally employs /k/ in words derived from Arabic spelled with the letter ق (Penzl, 1955).

## 4 Assessment technique

Precision and recall are the most common measures for assessing quality in the context of audio hotspotting (Hu et al., 2012). We employ these metrics in two scenarios: dialect-agnostic and dialect-specific search. In the dialect-agnostic case, one would search for an orthographic term, for example Lashkar Gah, and calculate precision (true positives/(true positives + false positives)) based on how many of the recalled terms were in fact Lashkar Gah, and calculate recall (true positives/(true positives + false negatives)) based on how many of the actual Lashkar Gah's in the file being searched were identified. This method provides a way of evaluating the efficacy of a given system to retrieve audio of interest when one's primary concern is the place or term in question, regardless of the pronunciation that was used.

We modify the scoring method in the dialect-specific case, in which we are focused on pronunciation. Consider for example, the two common pronunciations of Lashkar Gah in Pashto: [laxkargɑ] and [laʂkargɑ]. In this case, when calculating precision, if one searches for [laxkargɑ] and [laʂkargɑ] is retrieved, it is just as wrong as if Kabul were retrieved (variable scoring, by incorporation of approaches such as Nerbonne and Heeringa (2010), will be considered in the future). For calculating recall, the universe of Lashkar Gah's is limited to those whose pronunciation matches the search term.

There is some pronunciation variation that does not necessarily represent dialect variation, and should be considered "under the radar" for the purposes of a dialect-specific search. In the example above, either of the first two vowels could be [ə] instead of [a]. For this reason, we introduce the notion of equivalence classes to enable us to give equal "correct" scores for example to both [laxkargɑ] and [ləxkargɑ] when searching for [laxkargɑ].

This scoring method provides a way of evaluating a given system's sensitivity to pronunciation differences. If a system proves adept at such a task, it can be employed in two related tasks:

- Language-specific search: find tokens of a given word uttered in a particular language
- Dialect-specific search: find tokens of a given word uttered in a particular dialect or accent

There is a large literature on language, speaker and dialect identification (Biadsy, 2011). Most of these methods are designed to emit a judgment as to language, speaker or dialect, based on a given audio sample, which might be useful in various kinds of batch processing. Another approach to accent and nativeness judgment is described by Weinberger and Kunath (2011). In this approach, audio is first reduced to a human-made phonetic transcription that is then mined for clues as to dialect and accent.

The work described here may be situated between automatic techniques based on audio and post-hoc techniques focused on transcriptions. Our method is designed for users interacting with a given audio sample; one that is likely to contain a mix of speakers, languages or dialects. Also, in contrast to statistical approaches which may appear as a "black box" to end-users, our approach allows users to iteratively and interactively develop hypotheses as to the association of specific pronunciations with languages, dialects or speakers.

## 5 Dialect Search

In this section, we contrast performance on dialect-specific vs. dialect-agnostic searches. Suppose in Dari we are interested in finding speakers who use the pronunciation [qalɑɛnaw] instead of [qalaʔɛnaw] for the town Qalah-ye Now قلعه نو. In this case, we are focused on the application of the phonetic process /aʔ/ → [ɑ]. The most salient aspect of this is the presence of the vowel [ɑ] rather than [a] in the second syllable. Consequently, we are unconcerned about other forms of variation we may encounter, such as variation between [q] and [k], and [ɛ] and [e]. We therefore contrast the following two equivalence classes for this experiment as shown in Table 5:

| No compensatory lengthening | Compensatory lengthening |
|---|---|
| [qalaʔɛnaw] | [qalɑɛnaw] |
| [qalaʔenaw] | [qalɑenaw] |
| [kalaʔɛnaw] | [kalɑɛnaw] |
| [kalaʔenaw] | [kalɑenaw] |

Table 5: Equivalence classes for Qalah-ye Now Experiment

When we search for a "no compensatory lengthening" pronunciation, we have a correct answer when we retrieve any one of the "no compensatory lengthening" pronunciations, and equivalently for the "compensatory lengthening" pronunciations. Table 6 provides results for precision and recall on this search above two levels of phonetic recognizer confidence:

| Search Term | Confidence | Precision | Recall | True Pos. | False Pos. | False Neg. |
|---|---|---|---|---|---|---|
| [qalaʔɛnaw] | 80 | 0.88 | 0.50 | 7 | 1 | 7 |
| | 60 | 0.80 | 0.57 | 8 | 2 | 6 |
| [qalaɑɛnaw] | 80 | 0.33 | 1.00 | 1 | 2 | 0 |
| | 60 | 0.13 | 1.00 | 1 | 7 | 0 |

Table 6: Dialect-specific results on compensatory lengthening in Dari

As expected, recall is better with lower confidence and precision is better with higher confidence. Note that when searching for [qalaʔɛnaw], [qalaɑɛnaw] is not retrieved above confidence 60. However, when searching for [qalaɑɛnaw], [qalaʔɛnaw] is sometimes retrieved above that confidence level. This asymmetric performance is reflected in the higher precision values for [qalaʔɛnaw] as compared to [qal-aɑɛnaw].

Table 7 presents data for a dialect-agnostic search for Qalah-ye Now. For this search, we are not concerned about the particular pronunciation, so any pronunciation of the place in question will count as correct. As can be seen, this perspective causes precision to increase for [qalaɑɛnaw].

| Term | Confidence | Precision | Recall | True Positive | False Positive | False Negative |
|---|---|---|---|---|---|---|
| [qalaʔɛnaw] | 80 | 0.88 | 0.47 | 7 | 1 | 8 |
| | 60 | 0.80 | 0.53 | 8 | 2 | 7 |
| [qalaɑɛnaw] | 80 | 1.00 | 0.20 | 3 | 0 | 12 |
| | 60 | 0.75 | 0.40 | 6 | 2 | 9 |

Table 7: Dialect-agnostic results on Qalah-ye Now

Table 8 provides dialect-specific results on the diagnosis of southwest vs. northeast Pashto on the basis of the presence of [ʂ] or [x] for the Pashto letter ښ in the pronunciation of the town Lashkar Gah لښکر گاه. In the dialect-specific search, presence of [ʂ] or [x] must match between the search term and what is retrieved. The search with [x] is seen to be more precise.

| Term | Confidence | Precision | Recall | True Positive | False Positive | False Negative |
|---|---|---|---|---|---|---|
| [laʂkargɑ] | 80 | 0.50 | 0.50 | 1 | 1 | 1 |
| | 60 | 0.50 | 1.00 | 2 | 2 | 0 |
| [laxkargɑ] | 80 | 1.00 | 0.17 | 1 | 0 | 5 |
| | 60 | 0.75 | 0.50 | 3 | 1 | 3 |

Table 8: Dialect-specific results on /ʂ/ vs. /x/ in Pashto

Table 9 presents data for a dialect-agnostic search for *Lashkar Gah*. In this search, any pronunciation of the town will count as correct. Again, precision is seen to increase from this perspective.

| Term | Confidence | Precision | Recall | True Positive | False Positive | False Negative |
|---|---|---|---|---|---|---|
| [laʂkargɑ] | 80 | 1.00 | 0.25 | 2 | 0 | 6 |
| | 60 | 0.80 | 0.50 | 4 | 1 | 4 |
| [laxkargɑ] | 80 | 1.00 | 0.13 | 1 | 0 | 7 |
| | 60 | 1.00 | 0.50 | 4 | 0 | 4 |

Table 9: Dialect-agnostic results on /ʂ/ vs. /x/ in Pashto

## 6 Crosslingual Search

Crosslingual search is treated as a form of query expansion by Hu et al. (2012) and its efficacy as well as algorithms for its implementation in the domain of placenames are discussed by Joshi et al. (2008). We adduce crosslingual search as a tool for assessing language-specific search. For example, if we search for Kabul using the Pashto engine, to what extent will we retrieve Pashto utterances of that place as opposed to Dari utterances, and vice versa? If the Pashto engine is good at picking up Pashto to the exclusion of Dari utterances of a placename, it may be an effective tool for language-specific search.

We performed a set of experiments to assess this capability. First, we performed a search that was agnostic with respect to language and dialect. This means that in a search for Kabul in Pashto, we give credit for both Pashto and Dari tokens of Kabul that are retrieved, regardless of their particular pronunciations. Next, we performed language-specific searches in both Dari and Pashto. When searching in a given language, we only give credit for retrievals in that language. Note that when we performed language-specific search, we were dialect-agnostic. That is, we gave credit for a retrieval provided it was in the language being searched for, regardless of the particular pronunciation used.

The first term used for both language-agnostic and language-specific search was IPA [kɑbʊl]. Note that due to details of the Nexidia engine, the actual SAMPA strings used were [k A: b O l] for Dari and [k A b u l] for Pashto. The symbols for /ā/ and /ʊ/ in each language are arbitrarily different as indicated in Table 10. While IPA symbols (and their SAMPA equivalents) are theoretically absolute values in acoustic or articulatory space, in practice, they often adhere to arbitrary conventions for transcription of a particular language.

| Language | Orthographic symbol | IPA | SAMPA |
|---|---|---|---|
| Dari | ا | ɑ, ɒ | A: |
| Pashto | ا | ɑ | A |
| Dari | ◌ُ | ʊ | O |
| Pashto | ◌ُ | ʊ | u |

Table 10: Differences in phoneme symbols used for Dari and Pashto

Pashto exhibits pronunciation variation between [kɑbʊl] and [kɑbəl]. Table 11 compares performance on language-agnostic search performed for Kabul in each language.

| Language | Search | Confidence | Precision | Recall | True Pos. | False Pos. | False Neg. |
|---|---|---|---|---|---|---|---|
| Dari | [kɑbʊl] | 60 | 0.75 | 0.61 | 41 | 14 | 26 |
| Pashto | [kɑbʊl] | 60 | 0.80 | 0.24 | 16 | 4 | 51 |
| | [kɑbəl] | 60 | 0.82 | 0.21 | 14 | 3 | 53 |

Table 11: Language and dialect-agnostic search

Table 12 compares performance on language-specific search. Note that this search was still dialect-agnostic, so credit was given as long as the token was in the searched-for language, regardless of its pronunciation.

| Language | Search | Conf. | Prec. | Recall | True Pos. | False Pos. | False Neg. |
|---|---|---|---|---|---|---|---|
| Dari | [kɑbʊl] | 60 | 0.29 | 0.42 | 16 | 39 | 22 |
| Pashto | [kɑbʊl] | 60 | 0.70 | 0.37 | 14 | 6 | 24 |
| | [kɑbəl] | 60 | 0.82 | 0.37 | 14 | 3 | 24 |

Table 12: Language-specific search

As we can see from these results, the Dari engine has better precision and recall on the language-agnostic search, in contrast to the Pashto engine, whose recall is better on language-specific search. This can be interpreted as follows: the Dari engine is more versatile and can pick up Pashto, whereas the Pashto engine is more specific to Pashto and does not pick up Dari as well.

## 7 Conclusion

We have achieved some success searching for language and dialect-specific pronunciations using the Audio Gazetteer tool. A future challenge will be to identify dialect-specific toponyms automatically from a gazetteer. Our results are encouraging for the exploitation of pronunciation variation in toponym resolution and perhaps speaker identification. While dialect-specific results are often not as precise as searches that are agnostic as to language or dialect, in effect because we are "raising the bar" for what is correct, more data and more dialect and language-specific phenomena need to be collected and processed through the system in order to establish its capabilities more clearly.

## References


Fadi Biadsy. 2011. *Automatic dialect and accent recognition and its application to speech recognition.* Ph.D. dissertation, Columbia University.

Paul Boersma. 2001. Praat, a system for doing phonetics by computer. *Glot International* 5(9/10):341-345.

Davide Buscaldi. 2010. *Toponym disambiguation in information retrieval.* Ph.D. dissertation. Universidad Politécnica de Valencia.

Abd-ul-Ghafur Farhadi. 1955. *Le persan parlé en Afghanistan.* Klincksieck, Paris.

Klaus Forster. 1981. *A pronouncing dictionary of English place-names including standard local and archaic variants.* Routledge, London.

Michelle Annette Minnick Fox. 2006. *Usage-based effects in Latin American Spanish syllable-final /s/ deletion.* Ph.D. dissertation, University of Pennsylvania.

Marsal Gavalda and Jeff Schlueter. 2010. "The truth is out there": Using advanced speech analytics to learn why customers call help-line desks and how effectively they are being served by the call center agent. In Amy Neustein, editor, *Advances in speech recognition: Mobile environments, call centers and clinics,* pages 221-243. Springer, New York.

Qian Hu, Fred J. Goodman, Stanley M. Boykin, Randall K. Fish, Warren R. Greiff, Stephen R. Jones, and Stephen R. Moore. 2012. Automatic detection, indexing, and retrieval of multiple attributes from cross-lingual multimedia data. In M. T. Maybury, editor, *Multimedia information extraction,* pages 221-233. Wiley, Hoboken.

Tanuja Joshi, Joseph Joy, Tobias Kellner, Udayan Khurana, A Kumaran, A. and Vibhuti Sengar. 2008. Crosslingual Location Search. *SIGIR '08.*

Jochen Lothar Leidner. 2007. *Toponym resolution in text.* Ph.D. dissertation, University of Edinburgh.

D. N. MacKenzie. 1959. A Standard Pashto. *Bulletin of the School of Oriental and African Studies* 22(1/3):231-235.

Corey Miller, Rachel Strong, Evan Jones and Mark Vinson. 2013. Reflections on Dari linguistic identity through toponyms. In Rudolf Muhr et al., editors, *Exploring linguistic standards in non-dominant varieties of pluricentric languages,* pages 319-330. Peter Lang, Vienna.

Corey Miller. 2014. Pashto Dialects. In Anne Boyle David, *Descriptive grammar of Pashto and its dialects,* pages 32-44. Mouton De Gruyter, Berlin.

Mohammad Alam Miran. 1969. *Major problems of Dari speakers in mastering Pashto morphology.* M.A. Thesis, UT Austin.

John Nerbonne and Wilbert Heeringa. 2010. Measuring dialect differences. In J. E. Schmidt and P. Auer, editors, *Language and space: an international handbook of linguistic variation, volume 1, theories and methods.* Mouton de Gruyter, Berlin.

MITRE. 2012. The MITRE Corporation Annual Report.

Herbert Penzl. 1955. *A Grammar of Pashto.* American Council of Learned Societies, Washington.

Raytheon. 2012. BBN Broadcast Monitoring System. Retrieved from http://bbn.com/resources/pdf/bms.pdf

Steven H. Weinberger and Stephen A. Kunath. 2011. The speech accent archive: towards a typology of English accents. In J. Newman, H. Baayen, H., and S. Rice, editors, *Corpus-based studies in language use, language learning and language documentation,* pages 265-281. Rodopi, Amsterdam.

J. C. Wells. 1997. SAMPA computer readable phonetic alphabet. In D. Gibbon, R. Moore and R. Winski, editors, *Handbook of standards and resources for spoken language systems.* Mouton de Gruyter, Berlin.

Mirjam Wester, Judith M. Kessens, Catia Cucchiarini and Helmer Strik. 2001. Obtaining phonetic transcriptions: A comparison between expert listeners and a continuous speech recognizer. *Language and Speech* 44(3): 377-403.

# Part-of-Speech Tag Disambiguation by Cross-Linguistic Majority Vote

**Noëmi Aepli***
URPP Language and Space
University of Zurich

**Ruprecht von Waldenfels**†
Institute of Computer Science
Polish Academy of Sciences

**Tanja Samardžić***
URPP Language and Space
University of Zurich

## Abstract

In this paper, we present an approach to developing resources for a low-resource language, taking advantage of the fact that it is closely related to languages with more resources. In particular, we test our approach on Macedonian, which lacks tools for natural language processing as well as data in order to build such tools. We improve the Macedonian training set for supervised part-of-speech tagging by transferring available manual annotations from a number of similar languages. Our approach is based on multilingual parallel corpora, automatic word alignment, and a set of rules (majority vote). The performance of a tagger trained on the improved data set of 88% accuracy is significantly better than the baseline of 76%. It can serve as a stepping stone for further improvement of resources for Macedonian. The proposed approach is entirely automatic and it can be easily adapted to other language in similar circumstances.

## 1 Introduction

Developing natural language processing tools for various languages proves to be of great interest for both, practical applications and linguistic research. Speakers of various languages and varieties increasingly use social media to interact in their own varieties. To make use of these interactions as a relatively easily accessible source of data, we need to be able to process different varieties automatically. However, a great majority of languages of the world lack resources for natural language processing.

With a relatively small number of speakers and weak research infrastructure, Macedonian is one of the languages lacking basic tools for natural language processing. On the other hand, this language is in a convenient position in the sense that it is very similar to other Slavic languages for which more resources are available. We can take advantage of this fact to automatise and facilitate creation of linguistic resources necessary for building tools for automatic processing of Macedonian.

In this paper, we build a part-of-speech tagger for Macedonian. Part-of-speech tagging is a crucial component in a natural language processing pipeline and it is a logical starting point in developing resources for a new language. To obtain a good performance on this task, one needs a sufficiently large corpus with manually annotated tags which can then be used to train a tagger. This is exactly the kind of resource which is often missing (or not easily available) because its development is long, costly and language specific. The current state of language technology allows us to automatise this process to a large degree.

We improve a training set for Macedonian part-of-speech tagging by automatic projection of manual annotation available in other languages. The basis of our method is automatic word alignment, which is widely used in applications for machine translation.

Automatic word alignment has already been used for improving language resources and tools for part-of-speech tagging in the context of supervised (Yarowsky et al., 2001) and unsupervised (Snyder et al., 2008) learning. The success of these techniques strongly depends on the amount of available parallel

*{noemi.aepli|tanja.samardzic}@uzh.ch
†ruprecht.waldenfels@issl.unibe.ch





*Proceedings of the First Workshop on Applying NLP Tools to Similar Languages, Varieties and Dialects*, pages 76–84,
Dublin, Ireland, August 23 2014.

corpora for training models for both word alignment and part-of-speech tagging. It is also strongly influenced by the limitations of automatic word alignment which often produces alignment errors, even if it is trained on a large parallel corpus. Our approach to obtaining robust word alignment in a small corpus available for Macedonian is to use a multiple parallel corpus of similar languages. Lexical similarity between the languages is expected to make word alignment easier than for unrelated languages. Combining the information from different languages is expected to cancel out wrong alignments.

## 2 The Challenge of Developing Resources for Macedonian

Macedonian is an Indo-European language of the Slavic branch. It has around 1.7 million speakers.[1] It is one of the youngest Slavic standard languages, with most of its codification done after the formal declaration of Macedonian as the official language of the Yugoslav Republic of Macedonia in 1944 (Friedman, 2001). Its closest relative is Bulgarian, with whose dialects the Macedonian dialects form a continuum.

### 2.1 Linguistic Properties

Macedonian belongs to the "Balkan Sprachbund", a famous group of Balkan languages consisting of three Slavic languages (Bulgarian, Macedonian, and some dialects of Serbian), one Romance language (Romanian) and two Indo-European isolates (Greek, Albanian). The members of this group share important structural features developed as a result of areal linguistic contact. The "Sprachbund" features can distinguish the languages belonging to the group from the other languages of the same genetical branch. For example, the Slavic languages belonging to the group differ from all the other Slavic languages in that they do not distinguish cases. To express grammatical relations expressed by case in other Slavic languages, Macedonian and Bulgarian use prepositions (Tomić, 2006). This is an important property in the context of our project because it influences the choice of the direction of automatic word alignment across languages, as it will be shortly described in section 3.2. This property also influences our decision to include in our data set English as the only non-Slavic language (as described in section 2.3).

### 2.2 Sparse Resources

As far as we know, there is no publicly available part-of-speech tagger for Macedonian at the moment of writing. There are references to morphological resources developed using the NOOJ environment (Ivanovska-Naskova, 2006; Silberstein, 2003). Also, some work on automatic morphological analysis of Macedonian was done in the context of developing an open-source machine translation system (Rangelov, 2011; Peradin and Tyers, 2012).

Most importantly for the current project, a morphologically annotated Macedonian translation of Orwell's 1984 was made available as part of the MULTEXT-East resources (Erjavec, 2012). The annotation in this corpus, however, is incomplete. The main problem is that tokens are assigned all potential part-of-speech tags without disambiguation. Multiple potential tags are assigned to 44,387 tokens, which makes 39% of the whole corpus. Another important problem is missing annotation. There are 4,810 tokens (around 4%) for which there is no annotation at all. The proportion of 43% tokens which lack the crucial information makes this corpus inadequate for training processing tools. To obtain an adequate training set for Macedonian from this corpus, we add the missing information from other languages available in the MULTEXT-East resources with more complete annotation.

### 2.3 The Overview of our Approach

We take parallel texts for Macedonian (MK), Bulgarian (BG), Czech (CZ), Slovene (SL), Serbian (SR) and English (EN) from the MULTEXT-East corpus (see section 3.1). We select Bulgarian, Czech, Slovene and Serbian as languages closely related to Macedonian. Since these languages are related, they have similar lexicon, grammar and word order. As a result, it can be expected that many words in a parallel text can be aligned as a one-to-one relation, with less cross-linguistic transformations and reordering than in the case of distant languages. In addition to the Slavic languages we also include

[1]https://www.ethnologue.com/language/mkd, 17.04.2014

English because of the fact that Macedonian differs from other Slavic languages (except Bulgarian) in the use of cases. As mentioned above, Macedonian uses analytic prepositional phrases instead of Slavic cases, which makes it closer to languages such as English in this respect.

For each of the five selected languages, manually disambiguated part-of-speech tags are available as part of the MULTEXT-East resources. Moreover, the annotation in different languages can be automatically aligned since the MULTEXT-East corpus consists of translations of the novel "1984" into different languages. All the texts are manually aligned at the level of sentence. Given the sentence alignment, we automatically align Macedonian with the selected languages. We then use word alignments to transfer automatically the annotation found in the other languages to Macedonian. As a next step, we put together all the tags from all the languages, including the available Macedonian tags. This results in a set of part-of-speech candidates for each Macedonian token. We choose the best candidate by a majority vote: the most frequent tag in the set of candidates is chosen as the correct tag. This step relies on the intuition that tags which end up in the candidate set by mistake will not be frequent because their distribution does not depend on the token for which they are candidates. On the other hand, the tags which are truly related to the token in question should be frequent in the set.

The five languages included in the study are not equally close to Macedonian. In addition to the most related languages (Bulgarian and Serbian), we include the data from other Slavic languages (Czech and Slovene) and English to deal with the noise caused by potentially wrong word alignments. We expect that a correct word alignment is more likely to be found in an increased data set. On the other hand, including more languages is not expected to introduce more noise. If word alignments with other languages are wrong, they are not expected to result in repeated tags in the tag candidate set.

Although the general idea is rather intuitive and straightforward, actual realisation of the plan proved technically not trivial. The main difficulty lies in combining word alignment with the original annotation and in cross-linguistic mapping of the manual annotation.

To evaluate the results of the cross-linguistic disambiguation, we provide manual disambiguation for a small section of the Macedonian corpus, which serves as the gold standard. To evaluate how useful our cross-linguistic tag disambiguation is for automatic tagging, we train a tagger on the automatically disambiguated corpus and test it on the portion for which we have provided the gold standard annotation. In the following section, we describe in more detail the decisions taken at each step of our approach.

## 3 Materials and Methods

As shortly mentioned before, we work with the corpus of the MULTEXT-East resources (Erjavec, 2012), "Multilingual Text Tools and Corpora for Central and Eastern European Languages". The corpus contains the novel "1984" by George Orwell, annotated with part-of-speech tags and further morphosyntactic specifications. It is a parallel corpus available in Macedonian, Bulgarian, Czech, English, Slovene, Serbian and many more. Furthermore, the parallel texts are manually sentence-aligned. The Macedonian corpus was only added in version 4 in 2010. It consists of 113,158 tokens corresponding to 6,790 sentences.

### 3.1 Multilingual Morphosyntactic Specifications

Morphosyntactic specifications are assigned manually to each token in the corpus. They are similar and largely equivalent across the languages included in the resource, but they are not fully consistent.

Each morphosyntactic definition specifies a value for a number of categories. Each definition consists of a string of characters, where each character specifies the value for one category. These strings can be rather long for words for which many categories need to be encoded. For example, the tag *#Vmia2s--------e* specifies a Macedonian verb form with 15 categories: 1) ***V*** for ***Verb***, 2) ***main*** as *type*, 3) ***indicative*** as the verb *form*, 4) ***aorist*** as *tense*, 5) ***2nd*** *person*, 6) ***singular***, and 7) *perfective* (***e***) as *aspect*. In between, there are no specifications (-) for the subcategories 8) *gender*, 9) *voice*, and 10) *negative*, which could be specified in Macedonian, but have no value in this specific case. Furthermore, there are five subcategories which are not specified for Macedonian but only for other languages, they are marked with a dash too.

Detailed descriptions can be found on the web page of the MULTEXT-East resources.[2]

We notice that the cross-linguistic mapping of the morphosyntactic definitions is more straightforward towards the left-hand side of the definition than towards the right-hand side. For our purpose we only consider the first two letters: the main category and its type (in this example *Vm*). We ignore the information concerning the grammatical categories and reduce the morphosyntactic definitions to relatively coarse part-of-speech tags.

There are 14 main categories (e.g. noun, verb, etc.). Each of these categories can be further specified for the type, but not necessarily. All the combinations of the first two letters in the corpus give a tag set which consists of 58 tags.

Even though morphosyntactic definitions are more consistent across languages for the first two than for the subsequent characters, some variation is found in our tags too. The variations in the subcategories are due to differences in the languages as well as different annotation strategies.

Table 1 shows the categories with the corresponding subcategory *type* across the languages we use. The first and second column of table 1 specify the PoS category to which the types for the six languages are specified. The possible values for the type of the category in one language are separated by a slash (/). The dash (-) means that the type is not specified for that language. A missing entry shows that the whole category is not specified for the language. We can see, for example, that there are three kinds of adjectives in Macedonian: *Af*, *As*, and *Ao*. There are no types in Bulgarian, while the types in other languages overlap with Macedonian only partially. The types which are found in other languages, but not in Macedonian (e.g. *Ag* and *Ap* in Slovenian) cannot be transferred to Macedonian.

| | | **MK** | **BG** | **CS** | **SL** | **SR** | **EN** |
|---|---|---|---|---|---|---|---|
| N | Noun | c/p | c/p | c/p | c/p | c/p | c/p |
| V | Verb | m/a/o | m/a | m/a/o/c | m/a | m/a/o/c | m/a/o/b |
| A | Adjective | f/s/o | - | f/s | g/s/p | f/s/o | f |
| P | Pronoun | p/d/i/s/q r/x/z/g | p/d/i/s/q r/x/z/g | p/d/i/s q/r/x | p/s/d/r/x g/q/i/z | p/d/i/s/q r/x/z/g | p/s/q/r x/g/t |
| R | Adverb | g/a/v | g/a | g | g/r | g/z/a/v | m/s |
| S | Adposition | p | p | p | - | p | p/t |
| C | Conjunction | c/s | c/s | c/s | c/s | c/s | c/s |
| M | Number | c/o/l/s | c/o | c/o/m/s | c/o/p/s | c/o/m/l/s | c/o |
| I | Interjection | - | - | - | - | - | - |
| Y | Abbreviation | - | - | n/r | - | n/r | - |
| X | Residual | - | - | - | f/t/p | - | - |
| Q | Particle | s/c | z/g/c/v/q/o | z/q/o/r | - | c/a/o/r | |
| D | Determiner | | | | | | d/i/s/g |
| T | Article | | | | | | |

Table 1: Cross-linguistic mapping of part-of-speech tags in our data set.

### 3.2 Automatic Word Alignment

The MULTEXT-East corpus contains manual sentence alignment for each language pair. We extract the information about sentence alignment between Macedonian and the five languages included in our study.

Given the sentence alignment, we word align each of the parallel texts using GIZA++ (Och and Ney, 2003). As it is required by the input format for GIZA++, we remove sentence boundaries in the cases where sentence alignment is not one-to-one. For example, if two English sentences are aligned with one Macedonian sentence, we remove the boundary between the two English sentences. We then restore the sentence boundaries in the alignment output so that we can identify the sentences in the original annotated corpus and retrieve the annotation.

For each pair of languages, word alignment can be performed in two directions. One language is considered as the source and the other as target. The choice of the alignment direction can have an important influence on the resulting alignment (Och and Ney, 2003; Samardžić and Merlo, 2010). The influence of the alignment direction on the results follows from the formal definition of word alignment

[2] http://nl.ijs.si/ME/, 24.06.2014

in the practical implementation. Since alignment is a single-valued function which assigns to each target language word exactly one source language word, many-to-one alignments are only possible in one direction: multiple target language words can be aligned with one source language word, but not the other way around.

The performance of the programs for automatic word alignment is not perfect. To obtain more reliable alignment, researchers usually take the intersection of both directions as the resulting alignment. This technique yields very reliable alignments reaching a precision of 98.6%. However, since it allows only one-to-one alignment, it necessarily leaves a good proportion of words unaligned (recall as low as 52.9%) (Padó, 2007).

Since our corpus is small, we need to obtain as many word alignments as possible. Thus we do not use the intersection of both alignments, but we use the full output of one alignment direction. It follows from the formal definition of alignment that all target words need to be aligned, which necessarily increases the recall, but potentially at the cost of precision.

To obtain a better precision, we choose the more suitable direction of alignment. Since the many-to-one mappings are possible only from the target language to the source language, we choose the alignment direction for each pair of languages so that the target language is the more analytic one. In all Slavic pairs, Macedonian is the target, due to the fact that it uses analytic prepositional expressions where other Slavic languages use single words in a particular case. In the pair English-Macedonian, the target language is English, because its forms are more analytic than in Macedonian.

### 3.3 Combining Information from All Languages

Given the word alignment, we replace each word of the other languages (OL) which is aligned to a Macedonian word with its corresponding part-of-speech tag retrieved from the original manually annotated corpus. Table 2 illustrates the resulting data structure. The first column in the table is the sentence ID, the second the Macedonian word. In the next columns the part-of-speech information is stored: first the Macedonian tags and then the tags projected from other languages. Language code is given before "#" and the full morphosyntactic definition found in the language in question after "#".

As it can be seen in Table 2, none, one, or several tags can be specified for each language. In the first example, there is exactly one tag for every language. In the second example, the part-of-speech information in English is missing because there was no alignment between the Macedonian word "со" and any English word. This is the case for all five other languages in the last example, where the tags are specified only for Macedonian.[3] The third example shows the opposite, with one PoS tag for each other language, but none for Macedonian.

| ID | Word | MK PoS | OL PoS |
|---|---|---|---|
| 1.1.1.1 | јасен 'clear' | mk#Af | bg#AM cs#Af en#Af sl#Ag sr#Af |
| 1.1.1.2 | со 'with' | mk#Sp | bg#SP cs#Rg en sl#Si sr#Sp |
| 1.1.1.2 | Винстон 'Winston' | | bg#Np cs#Np en#Np sl#Np sr#Np |
| 2.7.2.3 | едно 'one' | mk#C- mk#Rg mk#Mc | bg#VM cs#Mc en#Di sl#Ap sr#Vm |
| 1.1.11.2 | што 'what' | mk#Pq mk#Pr mk#C- mk#Q- mk#Rg mk#I | bg cs en sl sr |

Table 2: Macedonian text with PoS tags of aligned words of other languages

### 3.4 Choosing the Best Candidate

Having collected sets of possible tags for each Macedonian word, the next step is to choose the best tag.

The general idea is to take into consideration all the tags of all languages that are given for one word and choose the most frequent of them as the correct tag for Macedonian. As the tags do not match

[3]Note that alignments are not missing in the technical sense in the case of Slavic languages. According to the formal definition of alignment discussed above, all Macedonian words need to be aligned in the direction that we chose. The fact that there is no alignment in our data means that the Macedonian word is aligned with the special "NULL" word in other Slavic languages in this case. This special word is added to each sentence of each source language in the process of alignment, so that the target language words for which there are no corresponding words in the source language can be aligned too.

completely (see section 3.1), the chosen tag has to be checked for validity. In other words, we check if the most frequent tag is a valid tag for Macedonian according to the MULTEXT-East specifications.

For the task of choosing the best tag, we define a set of if-then rules. We apply an outer structure of three if/else statements checking how many tags are given for Macedonian: one, zero or several. If exactly one tag is given, we choose it as the best candidate. The latter two cases include further checks taking into account the number of specified tags of the other languages (zero or several) as well as the number of most frequent tags (the maximum). The former check is necessary because of the cases where there are zero tags in Macedonian. If there are no tags in other languages either, we have to assign a "dummy tag". The dummy tag is the most frequently occurring tag in the original annotation for Macedonian. This is the *Nc* (common noun) tag in our case. The latter check, the number of maxima, is done because more than one tag could have the same frequency. In cases where the competition between the tags remains unresolved because of no matchings and/or sparse data, we reduce the tag to make it less specific. We ignore the type, that is, the second letter of the tag, which leaves us with only the category. Even this approach does not solve all the decision problems. If this is the case we have two procedures: if there is no tag information coming from any language, we assign a "dummy tag". In the second case, where we can not decide but we do have some information in Macedonian, we randomly choose one of the given Macedonian tags. The cases in which we had to apply some additional heuristics (comparing reduced tags, random choice and dummy tag) because there was not one single most frequent tag constitute around 10%. The decision process for choosing the best candidate is given in more detail in the pseudocode "Algorithm 1".

Consider, for example, the fourth entry in Table 2, "едно". There are three tags for Macedonian, which means it satisfies the third condition of the outer if/else structure (more than 1 MK PoS tag). Next, the most frequent tag considering all the given PoS tags of all the languages is searched. As described in Section 3.1, we only take into account the first two letters (category and type) of a given morphosyntactic definition. In this case, we have the following tags with the corresponding frequencies: (MC : 2), (VM : 2), (C : 1), (AP : 1), (DI : 1), (RG : 1). Looking for the maximum, we find two tags with the same frequency (2): MC and VM. Because there is more than one maximum, we check for each of the two tags if they are identical to one of the Macedonian tags. In this case, the test is true for MC (cardinal numeral). This is one of the maxima **and** one of the Macedonian tags, therefore the winner.

### 3.5 Training a Tagger

To asses whether disambiguating part-of-speech tags as described in the previous sections is useful for training a statistical part-of-speech tagger, we divide our data set into a training and test portion. We train a tagger on the training portion of the disambiguated corpus and we measure its performance on the test set. We use the BTagger (Gesmundo and Samardzic, 2012), since it has good generalisation capacities, which makes it suitable for small data sets. Furthermore, it does not need any manually constructed morphological dictionaries and it can be used for any language.

## 4 Evaluation

To evaluate both our disambiguation method and the performance of the tagger on the disambiguated corpus, we chose an arbitrary sample section of the corpus as the test set. The sample included 9,954 tokens (around 10% of the whole corpus), out of which 616 were missing annotation, and 3,231 were not disambiguated. We manually add the missing tags and disambiguate the ambiguous ones. In this way, we obtain the gold standard for the evaluation.

### 4.1 The baseline

We compare both, the success of our cross-linguistic disambiguation and the performance of the tagger with a baseline. To define the baseline, we use a simple heuristic which allows us to disambiguate Macedonian tags without cross-linguistic information: we take the first tag in the list as the correct one. In the case of missing tags, we add NC (common noun), which is the most frequent tag in the corpus. We run the tagger on the corpus disambiguated in this way, which gives us the baseline performance.

**Algorithm 1** Find the best PoS-tag for an MK word given MK, BG, CS, EN, SL and SR tags

```
if number of MK-PoS-tags = 1 then
    result ← this MK-PoS-tag
else if number of MK-PoS-tags = 0 then
    if number of OL-PoS-tags = 0 then
        result ← dummy-tag
    else if number of OL-PoS-tags > 0 then
        if 1 maximum then
            result ← maximum (→ to be checked whether it is a valid MK-tag)
        else if >1 maximum then
            result ← dummy-tag
        end if
    end if
else if number of MK-PoS-tags > 1 then
    if 1 maximum then
        if maximum = one of MK-PoS-tags then
            result ← maximum
        else if reduced PoS-tag = one of MK-PoS-tags then
            result ← MK-PoS-tag with the same category like the maximum
        else if maximum not in MK-PoS-tags then
            result ← random choice of available MK-PoS-tags
        end if
    else if > 1 maximum then
        for candidate in maxima do
            if candidate = one of MK-PoS-tags then
                result ← candidate
            else if candidate not one of MK-PoS-tags then
                reduce candidate to 1 letter
                if reduced candidate = one of reduced MK-PoS-tags then
                    result ← not-reduced MK-PoS-tags
                else
                    result ← random choice of available MK-PoS-tags
                end if
            end if
        end for
    else if number of OL-PoS-tags = 0 then
        result ← random choice of available MK-PoS-tags
    end if
end if
```

### 4.2 Results and Discussion

Table 3 shows the accuracy of cross-linguistic disambiguation and tagging in comparison with the baseline. The second column shows the agreement between manual disambiguation (the gold standard) and automatic disambiguation in the two settings.

We can see that our simple heuristics alone provide some correct disambiguation. Roughly half of the 43% of tags which are potentially wrong in the original corpus (because they are not disambiguated or because they miss annotation) are correctly disambiguated by the baseline heuristics. This gives the baseline disambiguation accuracy of 78%. Adding the information from other languages improves the accuracy of automatic disambiguation to 87%.

| Accuracy (%) | Disambiguation | BTagger | |
|---|---|---|---|
| Baseline | 78 | All | 77 |
| | | Known | 76 |
| | | Unknown | 77 |
| Cross-linguistic Majority Vote | 87 | All | 88 |
| | | Known | 88 |
| | | Unknown | 91 |

Table 3: The accuracy of disambiguation and tagging compared with the gold standard.

When trained on the corpus disambiguated in the baseline setting, the tagger's accuracy is 77%, while its accuracy is improved to 88% when it is trained on the corpus disambiguated using our cross-linguistic majority vote.

It is important to note that the tagger's performance improves more than the disambiguation accuracy compared to the baseline (77% to 88% vs. 78% to 87%). The tagger outperforms the direct disambiguation in the cross-linguistic setting. This means that eliminating wrong tags from the training set allows the tagger not only to learn better correct tags, but also to come up with generalisations and provide a more robust output. Although it assigns learned wrong tags to the words seen in the training set (accuracy on known words 88%), it uses the learned generalisations to predict more correct tags on the words unseen in the training set (accuracy on unknown words 91%).

## 5 Conclusion

We have presented a method for improving resources in a new language using the existing resources in similar languages and state-of-the art language technology. We evaluated our method as applied to Macedonian, a low-resource Slavic language, closely related to other Slavic languages with more available resources.

By cross-linguistic annotation projection, we improved the existing annotation, assigning the correct tag to two thirds of potentially wrong part-of-speech tags in the original corpus. The performance of a tagger trained on the disambiguated corpus reaches 88% accuracy. This is not a satisfying performance in itself, but this tagger is the first trained and evaluated tool for Macedonian. Another important outcome of our experiments is the fact that an improved training set allows a tagger to develop crucial generalisations and to provide a more robust output. This finding can be useful for further improvement of the resources not only in Macedonian, but in other low-resource languages too.

The presented approach to improving annotated language resources across languages is entirely automatic. It can be applied to any other language in similar circumstances. Instead of repeating the same kind of costly, time-consuming manual work in each new language, our approach makes use of available annotations by transferring them automatically from one language to another.

## Acknowledgements

The work presented in this paper is supported by the URPP Language and Space, University of Zurich and the Swiss National Science Foundation. Training data annotation was co-financed by the Slavic Institute of Bern University. Many thanks to Andrea Gesmundo for valuable comments and suggestions.

## References


Tomaž Erjavec. 2012. MULTEXT-East: Morphosyntactic Resources for Central and Eastern European Languages. In *Language Resources and Evaluation*, volume 46, pages 131–142.

Victor A. Friedman, 2001. *Facts About The World's Languages: An Encyclopedia of the World's Major Languages, Past and Present*, chapter Macedonian, pages 435 – 439. The H. W. Wilson Company New York and Dublin.

Andrea Gesmundo and Tanja Samardzic. 2012. Lemmatisation as a tagging task. In *Proceedings of the 50th Annual Meeting of the Association for Computational Linguistics (Volume 2: Short Papers)*, pages 368–372, Jeju Island, Korea, July. Association for Computational Linguistics.

Ruska Ivanovska-Naskova. 2006. Development of the First LRs for Macedonian: Current Projects. In *Proceedings of the Fifth International Conference on Language Resources and Evaluation (LREC'06)*, pages 1837–1841. European Language Resources Association (ELRA).

Franz Josef Och and Hermann Ney. 2003. A Systematic Comparison of Various Statistical Alignment Models. In *Computational Linguistics*, volume 29, pages 19–51.

Sebastian Padó. 2007. *Cross-Lingual Annotation Projection Models for Role-Semantic Information*. Ph.D. thesis, Saarland University.

Hrvoje Peradin and Francis Tyers. 2012. A rule-based machine translation system from Serbo-Croatian to Macedonian. In *Proceedings of the Workshop Free/Open-Source Rule-Based Machine Translation*, pages 55 – 62, Gothenburg, Sweden.

Tihomir Rangelov. 2011. Rule-based machine translation between Bulgarian and Macedonian. Universitat Oberta de Catalunya.

Tanja Samardžić and Paola Merlo. 2010. Cross-lingual variation of light verb constructions: Using parallel corpora and automatic alignment for linguistic research. In *Proceedings of the 2010 Workshop on NLP and Linguistics: Finding the Common Ground*, pages 52–60, Uppsala, Sweden. Association for Computational Linguistics.

Max Silberstein. 2003. NooJ Manual. Available at www.nooj4nlp.net.

Benjamin Snyder, Tahira Naseem, Jacob Eisenstein, and Regina Barzilay. 2008. Unsupervised Multilingual Learning for POS Tagging. In *Proceedings of the 2008 Conference on Empirical Methods in Natural Language Processing*, pages 1041–1050, Honolulu. Association for Computational Linguistics.

Olga Mišeska Tomić. 2006. *Balkan Sprachbund Morpho-syntactic Features*. Springer, Dordrecht, The Netherlands.

David Yarowsky, Grace Ngai, and Richard Wicentowski. 2001. Inducing multilingual text analysis tools via robust projection across aligned corpora. In *Proceedings of the 1st international conference Human Language Technology*, pages 161–168, San Diego, CA. Association for Computational Linguistics.

# Compilation of a Swiss German Dialect Corpus and its Application to PoS Tagging

**Nora Hollenstein**
University of Zurich
hollenstein@cl.uzh.ch

**Noëmi Aepli**
University of Zurich
noemi.aepli@uzh.ch

## Abstract

Swiss German is a dialect continuum whose dialects are very different from Standard German, the official language of the German part of Switzerland. However, dealing with Swiss German in natural language processing, usually the detour through Standard German is taken. As writing in Swiss German has become more and more popular in recent years, we would like to provide data to serve as a stepping stone to automatically process the dialects. We compiled *NOAH's Corpus of Swiss German Dialects* consisting of various text genres, manually annotated with Part-of-Speech tags. Furthermore, we applied this corpus as training set to a statistical Part-of-Speech tagger and achieved an accuracy of 90.62%.

## 1 Introduction

Swiss German is not an official language of Switzerland, rather it includes dialects of Standard German, which is one of the four official languages. However, it is different from Standard German in terms of phonetics, lexicon, morphology and syntax. Swiss German is not dividable into a few dialects, in fact it is a dialect continuum with a huge variety. Swiss German is not only a spoken dialect but increasingly used in written form, especially in less formal text types. Often, Swiss German speakers write text messages, emails and blogs in Swiss German. However, in recent years it has become more and more popular and authors are publishing in their own dialect. Nonetheless, there is neither a writing standard nor an official orthography, which increases the variations dramatically due to the fact that people write as they please with their own style.

So far, there are almost no natural language processing (NLP) tools for Swiss German (Scherrer and Owen, 2010). Considering the fact that the major part of communication between Swiss people of the German part is in dialect, we would like to start building NLP tools for Swiss German dialects.

Furthermore, it is an attempt to deal with dialect varieties directly instead of taking the detour through the standard of a language. Speakers of various dialects increasingly communicate through social media in their own varieties. These interactions are relatively easily accessible and could be used as a source of data. However, there is a lack of natural language processing tools for dialects, which need to be developed first in order to process these data automatically.

We start with training a model for a Swiss German Part-of-Speech tagger, which is one of the first steps dealing with the automatic processing of natural language. Based on a part-of-speech tagged corpus, further processes like semantical analysis, syntactical parsing or even applications like machine translation can be conducted.

In order to train a PoS tagger we need a corpus annotated with parts-of-speech. As such data does not exist yet, we compiled *NOAH's Corpus of Swiss German Dialects* containing Swiss German texts of different genres, and annotated it manually. This is an iterative process alternating between running/training a PoS tagger and manually annotating/correcting the output. The corpus we present in this paper consists of 73,616 manually annotated tokens covering many dialect variations of the German-speaking part of Switzerland.





*Proceedings of the First Workshop on Applying NLP Tools to Similar Languages, Varieties and Dialects*, pages 85–94, Dublin, Ireland, August 23 2014.

In the next section, we will mention some related work before we will have a closer look at the Swiss German dialects and its differences to Standard German in section 3. In section 4 we introduce our corpus including the adapted tagset before we present the application of our corpus to the Part-of-Speech tagging task in section 5.

## 2 Related Work

Most natural language processing applications focus on standardised, written language varieties, but from a methodological as well as a practical point of view, it is interesting to develop NLP methods for variational linguistics. Even though there are no other resources of this size and no studies on PoS tagging for written Swiss German, there have been a few approaches which share some common aspects with our work. While there are some corpora of spoken texts, such as the Archimob project (Dejung et al., 1999) which comprises transcribed interviews, it is difficult to find resources to build a written Swiss German corpus. One of the rare written resources is the *sms4science* project (Dürscheid and Stark, 2011), a collection of text messages in all official languages of Switzerland as well as Swiss German dialects.

Concerning Part-of-Speech tagging for non-standard dialects, there are some approaches addressing linguistic varieties in historical texts, Hinrichs and Zastrow (2012) and Rayson et al. (2007) for German and English respectively. Furthermore, Diab (2009), Habash and Rambow (2009) and Duh and Kirchhoff (2005) worked on PoS tagging for Arabic dialects. The latter developed a minimally supervised PoS tagger for an Egyptian Arabic dialect, which does not have a standard orthography either, without using any dialect-specific tools.

As far as Swiss German NLP goes, there are approaches to dialect identification (Scherrer and Owen, 2010), dialect machine translation (Scherrer, 2012) and morphology generation (Scherrer, 2013).

## 3 Swiss German

Swiss German belongs to the Alemannic group of dialects, a branch of the Germanic language family. This group can be split into three linguistic divisions; Low, High and Highest Alemannic, each of which contains a few regions of Switzerland. There is no strict border between the Swiss German dialects and the other Alemannic dialects, rather it is referred to as a dialect continuum. Unlike the continuum among Swiss German dialects, there is a strict separation between Swiss German and Standard German. When it comes to the dialects of Swiss German, one can find the concept of diglossia. Diglossia is defined as a situation in which two languages (or two varieties of the same language) are used under different conditions within a language community. In the case of the German language, Standard German is used in Switzerland nearly exclusively in written context while Swiss German is in daily use, mostly in spoken form but also in informal written contexts (Siebenhaar and Wyler, 1997). However, this distinction is becoming more and more blurred. Schools are one of a few environments where Standard German is expected to be used in spoken language. Unlike the situation in other languages, it is standard in Switzerland to use dialect even in formal situations. In Swiss media, both TV and radio, Swiss German is well represented and commonly used.

With the introduction of emails, text messages, blogs and chats, Swiss German is taking over more and more space in written contexts. Nowadays, especially for the younger generations, it is completely normal to write in Swiss German. However, it is not limited to the private communication. In fact, it is even becoming a cult status to write and publish in Swiss German. Many authors, among them for example Lenz (2013), Schobinger (2014) and Kaiser (2012) write books in their dialect, and newspaper agencies publish newspapers in Swiss German, e.g. *Blick am Abend* (Ringier AG, 2013, 2014). Even the Swiss company *Swatch* has published their annual report 2012 in addition to Standard German, French and English also Swiss German (The Swatch Group AG, 2012). This hype does not seem to cease, in the contrary. Speaking a certain dialect is part of the identification. Swiss are proud of their dialect, which makes it possible to identify their home region if they move to another canton. Despite the big differences, speakers of various dialects usually understand each other, except a few German varieties of the canton Valais which others usually have troubles understanding (Keller, 1961).

## 3.1 Differences to Standard German

Swiss German differs from Standard German in many aspects such as phonetics, lexicon, morphology and syntax. One of the most significant differences is the vocabulary, which even introduces a new word class not in use in Standard German (see section 4.2). In Swiss German, the Standard German words are sometimes used in a different manner. For instance, in some cases the genus may change: the word *Radio* (radio) as a masculine word (in Swiss German) instead of neutral (in Standard German). However, there are not merely differences between Swiss and Standard German, but also between the different dialectal regions. Scherrer (2011) differs between variations which apply for the whole Swiss German speaking area and differences which appear only in certain dialects and not outside of Allemanic dialects. The differences between the dialects are partly due to the influence from other languages. For instance dialects closer to the French speaking part of Switzerland use different grammatical constructions than Eastern Swiss dialects. In this section we describe some examples of disparities between the Swiss German dialects and Standard German.

In Swiss German there is no preterite tense ("Präteritum") and the pluperfect ("Plusquamperfekt") is used extremely rarely. Both of them are expressed using the present perfect ("Perfekt") or rather a duplication of it (for an example see table 1). Another difference exists with regards to verb tenses and the use of the auxiliary verbs *sein* (to be) and *haben* (to have). For instance, if you are cold, in Switzerland you would say *Ich ha chalt.*, where *ha* is the first person singular of "to have". However, to express yourself in this situation in Standard German, the auxilary verb "to be" is used: *Mir ist kalt.*

Furthermore, there is more freedom in the order of words of a sentence, especially concerning verbs (for an example see table 1) as well as more possibilities to correctly arrange phrases. The overt specification of the subject is another difference. In Swiss German the subject can be dropped in many cases, the information about the person is then usually given in the conjugation of the verb. In the question *Chunnsch au?* (Swiss German) vs. *Kommst du auch?* (Standard German) (Are you coming too?), the subject *du* is not explicitly expressed in the Swiss German version but only in the second person singular conjugation of the verb.

Regarding nouns, the four cases of Standard German (nominative, accusative, dative and genitive) are not all in use in the dialects (Siebenhaar and Voegeli, 1997). Swiss German speakers generally neither speak nor write in the genitive case, apart from a few exceptions e.g. in the dialect of the canton Valais. The genitive is replaced by a possessive dative or a phrase using prepositions. This means, in order to express the German phrase *die Ohren des Hasen* (the bunny's ears), either the possessive dative *am Haas sini Ohrä* or a preposition *d Ohrä vom Haas* (where *vom* is a fusion of an preposition *von* and an article *dem*) is used. Moreover, nominative and accusative forms only differ in personal pronouns, whereas the dative case, if used, is marked with its own determiner and endings for adjectives and nouns.

There are many phenomena, which are treated differently not only in regards to Standard German but also in different dialects. First of all, the lexicon varies a lot. The variations do not only include different pronunciation but also completely different words. For instance in some regions of Switzerland, the Standard German word *Butter* (butter) is used (even though with a masculine article instead of the feminine one, which is correct in Standard German). In other regions, however, different words such as *Anke* are used instead. Another variation concerns the order of verbs if there is more than one of them in a sentence. It is often inverted compared to Standard German, but this varies according to the dialect. To express a final clause with *um ... zu* (in order to) for instance, people in eastern Switzerland would use the concatenation *zum*. Closer to the French speaking part though, the construction *für ... z* is commonly used, which marks the similarity to the French *pour ...*.

The following sentences in table 1 contain examples of both kinds of differences. On the one hand, there are the Standard German preterite forms *liess* and *hatte*, which are expressed in the perfect tense across dialects: *hat ... (gehen) lassen* and *hat gehabt*. On the other hand, the order of the verbs in the perfect construction (*het gha* vs. *gha hät*) as well as the final clause with *um ... zu* differs from dialect to dialect.

Considering the way people write in Swiss German reveals another characteristic. The aforementioned lack of a spelling standard causes variations not only between different authors but also within texts of

| | |
|---|---|
| Dialect around Bern | Si **het** ne **la ga**, wü er ne gnue Gäud **het gha**, **für** es Billet **z'**löse. |
| Dialect around Zurich | Si **hät** ihn **gah lah**, wil er nöd gnueg Gäld **gha hät**, **zum** es Billet löse. |
| Standard German | Sie **liess** ihn gehen, weil er nicht genug Geld **hatte**, **um** ein Billet **zu kaufen**. |
| English | She **let** him go because he **did** not **have** enough money **to** buy a ticket. |

Table 1: Differences between dialects and Standard German

the same author. As people write how they speak, they are not consistent and may spell the same word differently in the same sentence. They are also free to merge any words, which is quite common. Joining words into compounds is not an unseen phenomena in Standard German either. However, a compound is a word consisting of more than one stem, which can act as one word with one corresponding part-of-speech (usually the one of the last part), e.g. *Skilift* (ski lift). In Swiss German, the process of merging words rather resembles the phenomena of clitics, i.e. phonologically bound to another word (Loos et al., 2004). For example *gömmer* is Swiss German for *gehen wir* (we go). *Gömmer* can not be split into verb and pronoun, as the separate occurrences would be *gönd* (first person plural of to go) and *mir* (we). Thus, such merged words are grammatically different words which, however, are phonologically bound and can not stand alone. One phonological word (realised as one alphabetic string limited by white spaces) can even contain the subject, an object and the finite verb of the sentence (see section 4.2 for an example). This means it can not be assigned to one part-of-speech. In section 4.2 we present how we deal with them in the part-of-speech tagging task.

To strengthen our argumentation for the necessity of a Swiss German PoS tagger we compare our results of the training with our corpus with the performance of a Standard German tagger. We run the German model of the most common tagger for Standard German, the TreeTagger (Schmid, 1995), on our Swiss German test set. The tagger reaches an accuracy of 50.8%, which is significantly lower than the result after the training with our corpus.

As we have shown in this section, the dialects of Swiss German differ in many aspects from Standard German. It is not only a different pronounciation or spelling with some variations in the vocabulary. It also involves syntactic differences and constructions which are ungrammatical when transferred to German. Therefore we argue against a normalisation of Swiss German as a mapping to Standard German, a frequently proposed approach dealing with varieties.

## 4 Corpus Creation

We compiled a Swiss German dialect corpus in order to provide resources to work with Swiss German. Furthermore, we applied the corpus to the basic natural language processing task of Part-of-Speech tagging as a first application. Therefore, we specified a tagset for Swiss German and annotated the corpus according to this tagset.

### 4.1 *NOAH's Corpus of Swiss German Dialects*

We present *NOAH's Corpus of Swiss German Dialects*, a unique resource for Swiss German. We compiled a Swiss German corpus containing manually annotated part-of-speech tags of 73,616 tokens. As the first annotated resource for written texts in Swiss German dialects, the goal is to cover various text genres as well as different dialects from all regions of Switzerland. *NOAH's Corpus* is freely available for research.[1]

In *NOAH's Corpus*, we include articles from the Alemannic Wikipedia (Wikipedia, The Free Encyclopedia, 2011) in five major dialects (Aarau, Basel, Bern, Zurich and the Eastern part of Switzerland) and a Swiss German special edition of the newspaper *"Blick am Abend"* (Ringier AG, 2013), which was published in 2013. In addition, we added sections of the Swiss German dialect version of the official annual report of the *Swatch* company from 2012 (The Swatch Group AG, 2012). Furthermore, we incorporated extracts of novels from the Swiss author Viktor Schobinger (Viktor Schobinger, 2013) which are written exclusively in the Zurich dialect. Finally, we also included three blogs from *BlogSpot* in various dialects as a web resource. The detailed token quantities for each text source are shown in table 2.

[1]http://www.cl.uzh.ch/research/downloads.html

| **Text source** | **No. of tokens** |
|---|---|
| Alemannic Wikipedia | 20,135 |
| Swatch Annual Report 2012 | 13,386 |
| Novels from Viktor Schobinger | 11,165 |
| Newspaper articles | 11,259 |
| Blogs | 17,671 |
| **Total** | **73,616** |

Table 2: Corpus composition

Manning (2011) suggests that the largest opportunities for improvement in part-of-speech tagging lies in improving the tagset and the accuracy of annotation, even though a perfect annotation of words into discrete lexical categories is not possible because some words do not fall clearly into one category. Thus, since the consistency of annotations in natural language corpora is of great importance for PoS tagging performance, we put great emphasis on the manual annotations. After the annotation of the corpus by native speakers, various consistency checks were conducted. For instance, we checked words with low probabilities in the tagging model and we also conducted random checks for cases of difficult tags.

### 4.2 Tagset

As the basic tagset we use the Stuttgart-Tübingen-TagSet (STTS), which is the standard for German (Schiller et al., 1999). Because of the differences between German and the Swiss German dialects we additionally introduced the tag *PTKINF* as well as the adding of a "+"-sign to any PoS tag.

The newly introduced tag *PTKINF* represents an infinitive particle suggested by Glaser (2003). It is a commonly used and therefore widely analysed phenomenon for Swiss German dialects with no corresponding word or construction in German. In Swiss German people say *Ich go go poschte.* (I'm going shopping.). The second *go* corresponds to the finite verb *gehen* (to go) in the according Standard German sentence *Ich gehe einkaufen.* The first *go*, however, does not exist in the Standard German version. This particle is probably originally derived from *gehen.* However, as a particle it exceeds the use in *gehen* (Glaser, 2003). This infinitive particle *go* (derived from *gehen*; to go) also comes in other forms like for instance *cho* (derived from *kommen*; to come) and *afa* (probably derived from *anfangen*; to begin). In our corpus we found 37 occurrences of this tag.

Furthermore, we introduce special tags for merged words. Since Swiss German does not have official spelling rules, words can be freely joined. Splitting these words in a pre-processing step would be one approach to deal with them. However, it is not always clear where to split them and would result in strange words as the words phonologically assimilate when merged with others (see section 3.1). Also Manning (2011) suggests that splitting tags seems to be largely a waste of time for the goal of improving PoS tagging numbers.

Instead of splitting, we identify these merged words by using the corresponding STTS-tag for the first part and add a plus sign to show that a given word consists of more than one simple word. There are sequences of words that are commonly joined, but also less common combinations can appear as it depends on the preferences of the writer. A commonly joined sequence is, for instance, *VAFIN+PPER*, a personal pronoun attached to a finite auxiliary verb, e.g. *hets* for German *hat es* (there is). An example for a less commonly joined sequence would be a concatenation of three different parts of speech *VVFIN+PIS+PPER* such as *bruchtmese* for the German words *braucht man sie* (one uses/needs it). Figure 3 shows some more examples of the most frequent combinations (e.g. a verb, a conjunction or a particle followed by a pronoun). We found 1008 occurrences of merged words, which represent 1.37% of all tokens in the corpus.

The STTS-tagset already contains one tag that is a combination of two, namely the *APPRART*, consisting of a preposition *APPR* and an article *ART*. This is used for words like *beim*, which is composed of *bei* and *dem*. However, these are "normal" Standard German prepositions. This is not the case with the word combinations in Swiss German writing habits, where any words of completely different parts-of-speech can be merged together. Using the approach of simply joining the corresponding part-of-speech tags of the words like the *APPRART*-case, we would end up with an infinite tagset. Thus, the approach

| PoS tag | Swiss German | Standard German | English |
|---|---|---|---|
| VAFIN+ | *isches* | ist es | is it |
| KOUS+ | *dasme* | dass man | that one |
| VMFIN+ | *chame* | kann man | can one |
| PTKZU+ | *zflügä* | zu fliegen | to fly |
| ADV+ | *deetobe* | dort oben | up there |

Table 3: PoS tags for compound words

of adding a plus sign allows us to have a clearly defined tagset. Another advantage is that it is possible to identify all the concatenated words easily, looking for PoS tags with a "+"-sign attached. Once the list of all occurrences is given, the corresponding tags can still be modified according to one's requirements for further processing in a text or corpus. Moreover, there is not a huge loss of information due to the omitted part-of-speech information for the other word part(s). For many combinations it is very clear which part of speech follows. Coming across a *PTKZU+* for example, the only possibility for the second part is a verb in the infinitive, a fact that can be inferred from the grammar.

## 5 Evaluation of PoS Tagging

In order to achieve the best results we trained different statistical, open source PoS taggers: TreeTagger (Schmid, 1995), hunpos tagger (Halácsy et al., 2007), RFTagger (Schmid and Laws, 2008), Wapiti CRF Tagger (Lavergne et al., 2010), TnT (*Trigrams'n'Tags*) tagger (Brants, 2000) and BTagger (Gesmundo and Samardžić, 2012). The BTagger and the TnT tagger reach the best results for our corpus, therefore we did a more detailed evaluation of the tagging results based on these two taggers.

### 5.1 Results

We evaluated the performance of the BTagger and the TnT tagger over our corpus with 10-fold cross validation. The folds we created are non-stratified, i.e. not contiguous sentences. This is because our corpus consists of diverse kinds of text. If we train the tagger on the whole corpus with diverse kinds of text and then evaluate only on blogs for instance, we will not get a fair result. Thus, in order to get balanced test sets, we chose the sentence for the 10 folds randomly. With the whole corpus as training set, we reach an accuracy of 90.62% with the BTagger and 90.14% with the TnT tagger (see table 4). Considering the 26.36% unknown tokens in average over all test sets, the accuracy for the unknown tokens is surprisingly high.

| Accuracy | BTagger | TnT tagger |
|---|---|---|
| Unknown tokens | 77.99% | 72.39% |
| Known tokens | 93.34% | 93.26% |
| Overall | **90.62%** | 90.14% |

Table 4: Accuracy of taggers over the whole corpus

As stated in section 4.1, our corpus contains texts from different genres. Therefore we additionally evaluated the different text genres individually. The results are shown in table 5. The Wikipedia articles score best with 90.92% accuracy. This is due to the fact that it is the biggest part of the corpus with 20,135 tokens (one third). In addition, the amount of unknown words is not as high as in other texts because the variety of different words is limited to one topic per article. The literary texts are on the second place. This corpus part is only half of the size of the Wikipedia articles. However, the texts are all extracted from the criminal novels of Viktor Schobinger. This means, they are written in one dialect by one person, which reduces the number of orthographic varieties and thus the number of unknown tokens. As table 5 shows, the novels have only 16% of unknown tokens, less than all the other parts.

Furthermore, we analysed the relation between the size of the corpus and the accuracy we achieved (see figure 1). In the case of Swiss German we found that the accuracy increases significantly until approximately 40,000 tokens. Increasing the size of the corpus beyond this amount of tokens is helpful

| Text type | Accuracy overall | Accuracy unknown tokens | Accuracy known tokens | Number of unknown tokens |
|---|---|---|---|---|
| Wikipedia articles | 90.92% | 75.64% | 94.60% | 22.7% |
| Literary texts (novels) | 89.37% | 70.41% | 92.89% | 16.0% |
| Annual report | 88.82% | 76.95% | 92.72% | 24.7% |
| Blogs | 88.10% | 71.69% | 91.73% | 18.2% |
| Newspaper articles | 87.17% | 71.19% | 93.15% | 27.4% |

Table 5: Results for the different text genres with the BTagger

to cover a larger amount of orthographic varieties and reducing the number of unknown words, but does not considerably improve the accuracy of known tokens.

Another fact that stands out in figure 1 is the difference of the tagger performances for a training set of 10,000 tokens. This is due to the fact that that the BTagger makes use of context information and thus emphasises the transition probability by learning sequences of tags. Therefore, not a huge amount of data is needed to get a comparably good performance (Gesmundo and Samardžić, 2012). The TnT tagger, on the other hand, emphasises the emission probability and does not generalise as well.

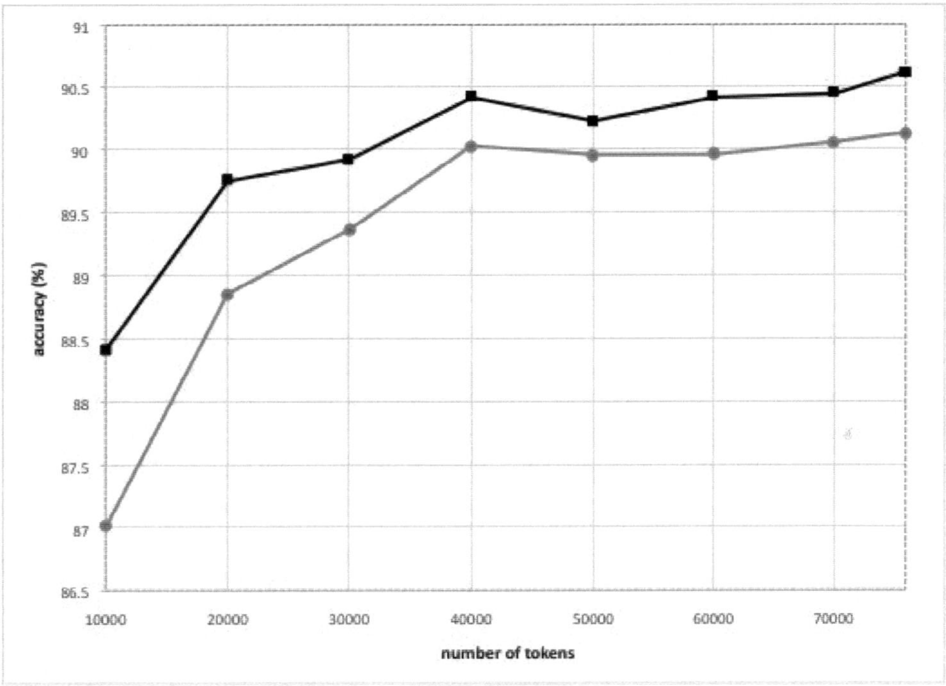


Figure 1: Relation between PoS tagging accuracy and corpus size for the TnT tagger (grey line) and the slightly better results from the BTagger (black line).

In section 3.1, discussing the differences between Standard German and Swiss German, we argue that Standard German tools are not capable of dealing with Swiss German dialects. As an additional experiment we extend our Swiss German corpus with a Standard German corpus to see if the addition of information of Standard German data improves the result. We combined our Swiss German corpus with the *TüBa-D/Z German Treebank* (Telljohann et al., 2006), which contains more than 1,300,000 tokens. The results on a 10-fold cross validation reached an accuracy of 87.6% which is lower than the results for the Swiss German corpus by itself. This implies that the addition of Standard German training data to our Swiss German corpus is not helpful for the training of a Swiss German PoS tagger.

### 5.2 Error Analysis

The most frequent errors were the confusion of nouns (*NN*) and proper names (*NE*), which represent ca. 15% of all errors. This is also a common problem for Standard German due to the capitalisation of nouns. The different kinds of adjectives and the adverbs as well as various types of verbs are also often mistaken, but these are confusions inside one part-of-speech category. Furthermore, there are many mistakes between articles and some types of pronouns, especially personal and demonstrative. However, this is not surprising as they often have the same form. For example the German indefinite article *ein* is often realised as *es* in Swiss German, the definite article *das* as *s*. The Swiss German *es* also stands for the German neutral personal pronoun *es* if it is not abbreviated to *s*. This issue is exemplified in table 6.

| **PoS tag** | **Swiss German example** | **Standard German** | **English** |
|---|---|---|---|
| ART (definite) | ***es** Buech* | **ein** Buch | a book |
| ART (indefinite) | ***s** Buech* | **das** Buch | the book |
| PPER | ***Es** isch rot.* | **Es** ist rot. | It is red. |
| PPER | ***S** rägnet.* | **Es** regnet. | It is raining. |

Table 6: Example of the same types with different PoS tags and meanings

### 5.3 Discussion & Future Work

We achieved reasonable PoS tagging results for the Swiss German dialects considering the low amount of available resources. As stated in section 3, we are dealing with a dialect continuum missing an orthography standard. We neither select one specific dialect (or region) of Switzerland nor do we normalise the data in any way. Thus, our data contains a high amount of hapax legomena, i.e. words which only appear once. This fact explains the considerably lower accuracy for unknown tokens compared to taggers for standardised languages. Furthermore, we include different sources and different text genres in one corpus, which does not simplify the work for a statistical PoS tagger. Thus, it is conceivable that accuracy improvements may be achieved by concentrating on one particular dialect.

In future work we will enlarge *NOAH's Corpus of Swiss German Dialects* by including more texts per dialect in order to reduce the number of unknown tokens. Another approach we are pursuing is to develop a procedure based on lexical distance measures and syntactical patterns in order to map the different orthographic version of a token, so that the tagger can benefit from these mappings. This procedure may also serve as a starting point towards the lemmatisation of Swiss German texts.

The goal of improving Part-of-Speech tagging for Swiss German as well as extending the corpus is to enable and facilitate the development of further NLP tasks, such as dependency parsing, opinion mining or deeper dialectology studies.

## 6 Conclusion

We have presented our work on compiling a corpus of Swiss German dialects and its application to the training of a Part-of-Speech tagger. As a first resource, our corpus is a stepping stone for natural language processing for the Swiss German dialect area. Training the BTagger on our corpus results in an accuracy of 90.62%. With little post processing effort on the tagger output, a PoS-annotated corpus for Swiss German can be obtained and thus resources extended.

*NOAH's Corpus of Swiss German Dialects* contains 73,616 tokens from texts of different genres in different dialects, manually annotated with PoS tags. We are happy to share it with interested parties. The corpus including the PoS tags can be downloaded in XML format.


## Acknowledgements

We are grateful to the Institute of Computational Linguistics of the University of Zurich for their support. We would like to thank Martin Volk and Simon Clematide for valuable comments and suggestions. Furthermore, many thanks to Tanja Samardžić for inputs concerning the PoS taggers and David Klaper for providing some of the raw data for the corpus.

## References


Thorsten Brants. TnT: a statistical part-of-speech tagger. In *Proceedings of the sixth conference on Applied natural language processing*, pages 224–231. Association for Computational Linguistics, 2000.

Christof Dejung, Thomas Gull, and Tanja Wirz. *Landigeist und Judenstempel: Erinnerungen einer Generation 19301945*. Limmat Verlag, 1999.

Mona Diab. Second generation AMIRA tools for Arabic processing: Fast and robust tokenization, POS tagging, and base phrase chunking. In *2nd International Conference on Arabic Language Resources and Tools*, 2009.

Kevin Duh and Katrin Kirchhoff. POS tagging of dialectal Arabic: a minimally supervised approach. In *Proceedings of the ACL Workshop on Computational Approaches to Semitic Languages*, pages 55–62. Association for Computational Linguistics, 2005.

Christa Dürscheid and Elisabeth Stark. SMS4science: An international corpus-based texting project and the specific challenges for multilingual Switzerland. *Digital Discourse: Language in the New Media*, pages 299–320, 2011.

Andrea Gesmundo and Tanja Samardžić. Lemmatisation as a tagging task. In *Proceedings of the 50th Annual Meeting of the Association for Computational Linguistics*, pages 368–372. ACL, 2012.

Elvira Glaser. Schweizerdeutsche Syntax: Phänomene und Entwicklungen. In Beat Dittli, Annelies Häcki Buhofe, and Walter Haas, editors, *Gömmer MiGro?*, pages 39–66, Freiburg, Schweiz, 2003.

Nizar Habash and Owen Rambow. Arabic tokenization, part-of-speech tagging and morphological disambiguation in one fell swoop. In *Proceedings of the 43rd Annual Meeting on Association for Computational Linguistics*, 2009.

Péter Halácsy, András Kornai, and Csaba Oravecz. HunPos - an open source trigram tagger. In *Proceedings of the 45th Annual Meeting of the Association for Computational Linguistics Companion Volume Proceedings of the Demo and Poster Sessions*, pages 209–212, Prague, Czech Republic, 2007.

Erhard Hinrichs and Thomas Zastrow. Linguistic annotations for a diachronic corpus of German. In *Proceedings of the 10th Workshop on Treebanks and Linguistic Theories*, Heidelberg, 2012.

Renato Kaiser. *UUFPASSÄ, NÖD AAPASSÄ!* Der gesunde Menschenversand, 2012.

R.E. Keller. *German dialects: phonology and morphology, with selected texts*. Manchester University Press, 1961.

Thomas Lavergne, Olivier Cappé, and François Yvon. Practical Very Large Scale CRFs. In *Proceedings the 48th Annual Meeting of the Association for Computational Linguistics (ACL)*, pages 504–513, Uppsala, Sweden, July 2010. Association for Computational Linguistics.

Pedro Lenz. *I bi meh aus eine*. Cosmos Verlag AG, 2013.

Eugene Loos, Susan Anderson, Day Dwight, Paul Jordan, and Douglas Wingate. *Glossary of linguistic terms*. http://www-01.sil.org/linguistics/GlossaryOfLinguisticTerms/WhatIsACliticGrammar.htm, 2004.

Christopher D. Manning. Part-of-speech tagging from 97% to 100%: is it time for some linguistics? *Computational Linguistics and Intelligent Text Processing*, pages 171–189, 2011.

Paul Rayson, Dawn Archer, Alistair Baron, Jonathan Culpeper, and Nicholas Smith. Tagging the Bard: Evaluating the accuracy of a modern POS tagger on Early Modern English corpora. 2007.

Ringier AG. Blick am Abig. http://epaper.blick.ch/webreader/baa/download/?doc=BAA280513ZH, May 2013.

Ringier AG. Blick am Abig. http://epaper.blick.ch/webreader/baa/download/?doc=BAA020614ZH, June 2014.

Yves Scherrer. Syntactic transformations for Swiss German dialects. In *First Workshop on Algorithms and Resources for Modelling of DIalects and Language Varieties*, Edinburgh, 2011. EMNLP.

Yves Scherrer. Machine translation into multiple dialects: The example of Swiss German. *7th SIDG Congress - Dialect 2.0*, 2012.

Yves Scherrer. Continuous variation in computational morphology - the example of Swiss German. In *TheoreticAl and Computational MOrphology: New Trends and Synergies (TACMO)*, Genève, Suisse, 2013. 19th International Congress of Linguists. URL `http://hal.inria.fr/hal-00851251`.

Yves Scherrer and Rambow Owen. Natural Language Processing for the Swiss German Dialect Area. In *Proceedings of the Conference on Natural Language Processing (KONVENS)*, pages 93–102, Saarbrücken, Germany, 2010.

Anne Schiller, Simone Teufel, Christine Stöckert, and Christine Thielen. Guidelines für das Taging deutscher Textkorpora mit STTS, August 1999.

Helmut Schmid. Improvements in Part-of-Speech Tagging with an Application to German. In *Proceedings of the ACL SIGDAT-Workshop*, Dublin, 1995.

Helmut Schmid and Florian Laws. Estimation of Conditional Probabilities with Decision Trees and an Application to Fine-Grained POS Tagging. *COLING*, 2008.

Viktor Schobinger. *Der Ääschmen und de schtùùrzmord*. Schobinger-Verlaag, 2014.

Beat Siebenhaar and Walter Voegeli. 6 Mundart und Hochdeutsch im Vergleich. In *Mundart und Hochdeutsch im Unterricht. Orientierungshilfen für Lehrer*, 1997.

Beat Siebenhaar and Alfred Wyler. *Dialekt und Hochsprache in der deutschsprachigen Schweiz*. 1997.

Heike Telljohann, Erhard W. Hinrichs, Sandra Kübler, Heike Zinsmeister, and Kathrin Beck. Stylebook for the Tübingen Treebank of Written German (TüBa-D/Z). Technical report, Universität Tübingen, 2006.

The Swatch Group AG. Swatch Group Geschäftsbericht 2012. http://www.swatchgroup.com/de/investor_relations/jahres_und_halbjahresberichte/fruehere_jahres_und_halbjahresberichte, 2012.

Viktor Schobinger. Viktor's züritü(ü)tsch. http://www.zuerituetsch.ch/index.html, 2013.

Wikipedia, The Free Encyclopedia. Alemannic Wikipedia. http://als.wikipedia.org/wiki/Wikipedia:Houptsyte, 2011.

# Automatically building a Tunisian Lexicon for Deverbal Nouns

**Ahmed Hamdi** **Núria Gala** **Alexis Nasr**
Laboratoire d'Informatique Fondamentale de Marseille, Aix-Marseille Université
{ahmed.hamdi,nuria.gala,alexis.nasr}@lif.univ-mrs.fr

## Abstract

The sociolinguistic situation in Arabic countries is characterized by diglossia (Ferguson, 1959) : whereas one variant Modern Standard Arabic (MSA) is highly codified and mainly used for written communication, other variants coexist in regular everyday's situations (dialects). Similarly, while a number of resources and tools exist for MSA (lexica, annotated corpora, taggers, parsers ...), very few are available for the development of dialectal Natural Language Processing tools. Taking advantage of the closeness of MSA and its dialects, one way to solve the problem of the lack of resources for dialects consists in exploiting available MSA resources and NLP tools in order to adapt them to process dialects. This paper adopts this general framework: we propose a method to build a lexicon of deverbal nouns for Tunisian (TUN) using MSA tools and resources as starting material.

## 1 Introduction

The Arabic language presents both a standard written form and a number of spoken variants (dialects). While dialects differ from one country to another, sometimes even within the same country, the written variety (Modern Standard Arabic, MSA), is the same for all the Arabic countries. Similarly, MSA is highly codified, and used mainly for written communication and formal spoken situations (news, political debates). Spoken varieties are used in informal daily discussions and in informal written communication on the web (social networks, blogs and forums). Such unstandardized varieties differ from MSA with respect to phonology, morphology, syntax and the lexicon. Linguistic resources (lexica, corpora) and natural language processing (NLP) tools for such dialects (parsers) are very rare.

Different approaches are discussed in the litterature to cope with Arabic dialects processing. A general solution is to build specific resources and tools. For example, (Maamouri et al., 2004) created a Levantine annotated corpus (oral transcriptions) for speech recognition research. (Habash et al., 2005; Habash and Rambow, 2006) proposed a system including a morphological analyzer and a generator for Arabic dialects (MAGEAD) used for MSA and Levantine Arabic. (Habash et al., 2012) also built a morphological analyzer for Egyptian Arabic that extends an existing resource, the Egyptian Colloquial Arabic Lexicon. Other approaches take advantage of the special relation (closeness) that exists betweeen MSA and dialects in order to adapt MSA resources and tools to dialects. To name a few, (Chiang et al., 2006) used MSA treebanks to parse Levantine Arabic. (Sawaf, 2010) presented a translation system for handling dialectal Arabic, using an algorithm to normalize spontaneous and dialectal Arabic into MSA. (Salloum and Habash, 2013) developped a translation system pivoting through MSA from some Arabic dialects (Levantine, Egyptian, Iraqi, and Gulf Arabic) to English. (Hamdi et al., 2013) proposed a translation system between Tunisian (TUN) and MSA verbs using an analyser and a generator for both variants.

Yet if the first kind of approach is more linguistically accurate because it takes into account specificities of each dialect, building resources from scratch is costly and extremely time consuming. In this paper we will thus adopt the second approach: we will present a method to automatically build a lexicon for Tunisian deverbal nouns by exploiting available MSA resources as well as an existing MSA-TUN lexicon





*Proceedings of the First Workshop on Applying NLP Tools to Similar Languages, Varieties and Dialects*, pages 95–102, Dublin, Ireland, August 23 2014.

for verbs (Boujelbane et al., 2013). We will use a root lexicon to generate possible deverbal nouns which will be later filtered through a large MSA lexicon.

This work is part of a larger project that aims at 'translating' TUN to an approximative form of MSA in order to use MSA NLP tools on the output of this translation process. The final lexicon for TUN deverbal nouns will be integrated into a morphological and syntactic parser for TUN.

The paper is organized as follows: in section 2 we describe and compare some morphological aspects of MSA and TUN, focusing on derivation. We then discuss in section 3 our approach to build a TUN lexicon for deverbal nouns from an existing MSA-TUN resource for verbs. Section 4 presents an evaluation of the results obtained and section 5 proposes some solutions to increase the coverage of the lexicon.

## 2 Arabic Morphology

Arabic words are built following two kinds of morphological operations: templatic and affixational. Functionally, both operations are used inflectionally or derivationally (Habash, 2010). In templatic morphology, a root and a pattern combine to form a word stem. A root is a sequence of three, four or five letters that defines an abstract notion while a pattern is a vocalized template which marks where the root radicals are inserted. To give an example, by combining the root ف ت ح *f t H*[1] with the verbal patterns 1a2a3 and ta1a22a3, two verbs are generated : (1) فتح *fataH* 'to open' and (2) تفتح *tafattaH* 'to bloom'. Derivation consists in replacing each digit of the pattern by the corresponding letter in the root.

Arabic verbs have ten basic triliteral patterns, which are conventionally noted with the Latin numbers I, . . . , X. and two basic quadriliteral patterns (XI, XII) (Habash, 2010). A verb is the combination of a root and a pattern.

Many deverbal nouns can be derived from verbs. Nine kind of deverbal nouns (1, 2, 3 ... 9) are defined in Arabic (Al-Ghulayaini, 2010), each of them corresponds to a semantic relationship between the verb and the deverbal noun (see table 1).

| | | |
|---|---|---|
| 1 | اسم الفاعل | active participle |
| 2 | اسم المفعول | passive participle |
| 3 | مصدر | infinitive form |
| 4 | اسم المكان | noun of place |
| 5 | اسم الزمان | noun of time |
| 6 | اسم الآلة | noun of instrument |
| 7 | صفة مشبهة | analogous adjective |
| 8 | اسم التفضيل | comparative adjective |
| 9 | صيغة المبالغة | exaggerate form |

Table 1: Arabic deverbal nouns

From the verbs (1) فتح *fataH* 'to open' and (2) تفتح *tafattaH* 'to bloom', many deverbal nouns can be derived, such as, فاتح *fAtiH* 'opener', مفتوح *maftuwH* 'opened' from (1), and متفتّح *mutfattiH* 'blooming', متفتّح *mutfattaH* 'blown' from (2). These deverbal nouns represent the active and the passive participles of these verbs. They are derived from the same root as the verb, using deverbal patterns which depend on the verbal pattern. Table 2 shows TUN and MSA patterns of the active and the passive participles for the first three verbal patterns.

Table 2 is just a sample of a larger table of deverbal nouns (henceforth called TUN-MSA deverbal table) that defines for every verbal pattern all deverbals which are derived from it in MSA and TUN.

[1]Arabic orthographic transliteration is presented in the Habash-Soudi-Buckwalter HSB scheme (Habash et al., 2007): (in alphabetical order)

| | | | | | | | | | | | | | | | | | | | | | | | | | | | |
|---|---|---|---|---|---|---|---|---|---|---|---|---|---|---|---|---|---|---|---|---|---|---|---|---|---|---|---|
| ا | ب | ت | ث | ج | ح | خ | د | ذ | ر | ز | س | ش | ص | ض | ط | ظ | ع | غ | ف | ق | ك | ل | م | ن | ه | و | ي |
| A | b | t | $\theta$ | j | H | x | d | ð | r | z | s | š | S | D | T | Ď | ς | $\gamma$ | f | q | k | l | m | n | h | w | y |

and the additional letters: ' ء, Â أ, Ǎ إ, Ā آ, ŵ ؤ , ŷ ئ , ¯h ة, ý ى.

| Verbal pattern | Deverbal noun | MSA patterns | TUN patterns |
|---|---|---|---|
| I | 1 | 1A2i3 | 1A2i3, 1A2a3 |
| | 2 | ma12uw3 | ma12uw3 |
| II | 1 | mu1a22i3 | m1a22i3, m1a22a3 |
| | 2 | mu1a22a3 | m1a22a3, mit1a22i3 |
| III | 1 | mu1A2i3 | mfA2i3, m1A2a3 |
| | 2 | mu1A2a3 | mfA2a3, mit1A2a3 |

Table 2: TUN-MSA Deverbal Table

This table has been created by a Tunisian native speaker. Unlike MSA, which defines a unique pattern for each participle with all verbal patterns, table 2 shows that TUN has often more than one pattern for participles. However, for some other cases, such as the infinitive forms and nouns of instruments, MSA defines several nominal patterns. The choice of the nominal pattern depends on the verbal pattern.

The Arabic nominal derivation system is not systematic and depends on the meaning of the verbs. In fact, for semantic reasons, most Arabic verbs cannot derive all deverbal nouns. The verb فتح *fataH* 'open', for example, cannot produce the noun of place and time. However, فتح *fataH* derives the active and the passive participles فاتح *fAtiH* 'opener' and مفتوح *maftuwH* 'opened', the noun of instrument مفتاح *miftAH* 'key' and an exaggerate form فتاح *fattAH* 'conqueror'...

## 3 Overview of the Method

Our method consists in generating TUN and MSA pairs of deverbal nouns simultaneously: in a first step, we use the TUN-MSA deverbal table and an existing MSA-TUN dictionary of verbs in order to generate candidate pairs of deverbal nouns ($NOUN_{MSA}$, $NOUN_{TUN}$). These candidates are then filtered on the MSA side using an available MSA resource.

### 3.1 Generating pairs of deverbal nouns

As shown in the TUN-MSA deverbal table (Table 2), every verbal pattern in MSA produces several patterns of deverbal nouns (i.e., pattern IX[2] yields for example the infinitive form Ai12i3A3). The same applies to TUN (i.e., pattern IX yields the infinitive form 12uw3iyy). A total of 54 MSA and 52 TUN nominal patterns were defined. To generate deverbal lexicon we have used an existing TUN-MSA lexicon (Boujelbane et al., 2013) of 1500 verbs composed of pairs of the form $(P_{MSA}, P_{TUN})$ where $P_{MSA}$ and $P_{TUN}$ are themselves pairs made of a root and a verbal pattern. The TUN side contains 920 distinct pairs and the MSA side 1,478 distinct pairs. This difference shows that MSA is lexically richer than TUN. For every pair (a pattern and a root) we combined the root with all the nominal patterns corresponding to the verbal pattern on both sides (MSA and TUN) as shown in figure 1.

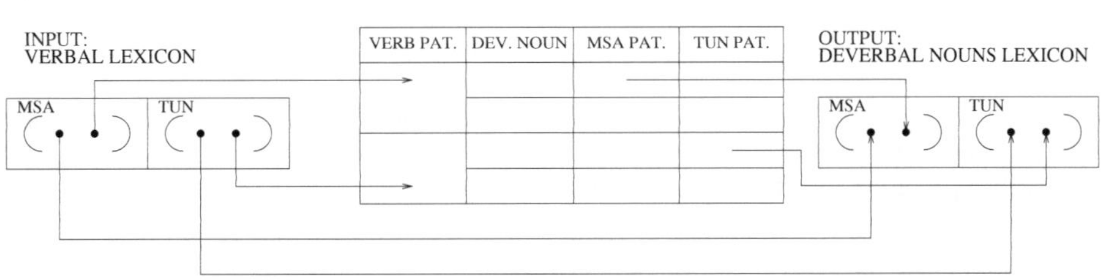


Figure 1: Generating TUN-MSA pairs of deverbal nouns using verbs

At this point, about twenty morphological and orthographic rules manually predefined are applied on the generated form in order to produce a lemma. For instance, the second root radical /y/ and /w/ changes to /ŷ/ for MSA active participle, while the second root radical /w/ changes to /y/ in the TUN side. Another

[2]The MSA and TUN IX patterns are respectively Ai12a33 and 12A3

rule which is common for MSA and TUN requires that the /t/ of the verbal pattern Ai1**t**a2a3 (VIII) and all nominal forms which derive from it, change to a /T/ if the first letter on the radical is /S/, /T/, /D/ or /Z/ : e.g. masdar اضتراب *AiDtirAb* becomes اضطراب *AiDTirAb* 'trouble'.

Following this step, a lexicon of $137,199$ nominal entries $(Noun_{MSA}, Noun_{TUN})$ was obtained.

## 3.2 Filtering

As it was expected, the generation method described above overgenerates: it can produce correct pairs as well as wrong pairs. Four cases have been identified:

1. Both TUN and MSA nouns are correct
2. TUN noun is wrong and MSA noun is correct
3. MSA noun is wrong and TUN noun is correct
4. Both forms are wrong

To give an example from the verbal lexicon entry (فتح, حلّ) $(fataH_{MSA}, Hall_{TUN})$ *'to open'*, we can generate these four situations :

1. passive participle : (مفتوح, محلول) $(maftuwH_{MSA}, maHluwl_{TUN})$ *'opened'*, both words are correct.
2. exaggerate form : (فتّاح, حلّال) $(fattAH_{MSA}, HallAl_{TUN})$, in this case TUN noun is wrong but the MSA noun is correct *'conqueror'*.
3. noun of place : (مفتح, محلّ) $(maftaH_{MSA}, mHall_{TUN})$, in this case TUN noun is correct *'shop, store'* while the MSA noun does not exist. The TUN noun is obtained after the application of the gemination[3] rule. The allows deleting the vowel between the second and the third radical.
4. analogous adjective : (فتيح, محلال) $(ftiyH_{MSA}, miHlAl_{TUN})$, both nouns are wrong.

Situations (3) and (4) can be handeled by filtering the MSA part using an MSA resource. In order to do so, we have used three resources :

- an Arabic corpus made of reports of the French Press Agency (AFP), which contains 1.5 million word forms. From these words, we have extracted $10,595$ types of nominal lemmas using the Arabic morphological analyser MADA (Habash et al., 2009). Only pairs that have the MSA noun in the corpus have been kept. At the end of this stage, we have obtained a lexicon of 20130 entries : 8441 MSA nouns and 2636 TUN nouns.
- an MSA large-scale lexicon SAMA (Graff et al., 2009) containing $36,935$ nominal lemmas. Our resulting lexicon contains $26,486$ entries : $4,712$ TUN nouns and $10,647$ MSA nouns.
- The union of these resources containing $40,172$ nominal lemmas. Using this resource, a lexicon made of $39,793$ was obtained : $5,017$ TUN nouns and $14,804$ MSA nouns. All results are given in section 4.

# 4 Evaluation

In order to evaluate the resource produced, we used a Tunisian corpus made of 800 sentences. In order to cover most spoken TUN varieties, the data was obtained from several sources: TV series, political debates, and a transcribed theater play (Dhouib, 2007). Once manually tokenized and annotated with morphological information (lemma and part-of-speech tag), the corpus contains $6,123$ tokens: $53.8\%$ $(3,295)$ of them are nouns, among which $52\%$ are deverbals.

We have divided the evaluation corpus into two different sets : a development corpus contaning 300 TUN sentences and a test corpus with 500 sentences.

Two metrics have been used to evaluate the deverbal lexicon produced. The first one is coverage, which is the part of the deverbal types of the evaluation corpus that are present in the lexicon. The second one is ambiguity which is the average number of target deverbals for a source deverbal.

There are two sources of ambiguity:

[3]The second and the third root radical are identical.

- The verbal lexicon can associate for one input verb many target verbs, for example the TUN verb مشى *mšý* matches with two different MSA verbs مشى *mšý 'to walk'* and ذهب *ðhb 'to go'*. The ambiguity is more important in the TUN → MSA sense. On average, a TUN pair corresponds to 1.78 MSA pairs, 1.11 in the opposite direction. The maximum ambiguity is equal to four in the MSA → TUN direction and sixteen in the opposite direction.
- the TUN-MSA deverbal table may define several patterns for a deverbal noun as shown in table 2.

The evaluation[4] of the deverbal lexicon on the test set is displayed in Table 3. The table shows that, without filtering the lexicon coverage is equal to 67.23%. Ambiguity (in the TUN→MSA direction) is equal to 12.58, which means that, on average, for a TUN deverbal, 12.58 MSA deverbals are produced. After filtering using AFP corpus, coverage drops to 60.04% and ambiguity to 6.99. Filtering with the SAMA lexicon yields a coverage of 62.66% and an ambiguity of 7.24. Finally, filtering using AFP ∪ SAMA, the coverage reaches 65.67% and the whith an ambiguity of 7.35.

| filtering method | number of entries | coverage | ambiguity rate MSA→TUN | ambiguity rate TUN→MSA |
|---|---|---|---|---|
| none | 173,407 | 67.23 | 7.65 | 12.58 |
| AFP | 17,896 | 60.04 | 2.36 | 6.99 |
| SAMA | 33,271 | 63.89 | 3.45 | 7.24 |
| AFP ∪ SAMA | 35,792 | 65.67 | 2.59 | 7.35 |

Table 3: Results on test set

As in the verbal lexicon, switching from TUN to MSA is more ambigous than the inverse direction. Ambiguity rates attests that MSA is lexically richer than TUN. The filtering step helps to significantly decrease ambiguity, but it also decreases coverage! The best result is the union of AFP∪SAMA, which enables us to obtain the best trade-off.

Table 4 summarizes the coverage and the ambiguity rate of the deverbal lexicon in the development and the test sets respectively :

| filtering method | number of entries | coverage | ambiguity rate MSA→TUN | ambiguity rate TUN→MSA |
|---|---|---|---|---|
| none | 173,407 | 66.12 | 7.65 | 12.58 |
| AFP | 17,896 | 59.23 | 2.36 | 6.99 |
| SAMA | 33,271 | 62.66 | 3.45 | 7.24 |
| AFP ∪ SAMA | 35,79 | 64.59 | 2.59 | 7.35 |

Table 4: Results in the development set

We have carried out an error analysis on the automatically generated lexical entries. There are three major causes that can explain a missing target deverbal:

1. Absence of the corresponding verb in the verbal lexicon: nouns deriving from a verb that is absent from the verb lexicon are not produced in the deverbal lexicon.
2. Missing entries in the TUN-MSA deverbal table
3. Missing morphological and orthographic rules.

In order to estimate the part of missing deverbals that is due to lack of coverage of the verbal lexicon, we have added verbs that derive missing deverbals of the development corpus. 92 verbal entries have been added. Table 5 shows results of coverage and ambiguity on the development set. This result, although artificial allows to compute an upper bound that can be attained with a more complete verbal lexicon.

As one can see in Table 5, coverage jumps from 66.12% to 87.33% before filtering and from 64.59% to 84.16% after filtering using AFP ∪ SAMA. The ambiguity rate increases slightly.

[4]In this paper, we don't use precision and recall measures because of the small size of the reference corpus.

| filtering method | number of entries | coverage | ambiguity rate | |
|---|---|---|---|---|
| | | | MSA→TUN | TUN→MSA |
| none | 195,917 | 87.33 | 7.93 | 12.86 |
| AFP | 20,130 | 81.46 | 2.24 | 7.17 |
| SAMA | 36,935 | 82.97 | 3.67 | 8.03 |
| AFP ∪ SAMA | 39,763 | 84.16 | 2.86 | 8.15 |

Table 5: Results in the development set after enriching the verbal lexicon

Table 6 gives the results obtained on the test set after enriching the verbal lexicon using the development set.

| filtering method | number of entries | coverage | ambiguity rate | |
|---|---|---|---|---|
| | | | MSA→TUN | TUN→MSA |
| none | 195,917 | 72.95 | 7.93 | 12.86 |
| AFP | 20,130 | 65.86 | 2.24 | 7.17 |
| SAMA | 36,935 | 68.41 | 3.67 | 8.03 |
| AFP ∪ SAMA | 39, 763 | 71.18 | 2.86 | 8.15 |

Table 6: Results in the test set after enriching the verbal lexicon

As shown in table 6, enriching the verbal lexicon improves significantly the coverage of the deverbal lexicon on the test set. In fact, it rises from 67% to 73% before filtering and from 65% to 71% after filtering using AFP∪SAMA, whereas ambiguity remains stable.

## 5 Root lexicon and pattern correspondance table

The previous section shows that a large portion of errors came from the lack of coverage of the verbal lexicon. By adding 92 verbal entries, the coverage jumps by about 6%. Among these 92 entries, there were 28 inexistent roots but for the 64 remaining, the root was already present in the verbal lexicon, we have just added new patterns to the roots (as the pair did not exist).

Sebsequently, we have divided the verbal lexicon into two independant resources : a root lexicon and a verbal pattern correspondance table.

The root lexicon is made of pairs of the form $(r_{MSA}, r_{TUN})$, where $r_{MSA}$ is an MSA root and $r_{TUN}$ is a TUN root. The root lexicon contains 1,357 entries. The MSA side contains 1,068 distinct roots and the TUN side 665 ones. 523 entries are composed of the same root on both sides. As in the verbal lexicon, the ambiguity is higher in the TUN → MSA direction. On average, a TUN root is paired with 2.07 MSA roots. In the opposite direction, 1.27 roots.

The verbal pattern correspondance table indicates, for a pattern in MSA or TUN, the most frequent corresponding pattern on the other side.

In this approach, the target pattern is selected by a lookup in the verbal pattern correspondance table but the target roots are selected by a root lexicon lookup. For each source root, we have combined it with all the nominal patterns corresponding to each verbal pattern. The target deverbal is made of the target root given by the lexicon root and the target nominal pattern depends on the target verbal pattern indicated in the verbal pattern correspondance table as shown in figure 2.

Results of this experiment on the test corpus show that using this method increase greatly the coverage. Although it also raises the number of generated entries and subsequently ambiguity.

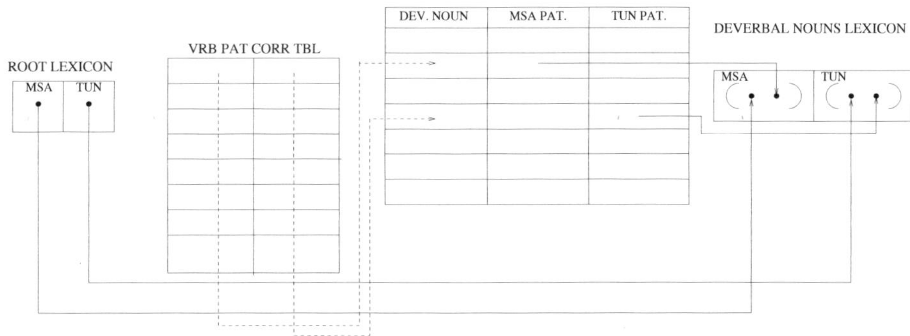


Figure 2: Generating TUN-MSA pairs of deverbal nouns using roots

| filtering method | number of entries | coverage | ambiguity rate | |
|---|---|---|---|---|
| | | | MSA→TUN | TUN→MSA |
| no filtering | 1,324,073 | 79, 13 | 18.47 | 36.42 |
| filtering by AFP | 122,315 | 71.33 | 6.66 | 31.04 |
| filtering by SAMA | 225,835 | 74.86 | 10.33 | 28.35 |
| filtering by AFP ∪ SAMA | 242, 104 | 76.83 | 6.57 | 28.68 |

Table 7: TUN-MSA Deverbal Table

## 6 Conclusion and Future Work

In this paper, we have presented a bilingual lexicon of deverbal nouns between MSA and TUN. Our method aims to extend an existing TUN verbal lexicon using a table of deverbal patterns to automatically generate pairs of TUN and MSA deverbal nouns. Several MSA resources were used to filter wrong pairs generated. The lexicon was evaluated using two metrics: coverage and ambiguity.

The coverage given by our lexicon is about 71%. Ambiguity is slightly high in TUN→MSA direction. It reaches 8.15. A contextual disambiguation process is therefore necessary for such a process to be of practical use.

In future work, we plan to include this lexicon into a system of translation from TUN to an approximative form of MSA which will be parsed using an MSA parser.

## References

Mustafa Al-Ghulayaini. 2010. جامع الدروس العربية *jAmς Aldrws Alςrbyħ Part II*. IslamKotob.

Rahma Boujelbane, Meriem Ellouze Khemekhem, and Lamia Hadrich Belguith. 2013. Mapping rules for building a tunisian dialect lexicon and generating corpora.

David Chiang, Mona Diab, Nizar Habash, Owen Rambow, and Safiullah Shareef. 2006. Parsing Arabic Dialects. In *Proceedings of the European Chapter of ACL (EACL)*.

Elmoncef Dhouib. 2007. *El Makki w-Zakiyya*. Publishing House Manshuwrat Manara, Tunis, Tunisia.

C.A. Ferguson. 1959. Diglossia. *Word*, 15(2).

David Graff, Mohamed Maamouri, Basma Bouziri, Sondos Krouna, Seth Kulick, and Tim Buckwalter. 2009. Standard Arabic Morphological Analyzer (SAMA) Version 3.1. Linguistic Data Consortium LDC2009E73.

N. Habash and O. Rambow. 2006. Magead: a morphological analyzer and generator for the arabic dialects. In *Proceedings of the 21st International Conference on Computational Linguistics and the 44th annual meeting of the Association for Computational Linguistics*, pages 681–688. Association for Computational Linguistics.

N. Habash, O. Rambow, and G. Kiraz. 2005. Morphological analysis and generation for arabic dialects. In *Proceedings of the ACL Workshop on Computational Approaches to Semitic Languages*, pages 17–24. Association for Computational Linguistics.

Nizar Habash, Abdelhadi Soudi, and Tim Buckwalter. 2007. On Arabic Transliteration. In A. van den Bosch and A. Soudi, editors, *Arabic Computational Morphology: Knowledge-based and Empirical Methods*. Springer.

Nizar Habash, Owen Rambow, and Ryan Roth. 2009. MADA+TOKAN: A toolkit for Arabic tokenization, diacritization, morphological disambiguation, POS tagging, stemming and lemmatization. In Khalid Choukri and Bente Maegaard, editors, *Proceedings of the Second International Conference on Arabic Language Resources and Tools*. The MEDAR Consortium, April.

N. Habash, R. Eskander, and A. Hawwari. 2012. A Morphological Analyzer for Egyptian Arabic. In *NAACL-HLT 2012 Workshop on Computational Morphology and Phonology (SIGMORPHON2012)*, pages 1–9.

Nizar Habash. 2010. *Introduction to Arabic Natural Language Processing*. Morgan & Claypool Publishers.

Ahmed Hamdi, Rahma Boujelbane, Nizar Habash, and Alexis Nasr. 2013. Un système de traduction de verbes entre arabe standard et arabe dialectal par analyse morphologique profonde. In *In proceedings of Traitement Automatique du Langage Naturel (TALN 2013)*.

Mohamed Maamouri, Tim Buckwalter, and Christopher Cieri. 2004. Dialectal Arabic Telephone Speech Corpus: Principles, Tool design, and Transcription Conventions. In *NEMLAR International Conference on Arabic Language Resources and Tools*.

Wael Salloum and Nizar Habash. 2013. Dialectal arabic to english machine translation: Pivoting through modern standard arabic. In *Proceedings of NAACL-HLT*, pages 348–358.

Hassan Sawaf. 2010. Arabic dialect handling in hybrid machine translation. In *Proceedings of the Conference of the Association for Machine Translation in the Americas (AMTA)*, Denver, Colorado.

# Statistical Morph Analyzer (SMA++) for Indian Languages

**Saikrishna Srirampur**
IIIT Hyderabad
saikrishna.srirampur
@research.iiit.ac.in

**Ravi Chandibhamar**
IIIT Hyderabad
chandibhamar.ravi
@students.iiit.ac.in

**Radhika Mamidi**
IIIT Hyderabad
radhika.mamidi
@iiit.ac.in

## Abstract

Statistical morph analyzers have proved to be highly accurate while being comparatively easier to maintain than rule based approaches. Our morph analyzer (SMA++) is an improvement over the statistical morph analyzer (SMA) described in Malladi and Mannem (2013). SMA++ predicts the gender, number, person, case (GNPC) and the lemma (L) of a given token. We modified the SMA in Malladi and Mannem (2013), by adding some rich machine learning features. The feature set was chosen specifically to suit the characteristics of Indian Languages. In this paper we apply SMA++ to four Indian languages viz. Hindi, Urdu, Telugu and Tamil. Hindi and Urdu belong to the Indic[1] language family. Telugu and Tamil belong to the Dravidian[2] language family. We compare SMA++ with some state-of-art statistical morph analyzers viz. Morfette in Chrupała et al. (2008) and SMA in Malladi and Mannem (2013). In all four languages, our system performs better than the above mentioned state-of-art SMAs.

## 1 Introduction

Morphological analysis for Indian Languages (ILs) is defined as the analysis of a word in terms of its lemma (L), gender (G), number (N), person (P), case (C), vibhakti[3], tense, aspect and modality. A tool which predicts Morph Analysis of a word is called a Morph Analyzer (MA).

Statistical Morph Analyzer (SMA) is an MA which uses machine learning to predict the morph information . Using the training data and the feature-set, statistical models are formed. These models help to predict the morph-analysis of the test data. This works for all words, including out of vocabulary (OOV) words. SMA is language independent. We chose Indian Languages for our study and built an SMA which is targeted for different ILs.

Indian languages are lexically and grammatically similar. Lexical borrowing[4] occurs between languages. Gramatically, there are many similarities. Indian languages are *synthetic*[5]; derivational and inflectional morphologies result in the formation of complex words by stringing two or more morphemes. ILs predominantly have *subject-object-verb (SOV)* word order. They show agreement[6] among words. We captured such type of characteristics, by building a robust feature set.

## 2 Related Work

Traditionally, morphological analysis for Indian languages has been done using the rule based approach. For Hindi, the MA by Bharati et al. (1995) is most widely used among the NLP researchers in the Indian Community. Goyal and Lehal (2008) and Kanuparthi et al. (2012) MAs are advanced versions of the Bharati et al. (1995)'s analyzer. Kanuparthi et al. (2012) built a derivational MA for Hindi by introducing a layer over the Bharati et al. (1995)'s MA .It identifies 22 derivational suffixes which help in providing derivational analysis for the word whose suffix matches with one of these 22 suffixes.



*Proceedings of the First Workshop on Applying NLP Tools to Similar Languages, Varieties and Dialects*, pages 103–109,
Dublin, Ireland, August 23 2014.

There have not been many updates in the rule based analyzers and the problem of not predicting OOV words is still a significant one. SMA in Malladi and Mannem (2013) is a data-driven MA which focuses primarily on Hindi.
For Urdu, Bögel et al. (2007) proposes an approach which uses Finite State Transducers. It introduces and discusses the issues that arise in the process of building finite-state MA for Urdu. For Telugu, Sunitha and Kalyani (2009) propose an approach of improving the existing rule based Telugu MA. They did this, using possible decompositions of the word, inflected by many morphemes. SMA in Malladi and Mannem (2013) evaluates the results for Urdu and Telugu as well. Not much research has been done in Morphological Analysis for Tamil.

## 3 Our Approach

### 3.1 Feature Set

The feature-set was chosen specifically to suit the Indian Languages. The following are the features used:
**(i) Suffixes** : Indian languages show inflectional morphology. The inflectional morphemes carry the G,N,P and C of a word. These morphemes generally occur in the form of suffixes. Hence, to capture the inflectional behaviour of ILs we considered the *suffixes* as a feature for the ML task. We considered suffixes whose length was maximum 7 characters.
**(ii) Previous morph tags**[7] and **next morph tags** : Agreement is an important characteristic of ILs. Through agreement, GNPC of a token may percolate to the other tokens. An example to this is, if the *subject* (noun) is masculine, then the verb form should also be masculine. To capture agreement, we considered features which carried the GNPC of the neighbouring words. *Previous morph tags* feature captures predicted morph tag of previous 3 tokens. *Next morph tags* feature captures the set of morph tags of the next token, if found in the training corpus.
**(iii) Word Forms**: ILs are morphologically rich languages. Words carry rich information regarding GNPC. To capture this characteristic we considered three features relating to word forms. *word_present* captures the word form of the present token. *word_previous* captures the word form of the previous token. *word_next* captures the word form of the next token.
**(iv) Part of Speech** (POS) : POS is one of the of the fundamental ML feature of any NLP task. Based on the POS of the word, the set of possible inflections can be found. For example, *verbs* have a set of inflections and *nouns* have another set. To capture such information we included POS in the feature-set.
**(v) Other features** : Features such as *length of the token* and *character types in the token* (eg. numbers, alphabets and so on) have also been considered.
The Support Vector Machine (SVM) (using linear classifier) was used for the ML task .

### 3.2 Choosing Class Labels

For the ML task, the class-labels for G, N, P, C were chosen from the training data itself. For lemma, the class-labels were formed based on the edit-distance[8] operations required to convert the given token to its lemma. This idea was inspired by Chrupała (2006), who introduced the concept of edit-operations[9] for lemmatization.
The Algorithm is explained using an example. Consider the token *crying*. The lemma for *crying* is *cry*.
**Step 1:** The token and its lemma are reversed. *crying* becomes *gniyrc* and *cry* becomes *yrc*.
**Step 2:** Note the edit operations required to convert reversed token to the reversed lemma. To convert *gniyrc* to *yrc* we need to delete the characters at the 1st, 2nd and 3rd indices. Hence the edit operations would be [d 1, d 2, d 3], where 'd' represents delete operation.
**Step 3:** The set of edit operations would form the class-label. [d 1, d 2, d 3] would be the class-label and would be added to the set of class-labels.

[7]The possible values of each G, N, P, C and L form the morph tags. eg. 'm' (masculine) is a morph tag for gender.
[8]Edit distance is a way of quantifying how dissimilar two strings (e.g., words) are to one another by counting the minimum number of operations required to transform one string into the other.
[9]The add, delete and replace operations required to convert one string to another

Similarly, the class-label for the token *playing* and the lemma *play* would be [d 1, d 2, d 3]. By this, *playing - play* and *crying - cry* have the same class label, because they have the common suffix *-ing*.

## 4 Experiments

Experiments were conducted for 4 ILs, viz. Hindi, Urdu, Telugu and Tamil. For Hindi, the Hindi Treebank (HTB) released as part of the 2012 Hindi Parsing Shared Task (Sharma et al., 2012) was used for the ML task. The statistical models were tuned on development data and evaluated on test data. Table 1. shows the HTB statistics.

For Urdu, the Urdu Treebank (UTB) released as a part of the 2012 Proceedings of TLT (Bhat and Sharma (2012)) was used for evaluation. Table 2. represents the UTB statistics. For Telugu, the Telugu Treebank (TTB) released for ICON 2010 Shared Task (Husain et al. (2010)) was used for evaluation. Table 3. represents the TTB statistics. For Tamil, the Tamil Treebank (TaTB) released by the The Indian Languages Machine Translation (ILMT)[10] project was used for evaluation. Table 4. represents the TaTB statistics.

| Data | #Sentences | #Words |
|---|---|---|
| Training | 12,041 | 268,096 |
| Development | 1,233 | 26,416 |
| Test | 1,828 | 39,775 |

Table 1: HTB Statistics.

| Data | #Sentences | #Words |
|---|---|---|
| Training | 5,700 | 159,743 |
| Test | 1,453 | 39,803 |

Table 2: UTB Statistics.

| Data | #Sentences | #Words |
|---|---|---|
| Training | 1300 | 5125 |
| Test | 150 | 600 |

Table 3: TTB Statistics.

[10]This consortium project is funded by Ministry of Communication and Information Technology, Technology Development for Indian Languages, Government Of India.

| Data | #Sentences | #Words |
|---|---|---|
| Training | 75 | 682 |
| Test | 25 | 271 |

Table 4: TaTB Statistics.

## 5 Results

The feature-set, which was specifically chosen for ILs, contributed to high accuracies. The results are shown for 4 Indian Languages. The results for each of L, G, N, P and C are shown individually, as well as in combination.

### 5.1 Hindi

The results are presented all five L ,G, N, P and C. The results are compared to 3 MAs viz. the traditional Rule Based MA (RBA) for Hindi, Morfette (M) in Chrupała et al. (2008) and SMA in Malladi and Mannem (2013) (SMA-M). There are two divisions for results. One for the Overall test data and other for the Out of Vocabulary (OOV) test data. SMA++ out performed other three MAs in almost all combinations. The results for OOV data are more pronounced. Table 5. shows the Hindi results.

| Analysis | Test Data - Overall (%) | | | | Test Data - OOV (%) | | | |
|---|---|---|---|---|---|---|---|---|
| | RBA | M | SMA-M | SMA++ | RBA | M | SMA-M | SMA++ |
| L | 86.69 | 94.14 | 95.84 | 98.43 | 82.48 | 90.30 | 89.51 | **93.07** |
| G | 79.59 | 95.05 | 96.19 | 96.21 | 44.06 | 72.03 | 82.65 | **83.11** |
| N | 80.50 | 94.09 | 95.37 | 95.47 | 47.56 | 84.89 | 90.44 | **92.81** |
| P | 84.13 | 94.88 | 96.38 | 96.28 | 53.89 | 84.76 | 94.85 | **96.17** |
| C | 81.20 | 93.91 | 95.32 | 95.43 | 47.36 | 80.21 | 88.52 | **89.45** |
| L+C | 72.06 | 88.56 | 91.39 | 94.01 | 44.66 | 72.89 | 79.09 | **82.92** |
| G+N+P | 73.81 | 88.36 | 91.11 | 90.36 | 38.58 | 62.33 | 76.52 | **77.24** |
| G+N+P+C | 70.87 | 84.43 | 87.78 | 88.51 | 35.95 | 55.74 | 69.99 | **72.36** |
| L+G+N+P | 66.28 | 83.44 | 87.51 | 89.26 | 38.46 | 57.85 | 69.13 | **72.82** |
| L+G+N+P+C | 63.41 | 79.73 | 84.25 | 85.87 | 38.49 | 51.52 | 63.06 | **65.96** |

Table 5: Hindi Results

### 5.2 Urdu

The results are presented for L, G, N, P and C. The results are compared to 2 MAs viz. Morfette (M) in Chrupała et al. (2008) and SMA in Malladi and Mannem (2013) (SMA-M). Results are shown for both Overall test data and OOV test data. Even in Urdu, SMA++ out performed other two MAs in most of the combinations. Table 6. presents the results in comparison with Morfette (M) and Table 7. presents the results in comparison with SMA-M.

| Analysis | Test Data - Overall (%) | | Test Data - OOV (%) | |
|---|---|---|---|---|
| | M | SMA++ | M | SMA++ |
| L | 93.65 | 95.34 | 87.54 | **89.21** |
| G | 90.39 | 93.79 | 79.40 | **90.35** |
| N | 92.38 | 95.66 | 85.36 | **94.50** |
| P | 93.93 | 97.07 | 86.56 | **98.39** |
| C | 87.99 | 90.92 | 76.08 | **84.07** |
| L+C | 82.94 | 86.93 | 67.25 | **75.66** |
| G+N+P | 84.52 | 89.43 | 70.32 | **86.09** |
| G+N+P+C | 77.01 | 82.17 | 58.54 | **73.69** |
| L+G+N+P | 80.12 | 86.07 | 64.14 | **78.93** |
| L+G+N+P+C | 73.11 | 79.16 | 53.30 | **67.98** |

Table 6: Urdu Results for SMA++ and M

| Analysis | Test Data - Overall (%) | | Test Data - OOV (%) | |
|---|---|---|---|---|
| | SMA-M | SMA++ | SMA-M | SMA++ |
| G | 89.14 | 93.79 | 88.18 | **90.35** |
| N | 91.62 | 95.66 | 91.35 | **94.50** |
| P | 93.37 | 97.07 | 95.53 | **98.39** |
| C | 85.49 | 90.92 | 79.01 | **84.07** |

Table 7: Urdu Results for SMA++ and SMA-M

### 5.3 Telugu

The results are presented for G, N, P and C. The results are compared to 2 MAs viz. Morfette (M) in Chrupała et al. (2008) and SMA in Malladi and Mannem (2013) (SMA-M). Results are presented for both Overall test data and OOV test data. SMA++ significantly out performed Morfette (M). The results of *Overall Data* for SMA++ and SMA-M are very close, but more importantly the results of *OOV data* for SMA++ are higher than SMA-M. Table 8. presents the results in comparison with Morfette (M) and Table 9. presents the results in comparison with SMA-M.

| Analysis | Test Data - Overall (%) | | Test Data - OOV (%) | |
|---|---|---|---|---|
| | M | SMA++ | M | SMA++ |
| G | 95.49 | 96.33 | 87.82 | **89.85** |
| N | 87.31 | 90.48 | 65.48 | **77.67** |
| P | 94.49 | 94.49 | 86.80 | 86.80 |
| C | 94.49 | 95.66 | 84.26 | **90.36** |
| G+N+P | 85.48 | 88.81 | 60.91 | **74.62** |
| G+N+P+C | 84.14 | 86.81 | 57.36 | **70.56** |

Table 8: Telugu Results for SMA++ and M

| Analysis | Test Data - Overall (%) | | Test Data - OOV (%) | |
|---|---|---|---|---|
| | SMA-M | SMA++ | SMA-M | SMA++ |
| G | 96.49 | 96.33 | 89.85 | 89.85 |
| N | 90.65 | 90.48 | 75.13 | **77.67** |
| P | 94.82 | 94.49 | 85.79 | **86.80** |
| C | 96.49 | 95.66 | 89.34 | **90.36** |

Table 9: Telugu Results for SMA++ and SMA-M

### 5.4 Tamil

The results are presented for G, N, P and C. The results are compared to Morfette (M) in Chrupała et al. (2008). SMA++ out performs Morfette (M). Table 10. presents the results in comparison with Morfette (M).

| Analysis | Test Data - Overall (%) | | Test Data - OOV (%) | |
|---|---|---|---|---|
| | M | SMA++ | M | SMA++ |
| G | 90.40 | 91.14 | 85.18 | **91.36** |
| N | 88.93 | 90.04 | 83.95 | **87.04** |
| P | 98.15 | 98.89 | 96.91 | **98.14** |
| C | 87.82 | 94.46 | 80.86 | **91.98** |
| G+N+P | 80.81 | 82.66 | 70.99 | **80.25** |
| G+N+P+C | 76.38 | 78.97 | 64.20 | **74.07** |

Table 10: Tamil Results

## 6 Conclusions and Future Work:

For all the four ILs, SMA++ out performs other SMAs. For Hindi, the L+G+N+P+C accuracy was **85.87%**. For Urdu, the L+G+N+P+C accuracy was **79.16%**. For Telugu, G+N+P+C accuracy was **86.81%** and for Tamil it was **78.97%**. These high values show that SMA++ is a marked improvement over the SMA in Malladi and Mannem (2013) . We studied two families of ILs, viz. Indic and Dravidian, because most of the ILs fall into these two groups. We plan to run SMA++ to predict Lemma in Telugu and Tamil. We plan to extend our work to European Languages such as Polish, German, French etc. We are currently working on the error analysis of our system. In future, we plan to deploy SMA++ for the ILMT project.

## References


Akshar Bharati, Vineet Chaitanya, Rajeev Sangal, and KV Ramakrishnamacharyulu. 1995. *Natural language processing: a Paninian perspective*. Prentice-Hall of India New Delhi.

Riyaz Ahmad Bhat and Dipti Misra Sharma. 2012. A dependency treebank of urdu and its evaluation. In *Proceedings of the Sixth Linguistic Annotation Workshop*, pages 157–165. Association for Computational Linguistics.

Tina Bögel, Miriam Butt, Annette Hautli, and Sebastian Sulger. 2007. Developing a finite-state morphological analyzer for urdu and hindi. *Finite State Methods and Natural Language Processing*, page 86.

Grzegorz Chrupała, Georgiana Dinu, and Josef Van Genabith. 2008. Learning morphology with morfette.

Grzegorz Chrupała. 2006. Simple data-driven contextsensitive lemmatization. *Procesamiento del Lenguaje Natural*, 37:121–127.

Vishal Goyal and Gurpreet Singh Lehal. 2008. Hindi morphological analyzer and generator. In *Emerging Trends in Engineering and Technology, 2008. ICETET'08. First International Conference on*, pages 1156–1159. IEEE.

Samar Husain, Prashanth Mannem, Bharat Ram Ambati, and Phani Gadde. 2010. The icon-2010 tools contest on indian language dependency parsing. *Proceedings of ICON-2010 Tools Contest on Indian Language Dependency Parsing, ICON*, 10:1–8.

Nikhil Kanuparthi, Abhilash Inumella, and Dipti Misra Sharma. 2012. Hindi derivational morphological analyzer. In *Proceedings of the Twelfth Meeting of the Special Interest Group on Computational Morphology and Phonology*, pages 10–16. Association for Computational Linguistics.

Deepak Kumar Malladi and Prashanth Mannem. 2013. Context based statistical morphological analyzer and its effect on hindi dependency parsing. In *Fourth Workshop on Statistical Parsing of Morphologically Rich Languages*, volume 12, page 119.

Dipti Misra Sharma, Prashanth Mannem, Joseph vanGenabith, Sobha Lalitha Devi, Radhika Mamidi, and Ranjani Parthasarathi, editors. 2012. *Proceedings of the Workshop on Machine Translation and Parsing in Indian Languages*. The COLING 2012 Organizing Committee, Mumbai, India, December.

KVN Sunitha and N Kalyani. 2009. A novel approach to improve rule based telugu morphological analyzer. In *Nature & Biologically Inspired Computing, 2009. NaBIC 2009. World Congress on*, pages 1649–1652. IEEE.

# Improved Sentence-Level Arabic Dialect Classification

**Christoph Tillmann** and **Yaser Al-Onaizan**
IBM T.J. Watson Research Center
Yorktown Heights, NY, USA
{ctill,onaizan}@us.ibm.com

**Saab Mansour***
Aachen University
Aachen, Germany
mansour@cs.rwth-aachen.de

## Abstract

The paper presents work on improved sentence-level dialect classification of Egyptian Arabic (ARZ) vs. Modern Standard Arabic (MSA). Our approach is based on binary feature functions that can be implemented with a minimal amount of task-specific knowledge. We train a feature-rich linear classifier based on a linear support-vector machine (linear SVM) approach. Our best system achieves an accuracy of 89.1 % on the Arabic Online Commentary (AOC) dataset (Zaidan and Callison-Burch, 2011) using 10-fold stratified cross validation: a 1.3 % absolute accuracy improvement over the results published by (Zaidan and Callison-Burch, 2014). We also evaluate the classifier on dialect data from an additional data source. Here, we find that features which measure the informalness of a sentence actually decrease classification accuracy significantly.

## 1 Introduction

The standard form of written Arabic is Modern Standard Arabic (MSA) . It differs significantly from various spoken varieties of Arabic (Zaidan and Callison-Burch, 2011; Zaidan and Callison-Burch, 2014; Elfardy and Diab, 2013). Even though these dialects do not originally exist in written form, they are present in social media texts. Recently a dataset of dialectal Arabic has been made available in the form of the **Arabic Online Commentary** (AOC) set (Zaidan and Callison-Burch, 2011; Zaidan and Callison-Burch, 2014). The data consists of reader commentary from the online versions of Arabic newspapers, which have a high degree of dialect content. Data for the following dialects has been collected: Levantine, Gulf, and Egyptian. The data had been obtained by a crowd-sourcing effort. In the current paper, we present results for a binary classification task only, where we predict the dialect of Egyptian Arabic ARZ vs. MSA sentences from the *Al-Youm Al-Sabe'* newspaper online commentaries [1]. Our ultimate goal is to use the dialect classifier for building a dialect-aware Arabic-English statistical machine translation (SMT) system. Our Arabic-English training data contains a significant amount of Egyptian dialect data only, and we would like to adapt the components of our hierarchical phrase-based SMT system (Zhao and Al-Onaizan, 2008) to that data.

Similar to (Elfardy and Diab, 2013), we present a sentence-level classifier that is trained in a supervised manner. Our approach is based on an Arabic tokenizer, but we do not use a range of specialized tokenizers or orthography normalizers. In contrast to the language-model (LM) based classifier used by (Zaidan and Callison-Burch, 2014), we present a linear classifier approach that works best without the use of LM-based features. Some improvements in terms of classification accuracy and 10-fold cross validation under the same data conditions as (Zaidan and Callison-Burch, 2011; Elfardy and Diab, 2013) are presented. In general, we aim at a smaller amount of domain specific feature engineering than previous related approaches.

The paper is structured as follows. In Section 2, we present related work on language and dialect identification. In Section 3, we discuss the linear classification model used in this paper. In Section 4, we evaluate the classifier performance in terms of classification accuracy on two data sets and present some

*Part of the work was done while the author was a student intern at the IBM T.J. Watson Research Center.

[1] We use the ISO 639-3 code ARZ for denoting Egyptian Arabic.





*Proceedings of the First Workshop on Applying NLP Tools to Similar Languages, Varieties and Dialects*, pages 110–119, Dublin, Ireland, August 23 2014.

error analysis. Finally, in Section 5, we discuss future work on improved dialect-level classification and its application to system adaptation for machine translation.

## 2 Related Work

From a computational perpective, we can view dialect identification as a more fine-grained form of language identification (ID). Previous work on language ID examined the use of character histograms (Cavnar and Trenkle, 1994; Dunning, 1994), and high accuracy prediction results have been reported even for languages with a common character set. (Baldwin and Lui, 2010) present a range of document-level language identification techniques on three different data sets. They use $n$-gram counting techniques and different tokenization schemes that are adopted to those data sets. Their classification task deals with several languages, and it becomes more difficult as the number of languages increases. They present an SVM-based multiclass classification approach similar to the one presented in this paper which performs well on one of their data sets. (Trieschnigg et al., 2012) generates $n$-gram features based on character or word sequences to classify dialectal documents in a dutch-language fairy-tale collection. Their baseline model uses $N$-gram based text classification techniques as popularised in the *TextCat* tool (Cavnar and Trenkle, 1994). Following (Baldwin and Lui, 2010), the authors extend the usage of $n$-gram features with nearest neighbour and nearest-prototype models together with appropriately chosen similarity metrics. (Zampieri and Gebre, 2012) classify two varieties of the same language: European and Brazilian Portuguese. They use word and character-based language model classification techniques similar to (Zaidan and Callison-Burch, 2014). (Huang and Lee, 2008) present simple bag-of-word techniques to classify varieties of Chinese from the Chinese Gigaword corpus. (Kruengkrai et al., 2005) extend the use of $n$-gram features to using string kernels: they may take into account all possible sub-strings for comparison purposes. The resulting kernel-based classifier is compared against the method in (Cavnar and Trenkle, 1994). (Lui and Cook, 2013) present a dialect classification approach to identify Australian, British, and Canadian English. They present results where they draw training and test data from different sources. The successful transfer of models from one text source to another is evidence that their classifier indeed captures dialectal rather than stylistic or formal differences. Language identification of related languages is also addressed in the DSL (Discriminating Similar Languages) task of the present Vardial workshop at COLING 14 (Tan et al., 2014).

While most of the above work focuses on document-level language classification, recent work on handling Arabic dialect data addresses the problem of sentence-level classification (Zaidan and Callison-Burch, 2011; Zaidan and Callison-Burch, 2014; Elfardy and Diab, 2013; Zaidan and Callison-Burch, 2014). The work is based on the data collection effort by (Zaidan and Callison-Burch, 2014) which crowdsources the annotation task to workers on Amazons Mechanical Turk. The classification results by (Zaidan and Callison-Burch, 2014) are based on $n$-gram language-models, where the $n$-grams are defined both on words and characters. The authors find that unigram word-based models perform best. The word-based models are obtained after a minimal amount of preprocessing such as proper handling of HTML entities and Arabic numbers. Classification accuracy is significantly reduced for shorter sentences. (Elfardy and Diab, 2013) presents classifcation result based on various tokinization and orthographic normalization techniques as well as so-called *meta* features that estimate the informalness of the data. Like our work, the authors focus on a binary dialect classification based on the ARZ-MSA portion of the dataset in (Zaidan and Callison-Burch, 2011).

## 3 Classification Model

We use a linear model and compute a score $s(t_1^n)$ for a tokenized input sentence consisting of $n$ tokens $t_i$:

$$s(t_1^n) \ = \ \sum_{s=1}^{d} w_s \cdot \sum_{i=1}^{n} \phi_s(c_i, t_i) \qquad (1)$$

where $\phi_s(c_i, t_i)$ is a binary feature function which takes into account the context $c_i$ of token $t_i$. $\mathbf{w} \in \mathbb{R}^d$ is a high-dimensional weight vector obtained during training. In our experiments, we classify a tokenized

| Description | MSA | | ARZ | |
|---|---|---|---|---|
| | # sentences | # words | # sentences | # words |
| ARZ-MSA portion of AOC | $13,512$ | $334K$ | $12,527$ | $327K$ |
| DEV12 tune set | 585 | $8.4K$ | 634 | $9.3K$ |

Table 1: We used the following dialect data: 1) the ARZ-MSA portion of the AOC data from commentaries of the Egyptian newspaper Al-Youm Al-Sabe', and 2) the DEV12 tune set (1219 sentences) which is the LDC2012E30 corpus BOLT Phase 1 dev-tune set. The DEV12 tune set was annotated by a native speaker of Arabic.

sentence as being Egyptian dialect (ARZ) if $s(t_1^n) > 0$. To train the weights $\mathbf{w}$ in Eq. 1, we use a linear SVM approach (Hsieh et al., 2008; Fan et al., 2008). The trainer can easily handle a huge number of instances and features. The training data is given as instance-label pairs $(x_i, y_i)$ where $i \in \{1, \cdots, l\}$ and $l$ is the number of training sentences. The $x_i$ are $d$-dimensional vectors of integer-valued features that count how often a binary feature fired for a tokenized sentence $t_1^n$. $y_i \in \{+1, -1\}$ are the class labels where a label of '+1' represents Egyptian dialect. During training, we solve the following optimization problem:

$$\min_{w} ||\mathbf{w}||_1 \; + \; C \sum_{i=1}^{l} \max(0, 1 - y_i \, \mathbf{w}^{\mathbf{T}} \, x_i \,) \;, \tag{2}$$

i.e. we use $L1$ regularized $L2$-loss support vector classification. We set the penalty term $C = 0.5$. For our experiments, we use the data set provided in (Zaidan and Callison-Burch, 2011) which also has been used in the experiments in (Elfardy and Diab, 2013; Zaidan and Callison-Burch, 2014). We focus on the binary classification between MSA and ARZ. Details on the data sources can be found in Table 1. We present accuracy results in terms of 10-fold stratified cross-validation which are comparable to previously published work.

### 3.1 Tokenization and Dictionaries

The Arabic tokenizer used in the current paper is based on (Lee et al., 2003). It is a general purpose tokenizer which has been optimized towards improving machine translation quality of SMT systems rather than dialect classification. Together with the tokenized text, a maximum-entropy based tagger provides the part-of-speech (PoS) tags for each token. In addition, we have explored a range of features that are based on the output of the AIDA software package (Elfardy and Diab, 2012; Mona Diab et al., 2009 2011). The AIDA software has been made available to the participants of the DARPA-funded Broad Operational Language Translation (BOLT) project. AIDA is a system for dialect identification, classification and glossing on the token and sentence level for written Arabic. AIDA aggregates several components including dictionaries and language models in order to perform named entity recognition, dialect identification classification, and MSA English linearized glossing of the input text. We created a dictionary from AIDA resources that includes about 41 000 ARZ tokens. In addition, we obtained a second small dictionary of about 70 ARZ dialect tokens with the help of a native speaker of Arabic. The list was created by training two IBM Model 1 lexicons, one on Egyptian Arabic data and another on MSA data. We then inspected the ARZ lexicon entries with the highest cosine distance to their MSA counterparts and kept the ones that are strong ARZ words. The tokens in both dictionaries are not ARZ exclusive, but could occur in MSA as well.

### 3.2 Feature Set

In our work, we employ a simple set of binary feature functions based on the tokenized Arabic sentence. For example, we define a token bigram feature as follows:

$$\phi_{Bi}(t_k, t_{k-1}) \;=\; \begin{cases} 1 & t_k = \text{`قوي' and } t_{k-1} = \text{`حلو'} \\ 0 & \text{otherwise} \end{cases} \;. \tag{3}$$

Token unigram and trigram features are defined accordingly. We also define unigram, bigram, and trigram features based on PoS tags. Currently, just PoS unigrams are used in the experiments. We define dictionary-based features as follows:

$$\phi_{Dict_l}(t_k) \quad = \quad \begin{cases} 1 & t_k = \text{`دلوقت' and } t_k \in Dict_l \\ 0 & \text{otherwise} \end{cases} , \tag{4}$$

where we use the two dictionaries $Dict_1$ and $Dict_2$ as described in Section 3.1. The dictionaries are handled as token sets and we generate separate features for each of them. We generate some features based on the AIDA tool output. AIDA provides a dialect label for each input token $t_k$ as well as a single dialect label at the sentence level. A sentence-level binary feature based on the AIDA sentence level classification is defined as follows:

$$\phi_{\text{AIDA}}(t_1^n) \quad = \quad \begin{cases} 1 & AIDA(t_1^n) \text{ is ARZ} \\ 0 & \text{otherwise} \end{cases} \tag{5}$$

where $AIDA(t_1^n)$ is the sentence-level classification of the AIDA tool. A word-level feature $\phi_{\text{AIDA}}(t_k)$ is defined accordingly. These features improve the classification accuracy of our best system significantly.

We have also experimented with some real-valued feature. For example, we derived a feature from dialect-specific language model probabilities:

$$\phi_{LM}(t_1^n) \quad = \quad 1/n \cdot [\, log(p_{\text{MSA}}(t_1^n)) \; - \; log(p_{\text{ARZ}}(t_1^n))] \, ,$$

where $log(p_{\text{ARZ}}(t_1^n))$ is the language-model log probability for the dialect class ARZ . We used a trigram language model. $p_{\text{MSA}}(\cdot)$ is defined accordingly. In addition, we have implemented a range of so-called 'meta' features similar to the ones defined in (Elfardy and Diab, 2013). For example, we define a feature $\phi_{Excl}(t_1^n)$ which is equal to the length of the longest consecutive sequence of exclamation marks in the tokenized sentence $t_1^n$ . Similarly, we define features that count the longest sequence of punctuation marks, the number of tokens, the averaged character-length of a token in the sentence, and the percentage of words with word-lengthening effects. These features do not directly model dialectalness of the data but rather try to capture the degree of in-formalness. Contrary to (Elfardy and Diab, 2013) we find that those features do not improve accuracy of our best model in the cross-validation experiments. On the DEV12 set, the use of the meta features results in a significant drop in accuracy.

## 4 Experiments

In this section, we present experimental results. Firstly, Section 4.1 demonstrates that our data is annotated consistently. In Section 4.2, we present dialect prediction results in terms of accuracy and F-score on our two data sets. In Section 4.3, we perform some qualitative error analysis for our classifier. In Section 4.4, we present some preliminary effects on training a SMT system.

### 4.1 Annotator Agreement

To confirm the consistent annotation of our data, we have measured some inter-annotator and intra-annotator agreement on it. A native speaker of Arabic was asked to classify the ARZ-MSA portion of the dialect data using the following three labels: ARZ, MSA, Other. We randomly sampled 250 sentences from the ARZ-MSA portion of the Zaidan data maintaining the original dialect distribution. The confusion matrix is shown in Table 2. It corresponds to a kappa value of 0.84 (using the definition of (Fleiss, 1971)), which indicates a very high agreement. In addition, we did re-annotate a sub-set of 200 sentences from the DEV12 set over a time period of three months using our own annotator. The kappa value of the corresponding confusion matrix is 0.93, indicating very high agreement as well.

### 4.2 Classification Experiments

Following previous work, we present dialect prediction results in terms of accuracy:

$$\textbf{ACC} \quad = \quad \frac{\text{\# sent correctly tagged}}{\text{\# sent}} , \tag{6}$$

| | | Predicted Class (IBM) | | |
|---|---|---|---|---|
| | | ARZ | MSA | Other |
| Actual | ARZ | 125 | 4 | 1 |
| Class | MSA | 14 | 105 | 1 |
| (AOC) | Other | 0 | 0 | 0 |

Table 2: Inter annotator agreement on 250 randomly selected AOC sentences from the data in Table 1. An in-lab annotator's dialect prediction is compared against the AOC data gold-standard dialect labels.

where '# sent' is the number of sentences. In addition, we present dialect prediction results in terms of precision, recall, and F-score. They are defined as follows:

$$\begin{aligned} \textbf{Prec} &= \frac{\text{\# sent correctly tagged as ARZ}}{\text{\# sent tagged as ARZ}} \\ \textbf{Recall} &= \frac{\text{\# sent correctly tagged as ARZ}}{\text{\# ref sent tagged as ARZ}} \\ \textbf{F} &= \frac{2 \cdot Prec \cdot Recall}{(Prec + Recall)}. \end{aligned} \quad (7)$$

MSA prediction F-score is defined analogously. Experimental results are presented in Table 3, where we present results for different sets of feature types and the two test sets in Table 1. In the top half of the table, results are presented in terms of 10-fold cross validation on the ARZ-MSA portion of the AOC data. In the bottom half, we present results on DEV12 tune set, where we use the entire dialect data in Table 1 for training (about $26K$ sentences).

As our baseline we have re-implemented the language-model-perplexity based approach reported in (Zaidan and Callison-Burch, 2011). We train language models on the dialect-labeled commentary training data for each of the dialect classes $c \in \{\text{MSA}, \text{ARZ}\}$. During testing, we compute the language model probability of a sentence $s$ for each of the classes $c$. We assign a sentence to the class $c$ with the highest probability (or the lowest perplexity) . For the 10-fold cross validation experiments, 10 language models are built and perplexities are computed on 10 different test sets. The resulting (averaged) accuracy is $83.3$ % for cross-validation and $82.2$ % on the DEV12 tune set. In comparison, (Elfardy and Diab, 2013) reports an accuracy of $80.4$ % as perplexity-based baseline. We have carried out additional experiments with a simple feature set that consists of only unigram token and bigram token features as defined in Eq. 3. Such a system performs surprisingly well under both testing conditions: we achieved an accuracy of $87.7$ % on the AOC data and an accuracy of $83.4$ % on the DEV12 test set. On the AOC set using 10-fold cross validation, we achieve only a small improvement from using the dictionary features defined in Eq. 4. The accuracy is improved from $87.7$ % to $88.0$ %. On the DEV12 set, we obtain a much larger improvement from using these features. Furthermore, we have investigated the usefulness of the AIDA-based features. The stand-alone sentence-level classification of the AIDA tool performs quite poorly. On the DEV12 set, it achieves an accuracy of just $77.9$ %. But using the AIDA assigned sentence-level and token-level dialect labels based on the binary features defined in Eq. 5 improves accuracy significantly, e.g. from $85.3$ % to $87.8$ % on the DEV12 set. In the current experiments, the so-called meta features which are computed at the sentence level do not improve classification accuracy. The meta features are only useful in classifying dialect data based on the in-formalness of the data, i.e. the ARZ news commentaries tend to exhibit more in-formalness than the MSA commentaries. Finally, the sentence-level perplexity feature defined in Eq. 6 did not improve accuracy as well (no results for this feature are presented in Table 3).

### 4.3 Classifier Analysis

In this section, we perform a simple error analysis of the classifier performance on some dialect data for which the degree of dialectalness is known. The data comes from news sources that differ from the data used to train the classifier. The classifier is evaluated on data from the DARPA-funded BOLT project.

| | Feature Types | | MSA | | | ARZ | | |
|---|---|---|---|---|---|---|---|---|
| | | ACC [%] | PREC | REC | F | PREC | REC | F |
| 10-fold AOC | language-model | 83.3 | 86.7 | 90.2 | 88.4 | 89.0 | 85.0 | 86.9 |
| | aida-sentence label | 81.0 | 84.2 | 78.0 | 81.0 | 78.0 | 84.3 | 81.0 |
| | uni,bi | 87.7 | 86.6 | 90.2 | 88.4 | 89.0 | 85.0 | 86.9 |
| | uni,bi,dict,pos | 88.0 | 86.9 | 90.4 | 88.6 | 89.2 | 85.3 | 87.2 |
| | uni,bi,dict,pos,aida | 89.1 | 87.5 | 92.2 | 89.8 | 91.1 | 85.7 | 88.3 |
| | uni,bi,dict,pos,aida,meta | 88.8 | 87.4 | 91.7 | 89.5 | 90.6 | 85.7 | 88.1 |
| DEV12 | language-model | 82.2 | 85.1 | 76.2 | 80.4 | 80.0 | 87.7 | 83.7 |
| | aida-sentence label | 77.9 | 80.9 | 70.8 | 75.5 | 75.8 | 84.5 | 79.9 |
| | uni,bi | 83.4 | 81.1 | 85.1 | 83.1 | 85.6 | 81.7 | 83.6 |
| | uni,bi,dict,pos | 85.3 | 83.5 | 87.5 | 85.5 | 88.0 | 84.1 | 86.0 |
| | uni,bi,dict,pos,aida | 87.8 | 83.4 | 93.0 | 88.0 | 92.8 | 83.0 | 87.6 |
| | uni,bi,dict,pos,aida,meta | 68.3 | 61.8 | 90.8 | 73.5 | 85.0 | 48.3 | 61.6 |

Table 3: Arabic Dialect Classification Results: predicting MSA vs. (ARZ) dialect in terms of 10-fold cross-validation on the AOC data and on the DEV12 set using all the AOC data for training.

| Corpus | #Sent | #Sent [ARZ] | %[ARZ] |
|---|---|---|---|
| ARZ web forum | 299K | 183K | 61% |
| Broadcast | 169K | 18K | 11% |
| Newswire | 885K | 29K | 3% |

Table 4: Sub-corpora together with total number as well as percentage of sentences that are classified as ARZ.

The BOLT data consists of several corpora collected from various resources. These resources include newswire, web-logs, ARZ web forum data and others. Classification statistics are presented in Table 4, where we report the number of sentences along with the percentage of those sentences classified as ARZ. The distribution of the dialect labels in the classifier output appears to correspond to the expected origin of the data. For example, the ARZ web forum data contains a majority of ARZ sentences, but quite a few sentences are MSA such as greetings and quotations from Islamic resources (Quran, Hadith ...). The broadcast conversation data is mainly MSA, but sometimes the speaker switches to dialectal usage for a short phrase and then switches back to MSA. Lastly, the newswire data has a vast majority of MSA sentences. Examining a small portion of newswire sentences classified as ARZ, the sentences labeled as ARZ are mostly classification errors.

Example sentence classifications from the BOLT data are shown in Table 5. The first two text fragments are taken from the Egyptian Arabic (ARZ) web forum data. In the first document fragment, the user starts with MSA sentences, then switches to Egyptian (ARZ) dialect marked by the ARZ indicator اللي and using the prefix # ب before a verb which is not allowed in MSA. The user then switches back to MSA. The classifier is able to classify the Egyptian Arabic (ARZ) sentence correctly. In the second document fragment, the user uses several Egyptian Arabic (ARZ) words. In the forth sentence no ARZ words exist, and the classifier correctly classifies the sentence as MSA. The third text fragment shows

| Predicted Dialect | Arabic | English |
|---|---|---|
| MSA | انا قرات الموضوع و الردود . | i read the topic and the replies . |
| MSA | الموضوع فكرة حلوة . | the topic is great ! |
| ARZ | و # انا مع الاخ **اللي** ب # **يقول** | i agree with the brother **who said** |
| MSA | الدين مهم في كل حاجة | Islam is significant in all |
| ARZ | **علشان** الناس **دي** صبرت علي البلاء | **because they** accept affliction with patience |
| ARZ | و **اللي** عملت +ه حماس **دة** اكبر انتصار | **what** Hamas did was a victory |
| ARZ | زي حماس وقفوا في **وش** احتلال | who encountered the occupation |
| MSA | و صبروا علي حصار | and they were patient despite the siege |
| ARZ | **علشان كده** رب +نا كافئ +هم | **that 's why** Allah rewarded them |
| ARZ* | و # قد قادت تي **دي** كه | **tdk** ... led |
| ARZ* | و # ينحو خبراء النقل ب #اللائمة | transport experts blame |
| ARZ* | لا استطيع تذكر ما قال +ه ل # +ي . | i cannot remember what he told me |

Table 5: Automatic classification examples for the dialect classes ARZ and MSA. Arabic source and English target sentences are given. Dialectal words are in **bold**. Incorrect predictions are marked by an asterisk (*).

some sentences from the newswire corpus that are mis-classified. The first sentence contains the word دي which corresponds to the letter 'd' in the abbreviation 'tdk'. The word is contained in one of our ARZ dictionaries such that the binary AIDA-based feature in Eq. 5 fires and triggers a mis-classification. In this context, the word is part of an abbreviation which is split in the Arabic text. In the other examples, only a few of the binary features defined in Section 3.2 apply and features that correspond to Arabic prefixes tend to support a classification as ARZ dialect.

### 4.4 Preliminary Application for SMT

The dialect classification of Arabic data for SMT can be used in various ways. Examples include domain-specific tuning, mixture modeling, and the use of so-called provenance features (Chiang et al., 2011) among others . As a motivation for the future use of the dialect classifier in SMT, we classify the BOLT bilingual training data into ARZ and MSA parts and examine the effect on the phrase table scores. Phrase translation pairs demonstrating the use of the classified training data are shown in Table 6. The ARZ web forum data is split into an ARZ part and an MSA part and two separate phrase probability tables are trained on these two splits. The ARZ web forum data is highly ambiguous with respect to dialect and it is difficult to obtain good dialect-dependent splits of the data. In the first example in the table, the word العربية could mean 'Arab' in MSA, but in ARZ it could also mean 'car'. The phrase table scores obtained from the classifier-split training data correctly reflect this ambiguity. The phrase pair with 'car' has the lowest translation score for the BOLT.ARZ phrase table, while it has a higher cost in the BOLT.MSA phrase table. In the full phrase table (BOLT), 'car' is the fifth translation candidate with a score of 2.09.

| f | BOLT.ARZ | | BOLT.MSA | |
|---|---|---|---|---|
| | e | cost | e | cost |
| العربية | the car | 1.20 | arab | 0.80 |
| | arab | 1.25 | the arab | 1.32 |
| | the arab | 1.70 | Arabic | 1.52 |
| مرسي | merci | 1.53 | marsa | 1.99 |
| | marsa | 1.63 | thanks | 2.01 |
| | mursi | 1.91 | morcy | 2.13 |

Table 6: Phrase tables based on classified training data. BOLT.ARZ is trained on the ARZ portion of the ARZ web forums data, while BOLT.MSA is trained on the MSA part. The table includes Arabic words and the top three phrase translation candidates, sorted (first is best) by the phrase model cost (cost= $-log(p(f|e))$ ).

In the second example, the word مرسي could function as a proper noun with its English translation 'mursi' or 'marsa', but only in ARZ it could also be translated as 'thanks' ('merci'). In this case, the classifier is unable to distinguish between the ARZ dialect and the MSA usage. We found out that the word token 'merci' appears only 4 times in the training data, rendering its binary features unreliable reliable. In general we note that the phrase tables build on the classified data become more domain-specific, and it is left to future work to check whether improvements could carry over to the translation quality.

## 5 Discussion and Future Work

The ultimate goal is to use the ARZ vs. MSA dialect classifier for training an adapted SMT system. We split the training data at the sentence level using our classifier and train dialect-specific systems on each of these splits along with a general dialect-independent system. We will be using techniques similar to (Koehn and Schroeder, 2007; Chiang et al., 2011; Sennrich, 2012; Chen et al., 2013) to adapt the general SMT system to a target domain with a predominant dialect. Or, we will be adopting an SMT system to a development or test set where we use the classifier to predict the dialect for each sentence and use a dialect-specific SMT system on each of them individually. Our approach of using just binary feature functions in connection with a sentence-level global linear model can be related to work on PoS-tagging (Collins, 2002). (Collins, 2002) trains a linear model based on Viterbi decoding and the perceptron algorithm. The gold-standard PoS tags are given at the word-level, but the training uses a global representation at the sentence level. Similarly, we use linear SVMs (Hsieh et al., 2008) to train a classification model at the sentence level without access to sentence length statistics, i.e. our best performing classifier does not compute features like the percentage of punctuation, numbers, or averaged word length as has been proposed previously (Elfardy and Diab, 2013). All of our features are actually computed at the token level (with the exception of a single sentence-level AIDA-based feature). An interesting direction for future work could be to train the dialect classifier at the sentence level, but use it to compute token-level predictions for a more fine-grained analysis. Even though the token-level prediction task corresponds to a word-level tag set of just size 2, Viterbi decoding techniques could be used to introduce novel context-dependent features, e.g. dialect tag $n$-gram features. Such a token-level predictions might be used for weighting each phrase pair in an SMT system using methods like the instance-based adaptation approach in (Foster et al., 2010).


## Acknowledgement

The current work has been funded through the Broad Operational Language Translation (BOLT) program under the project number DARPA HR0011-12-C-0015.

## References


Timothy Baldwin and Marco Lui. 2010. Language Identification: The Long and the Short of the Matter. In *Proc. of HLT'10*, pages 229–237, Los Angeles, California, June.

William Cavnar and John M. Trenkle. 1994. N-gram-based Text Categorization. In *In Proceedings of SDAIR-94, 3rd Annual Symposium on Document Analysis and Information Retrieval*, pages 161–175.

Boxing Chen, George Foster, and Roland Kuhn. 2013. Adaptation of reordering models for statistical machine translation. In *Proc. of HLT'13*, pages 938–946, Atlanta, Georgia, June.

David Chiang, Steve DeNeefe, and Michael Pust. 2011. Two Easy Improvements to Lexical Weighting. In *Proc. of HLT'11*, pages 455–460, Portland, Oregon, USA, June.

Michael Collins. 2002. Discriminative Training Methods for Hidden Markov Models: Theory and Experiments with Perceptron Algorithms. In *Proceedings of EMNLP'02*, pages 1–8, Philadelphia,PA, July.

Ted Dunning. 1994. Statistical Identification of Language. technical report mccs 94-273. Technical report, New Mexico State University.

Heba Elfardy and Mona Diab. 2012. Aida: Automatic Identification and Glossing of Dialectal Arabic. In *Proceedings of the 16th EAMT Conference (Project Papers)*, pages 83–83, Trento, Italy, May.

Heba Elfardy and Mona Diab. 2013. Sentence level dialect Identification in arabic. In *Proc. of the ACL 2013 (Volume 2: Short Papers)*, pages 456–461, Sofia, Bulgaria, August.

Rong-En Fan, Kai-Wei Chang, Cho-Jui Hsieh, Xiang-Rui Wang, and Chih-Jen Lin. 2008. LIBLINEAR: a Library for Large Linear Classification. *Machine Learning Journal*, 9:1871–1874.

Joseph L Fleiss. 1971. Measuring nominal scale agreement among many raters. *Psychological Bulletin*, 76(5):378.

George Foster, Cyril Goutte, and Roland Kuhn. 2010. Discriminative Instance Weighting for Domain Adaptation in Statistical Machine Translation. In *Proc. of EMNLP'10*, pages 451–459.

C.-J. Hsieh, K.-W. Chang, C.-J. Lin, S.S. Keerthi, and S.Sundararajan. 2008. A Dual Coordinate Descent Method for Large-scale linear SVM. In *ICML*, pages 919–926, Helsinki,Finland.

Chu-Ren Huang and Lung-Hao Lee. 2008. Contrastive Approach towards Text Source Classication based on top-bag-of-word Similarity. In *PACLIC 2008*, pages 404–410, Cebu City, Philippines.

Philipp Koehn and Josh Schroeder. 2007. Experiments in Domain Adaptation for Statistical Machine Translation. In *Proceedings of the Second Workshop on Statistical Machine Translation (WMT07)*, pages 224–227.

Canasai Kruengkrai, Prapass Srichaivattana, Virach Sornlertlamvanich, and Hitoshi Isahara. 2005. Language Identification based on string kernels. In *In Proceedings of the 5th International Symposium on Communications and Information Technologies (ISCIT-2005*, pages 896–899.

Young-Suk Lee, Kishore Papineni, Salim Roukos, Ossama Emam, and Hany Hassan. 2003. Language Model Based Arabic Word Segmentation. In *Proc. of the 41st Annual Conf. of the Association for Computational Linguistics (ACL 03)*, pages 399–406, Sapporo, Japan, July.

Marco Lui and Paul Cook. 2013. Classifying English Documents by National Dialect. In *Proc. Australasian Language Technology Workshop*, pages 5–15.

Mona Mona Diab, Heba Elfardy, and Yassine Benajiba. 2009–2011. AIDA Automatic Identification of Arabic Dialectal Text. a Tool for Dialect Identification & Classification, Named Entity Recognition, English and Modern Standard Arabic Glossing and Normalization.

Rico Sennrich. 2012. Perplexity minimization for translation model domain adaptation in statistical machine translation. In *Proc. of EACL'12*, pages 539–549.

Liling Tan, Marcos Zampieri, Nicola Ljubešić, and Jörg Tiedemann. 2014. Merging Comparable Data Sources for the Discrimination of Similar Languages: The DSL Corpus Collection. In *7th Workshop on Building and Using Comparable Corpora at LREC'14*, Reykjavik, Iceland, September.

D. Trieschnigg, D. Hiemstra, M. Theune F. Jong, and T. Meder. 2012. An Exploration of Language Identication Techniques for the Dutch Folktale Database. In *Adaptation of Language Resources and Tools for Processing Cultural Heritage Workshop (LREC 2012)*, Istanbul, Turkey, May.

Omar F. Zaidan and Chris Callison-Burch. 2011. Crowdsourcing translation: Professional quality from non-professionals. In *Proc. of ACL / HLT 11*, pages 1220–1229, Portland, Oregon, USA, June.

Omar F. Zaidan and Chris Callison-Burch. 2014. Arabic Dialect Classification. *CL*, 40(1):171–202.

Marcos Zampieri and Binyam Gebrekidan Gebre. 2012. Automatic Identication of Language Varieties: The case of Portuguese. In *Konvens 12*, pages 233–237, Vienna, Austria.

Bing Zhao and Yaser Al-Onaizan. 2008. Generalizing Local and Non-Local word-reordering patterns for syntax-based machine translation. In *Proc. of EMNLP'08*, pages 572–581, Honolulu, Hawaii, October.

# Using Maximum Entropy Models to Discriminate between Similar Languages and Varieties

**Jordi Porta** and **José-Luis Sancho**
Departamento de Tecnología y Sistemas
Centro de Estudios de la Real Academia Española
c/ Serrano 187-189, 28002 Madrid
{porta, sancho}@rae.es

## Abstract

DSLRAE is a hierarchical classifier for similar written languages and varieties based on maximum-entropy (maxent) classifiers. In the first level, the text is classified into a language group using a simple token-based maxent classifier. At the second level, a group-specific maxent classifier is applied to classify the text as one of the languages or varieties within the previously identified group. For each group of languages, the classifier uses a different kind and combination of knowledge-poor features: token or character n-grams and 'white lists' of tokens. Features were selected according to the results of applying ten-fold cross-validation over the training dataset. The system presented in this article[1] has been ranked second in the Discriminating Similar Language (DSL) shared task co-located within the VarDial Workshop at COLING 2014 (Zampieri et al., 2014).

## 1 Introduction

Language identification (LI) can be defined as the task of determining the language of a written text. LI is also a cross-cutting technology supporting many other text analysis tasks: sentiment analysis, political tendency or topic classification. There are some interesting problems around written language identification that have attracted some attention recently, as native language identification (NLI, Tetreault et al., 2013), the identification of the country of origin or the discrimination between similar or closely related languages (DSL, Tiedemann and Ljubešić, 2012).

LI has reached a great success in discriminating between languages with unique character sets and languages belonging to different language groups or typologically distant. However, according to Zampieri (2013), multilingualism, noisy or non-standard features in text and discrimination between similar languages, varieties or dialects remain as the major known bottlenecks in language identification. For this reason, DSL can be considered as a sub-task in language identification. Interestingly enough, LI seems to work well with what Kloss (1967) called *abstandsprache* or language by distance (because Basque is an isolate, it is generally regarded as a distant language) but fails in dealing with *ausbausprache* or language by development (a standard variety together with all varieties heteronomous with respect to it, e. g. Basque Batua koiné and the various vernacular dialects).

Mass media, educational centres, administrations and communications favour standard languages instead of other varieties. Standard varieties of languages are then seen by sociolinguists and dialectologists as political and cultural constructs (Trudgill, 2004). However, languages and varieties are not just systems for communication between individuals, they are also used by groups and they are a crucial part of their identity and culture. Language variation is systematic, both inter- and intra-personal. It can be related to political, social, geographical, situational, communicative or instrumental factors. Variation within a language can be found at different levels: alphabet, orthography (diacritics), word structure (syllable composition, morphology), lexical choice or even syntax. Similar or closely related languages often reflect a common origin and are members of a dialect continuum (Bloomfield, 1935).

[1]We wish to thank an anonimous reviewer for her valuable comments and suggestions.




*Proceedings of the First Workshop on Applying NLP Tools to Similar Languages, Varieties and Dialects*, pages 120–128, Dublin, Ireland, August 23 2014.

Solutions to language identification are often based either on generative or discriminative character n-gram language models. While character-based methods provide a means to distinguish between different languages on the basis of coarse-grained statistics on n-grams, it seems that discriminating between similar languages needs more fine-grained distinctions not always reflected by n-gram character distributions. According to Tiedemann and Ljubešić (2012), character-based n-gram methods fail for languages with a high lexical overlap, since the more shared words between two languages, the more similar will their n-gram character frequency profiles be.

| Group | Model | Lang/Var | Precision | Recall | $F_1$-score |
|---|---|---|---|---|---|
| | | *bs* | 0.930 | 0.889 | 0.909 |
| A | C 1-5 | *hr* | 0.924 | 0.941 | 0.932 |
| | | *sr* | 0.929 | 0.953 | 0.941 |
| B | L 1 | *id* | 0.988 | 0.994 | 0.991 |
| | | *my* | 0.994 | 0.988 | 0.991 |
| C | T 1-2 | *cz* | 1.000 | 0.999 | 0.999 |
| | | *sk* | 0.999 | 1.000 | 0.999 |
| D | T 1-2 | *pt-BR* | 0.933 | 0.964 | 0.948 |
| | | *pt-PT* | 0.963 | 0.930 | 0.946 |
| E | T 1-2 | *es-AR* | 0.942 | 0.816 | 0.874 |
| | | *es-ES* | 0.837 | 0.949 | 0.890 |
| F | L 1 | *en-GB* | 0.959 | 0.411 | 0.575 |
| | | *en-US* | 0.643 | 0.932 | 0.761 |
| | | **Overall without F** | 0.949 | 0.947 | 0.947 |
| | | **Overall** | 0.926 | 0.932 | 0.928 |

Table 1: Macro-averaged Precision, Recall and $F_1$-score on the DSL training dataset resulting from 10-fold cross-validation using the best model for each group of languages o varieties. Model has a letter code indicating the kind of elements considered: C (characters), T (tokens), L (tokens from the list of the 10,000 most frequent tokens), and a number indicating how many consecutive elements have been taken in a feature: 1 (unigrams), 1-2 (unigrams and bigrams), 1-5 (sequences of length one to five).

## 2 Previous Approaches

Although focused on formal languages, Gold (1967) is usually credited as the first to attempt computational language identification. In particular, two common LI approaches, namely n-gram language models and white (or black) lists, echo Gold's information presentation methods. In the 1990s, language identification was formulated as a sub-task of text categorization and varied approaches were explored. Beesley (1988) pioneered the use of character n-grams models, which were also used by Dunning (1994) and Cavnar and Trenkle (1994). Grefenstette (1995) compared this approach to Ingle (1978), based on the frequency of short words. The interested reader is referred to Zampieri (2013) for a review of some statistical and machine learning proposals and to both Baldwin and Lui (2010) and Lui and Baldwin (2011) for an overview of some linguistically motivated models.

As Baldwin and Lui (2010) or Tiedemann and Ljubešić (2012) point out, language identification is erroneously considered an easy and solved problem[2], in part because of some general purpose systems being available, notably TextCat[3], Xerox Language Identifier[4] and, more recently, `langid.py` (Lui and Baldwin, 2012). While it is true that it is possible to obtain brilliant results for a small number of languages (Baldwin and Lui, 2010) or typologically distant languages (Zampieri et al., 2013), accurately discriminating among closely related languages or varieties of the same language has been repeatedly reported as a bottleneck for language identification systems, in particular for those based on n-grams.

[2]See McNamee (2005) eloquent title.

[3]http://odur.let.rug.nl/vannoord/TextCat

[4]http://open.xerox.com/Services/LanguageIdentifier

Back in 2004, Padró and Padró concluded that "since the tested systems tend to fail when distinguishing similar languages (e.g. Spanish and Catalan), further research could be done to solve these cases." Martins and Silva (2005) report similar difficulties in discriminating among European and Brazilian Portuguese. Ranaivo-Malançon (2006) motivates her work on the unsatisfactory performance of (then) available language identifiers when dealing with close languages such as Malay and Indonesian. Ljubešić et al. (2007) do not even attempt to distinguish Bosnian from Croatian when developing a Croatian identifier because of their closeness. Trieschnigg et al. (2012) come as an exception as they report satisfactory results in identifying sixteen varieties of Dutch with TextCat.

Ranaivo-Malançon (2006) presents a cascaded language identifier for Malay and Indonesian. It first distinguishes Malay or Indonesian from other four European languages using trigrams extracted from the most frequent words from each language. Texts classified as Malay or Indonesian are subsequently scanned for some linguistic features (format of numbers and exclusive words), yielding a more precise performance than TextCat.

Ljubešić et al. (2007) also propose a cascaded identifier that relies on 'black lists' to discard non-Balkan languages and a second order Markov model on n-grams to discriminate among them, augmented with a 'black list' component that raises accuracy up to 0.99 when dealing with the most difficult pair (Croatian and Serbian). This work is followed up in Tiedemann and Ljubešić (2012) where 9% of improvement over standard approaches is reported and where support for Bosnian discrimination is included.

Huang and Lee (2008) use a bag of the most frequent words to build a voting identifier for three Chinese varieties with a top accuracy of 0.929. More recently, Zampieri (2013) compares the performance of n-gram based models to machine learning methods using bag of words when discriminating similar languages and varieties obtaining comparable performance with both approaches.

Grouin et al. (2010) present the shared task DEFT 2010. Participants were challenged to identify the decade, country (France and Canada) and newspaper for a set of journalistic texts. As far as the country labeling is concerned, they report an upper 0.964 $F_1$-measure and an average of 0.767. Very brief descriptions of the systems are also offered.

Zampieri and Gebre (2012) present a log-likelihood estimation method for language models built on orthographical (character n-grams), lexical (word unigrams) and lexico-syntactic (word bigrams) features. They report a 0.998 accuracy distinguishing European and Brazilian Portuguese with a language model based on character 4-grams. This approach is adapted in Zampieri et al. (2013) to deal with Spanish varieties, where the role of knowledge-rich features (POS tags) is also explored. They report a 0.99 accuracy when binarily distinguishing Argentinean and Mexican Spanish with single words or bigrams.

Trieschnigg et al. (2012) compare the performance of TextCat to the nearest neighbour and nearest prototype in combination with a cosine distance when distinguishing among sixteen varieties of Dutch. They report a micro-average $F_1$-score of 0.799 (and a macro-average $F_1$-score of 0.527) with a top $F_1$-score of 0.987 when dealing with Frisian.

Lui and Cook (2013) report experiments with different classifiers to map English documents to their country of origin. An SVM classifier with bag of words is top ranked with a macro-average 0.911 $F_1$-score in a cross-domain setting and 0.975 in an in-domain setting.

All these previous works (with the sole exception of Trieschnigg et al. (2012), where a general purpose LI system yields a satisfactory performance) agree in the specificity of DSL regarding LI. Maybe because of that, two level approaches are not uncommon. Features used to discriminate seem to be language-group specific, altough word rather than character features seem to perform better (Zampieri and Gebre (2012) report best results for character 4-grams, however, given that European and Brazilian Portuguese do not completely share ortography).

## 3 Maximum Entropy Models and Feature Engineering

Maximum Entropy modelling is a general purpose machine learning framework that has proven to be highly expressive and powerful in many areas. Maximum Entropy (maxent) was first introduced into natural language processing by Berger et al. (1996) and Della Pietra et al. (1997). Since its introduction,

Maximum Entropy techniques and the more general framework of Random Fields have been applied extensively to natural language processing problems, where maxent classifiers are commonly used as an alternative to Naïve Bayes classifiers. In maxent modelling, the probability that an example $x$ is in a class $c$ is estimated from its bag of words (or n-grams) as:

$$p(c|x) = \frac{1}{Z} \exp \sum_{y \in bow(x)} \sum_{i=1}^{N} w_{ci} \cdot f_i(c, y)$$

where $f_i(c, y)$ are indicator functions, $w_{ci}$ is the weight assigned to feature $i$ in class $c$, and $Z$ is a normalization factor. Features are modelled by indicator functions $f_i(c, y)$, which are evaluated to one when the feature $i$ for a particular class $c$ is true for a word $y$ and zero otherwise. The following is an example of an indicator function modelling the presence of a particular word in a class:

$$f_1(c, y) = \begin{cases} 1, & c = \textit{en-GB} \wedge y = \text{`colour'} \\ 0, & \text{otherwise} \end{cases}$$

The class assigned to an example $x$ is the most probable one:

$$\hat{c} = \arg\max_{c \in C} p(c|x)$$

The maxent classifiers are implemented with the toolkit of Zhang Le (2004), and the parameters of the model are estimated using Generalized Iterative Scaling (Darroch and Ratcli, 1972).

Having chosen a closed approach to the DSL shared task, no other resources than the text samples given as training and development datasets have been used in features design. In this knowledge-poor approach to the problem, the maxent classifier has been trained with token and character n-gram features. Character-based features are obtained with a simple character tokenizer. However, for token-based features, texts are tokenized using an orthographic tokenizer which splits punctuation from words. Several bags of features have been considered during the experiments: single tokens (T1), single words from the list of the 10,000 most frequent tokens (L1), token bigrams (T2), and n-grams of character sequences of length from one to five (C1-5). We will also refer to the lists of the 10,000 most frequent words as 'white list', which have a complementary role to the 'black lists' of Tiedemann and Ljubešić (2012).

To determine which features are best suited to each group, we measured their performance using ten-fold cross-validation on the training dataset and using the development dataset for testing. For group A, best results were obtained using bag of features consisting of variable length character n-grams ranging from one to five (C1-5). On group B, token bigrams (T2) performed slightly better in the development set than in the training set than the 'white list' of tokens (L1), which seems to indicate a better generalisation of the former on unseen examples. Results for group C were similar for all features considered. Regarding groups D and E, token-based features got similar results, with slightly better results for token bigrams. Finally, for English (group F) results were generally bad, reaching the 'white list' the better results. Group F is known to contain more than a few misclassifications due to news cross citing between American and British press. Results for each group's best model using ten-fold cross-validation on the training dataset are shown in Table 1. All figures have been macro averaged, i.e., they have been computed averaging the ten folds.

Because best results for each group are obtained with different feature sets, a new classifier is introduced. This classifier determines the language/variety group of each example before applying its particular group classifier. As can be seen in Table 2, the degree of token overlap between languages and varieties of different groups is rather low compared with the degree of overlap within the same group. Using only tokens, total accuracy is reached on the training dataset using cross validation. A classifier applying several classifiers in the way we propose is known as a hierarchical two-level classifier.

## 4 Evaluation and Error Analysis

Having as a goal to assess the performance of the hierarchical maxent classifier with the DSL task dataset, models were trained using all the examples provided in the training and development datasets.

| | *bs* | *hr* | *sr* | *id* | *my* | *sk* | *cz* | *pt-BR* | *pt-PT* | *es-AR* | *es-ES* | *en-GB* | *en-US* |
|---|---|---|---|---|---|---|---|---|---|---|---|---|---|
| *bs* | | **35.51** | **31.29** | 2.25 | 2.05 | 2.09 | 1.95 | 1.91 | 2.00 | 1.92 | 1.99 | 2.09 | 2.10 |
| *hr* | | | **41.18** | 2.47 | 2.21 | 2.15 | 2.04 | 2.08 | 2.20 | 2.12 | 2.16 | 2.42 | 2.39 |
| *sr* | | | | 2.06 | 1.74 | 1.95 | 1.79 | 1.63 | 1.72 | 1.69 | 1.69 | 1.68 | 1.68 |
| *id* | | | | | **19.02** | 2.36 | 2.47 | 4.00 | 4.14 | 4.35 | 4.21 | 6.81 | 6.74 |
| *my* | | | | | | 1.91 | 2.00 | 3.43 | 3.61 | 3.75 | 3.52 | 6.40 | 6.23 |
| *sk* | | | | | | | **9.45** | 2.12 | 2.15 | 2.20 | 2.22 | 2.55 | 2.56 |
| *cz* | | | | | | | | 2.18 | 2.25 | 2.24 | 2.27 | 2.73 | 2.70 |
| *pt-BR* | | | | | | | | | **29.17** | 12.04 | 11.63 | 4.62 | 4.60 |
| *pt-PT* | | | | | | | | | | 12.14 | 12.50 | 4.92 | 4.94 |
| *es-AR* | | | | | | | | | | | **30.91** | 5.52 | 5.52 |
| *es-ES* | | | | | | | | | | | | 4.89 | 4.90 |
| *en-GB* | | | | | | | | | | | | | **32.76** |
| *en-US* | | | | | | | | | | | | | |

Table 2: Lexical overlap between pairs of languages as a percentage. Only orthographic forms and punctuation signs appearing more than once in the training dataset has been considered.

| Group | Model | Lang/Var | Precision | Recall | $F_1$-score |
|---|---|---|---|---|---|
| A | C 1-5 | *bs* | 0.903 | 0.875 | 0.889 |
| | | *hr* | 0.923 | 0.931 | 0.927 |
| | | *sr* | 0.928 | 0.951 | 0.939 |
| B | L 1 | *id* | 0.991 | 0.996 | 0.993 |
| | | *my* | 0.996 | 0.991 | 0.993 |
| C | T 1-2 | *cz* | 1.000 | 1.000 | 1.000 |
| | | *sk* | 1.000 | 1.000 | 1.000 |
| D | T 1-2 | *pt-BR* | 0.933 | 0.964 | 0.948 |
| | | *pt-PT* | 0.962 | 0.931 | 0.946 |
| E | T 1-2 | *es-AR* | 0.950 | 0.819 | 0.879 |
| | | *es-ES* | 0.840 | 0.957 | 0.895 |
| F | L 1 | *en-GB* | 0.486 | 0.713 | 0.578 |
| | | *en-US* | 0.463 | 0.247 | 0.322 |
| | | **Overall without F** | 0.948 | 0.948 | 0.947 |
| | | **Overall** | 0.875 | 0.870 | 0.872 |

Table 3: Macro-averaged Precision, Recall and $F_1$-score on the DSL test dataset. Models are described in Table 1.

Table 4 shows the confusion matrix for the classifier on the test dataset and Table 1 the results in terms of precision, recall and $F_1$-score for each language and variety. As can be seen in Table 4, no example has been classified outside in a wrong group.

Tan et al. (2014) provide a baseline using a Naïve Bayes classifier on character 5-grams. As can be seen if Table 3 is compared with Table 4 of Tan et al. (2014), figures for group A are slightly below the baseline, groups B and C achieve the same results, D and E groups get slightly better results with the maxent classifier, and the biggest difference is found in group F, having better results Naïve Bayes. The overall result without group F is similar: an $F_1$-score of 0.947 for maxent and 0.942 for Naïve Bayes.

The DSL Corpus is composed of journalistic comparable texts to make the corpus suitable for discriminating similar languages and languages varieties but not text types or genres. Tiedemann and Ljubešić (2012) avoid biases towards topic and domain by experimenting with parallel texts reaching an overall accuracy of 90.3% for group A (*br*, *hr*, *sr*) using a 'black list' classifier and comparing its results with a Naïve Bayes approach. They found that the 'black list' classifier generalise better than the Naïve Bayes approach when moving from parallel to comparable corpora, since the former classifier is based on more informative features than the later.

Results of ten-fold cross-validation on the training dataset for different feature settings for group E (Spanish) were consistent with those of Zampieri et al. (2013), where word bigrams are reported to

| | *bs* | *hr* | *sr* | *id* | *my* | *cz* | *sk* | *pt-BR* | *pt-PT* | *es-AR* | *es-ES* | *en-GB* | *en-US* |
|---|---|---|---|---|---|---|---|---|---|---|---|---|---|
| *bs* | 875 | 61 | 64 | 0 | 0 | 0 | 0 | 0 | 0 | 0 | 0 | 0 | 0 |
| *hr* | 60 | 931 | 9 | 0 | 0 | 0 | 0 | 0 | 0 | 0 | 0 | 0 | 0 |
| *sr* | 33 | 16 | 951 | 0 | 0 | 0 | 0 | 0 | 0 | 0 | 0 | 0 | 0 |
| *id* | 0 | 0 | 0 | 996 | 4 | 0 | 0 | 0 | 0 | 0 | 0 | 0 | 0 |
| *my* | 0 | 0 | 0 | 9 | 991 | 0 | 0 | 0 | 0 | 0 | 0 | 0 | 0 |
| *cz* | 0 | 0 | 0 | 0 | 0 | 1,000 | 0 | 0 | 0 | 0 | 0 | 0 | 0 |
| *sk* | 0 | 0 | 0 | 0 | 0 | 0 | 1,000 | 0 | 0 | 0 | 0 | 0 | 0 |
| *pt-BR* | 0 | 0 | 0 | 0 | 0 | 0 | 0 | 964 | 36 | 0 | 0 | 0 | 0 |
| *pt-PT* | 0 | 0 | 0 | 0 | 0 | 0 | 0 | 69 | 931 | 0 | 0 | 0 | 0 |
| *es-AR* | 0 | 0 | 0 | 0 | 0 | 0 | 0 | 0 | 0 | 819 | 181 | 0 | 0 |
| *es-ES* | 0 | 0 | 0 | 0 | 0 | 0 | 0 | 0 | 0 | 43 | 957 | 0 | 0 |
| *en-GB* | 0 | 0 | 0 | 0 | 0 | 0 | 0 | 0 | 0 | 0 | 0 | 571 | 229 |
| *en-US* | 0 | 0 | 0 | 0 | 0 | 0 | 0 | 0 | 0 | 0 | 0 | 602 | 198 |

Table 4: Confusion matrix for the hierarchical maxent classifier on languages and varieties in the DSL test dataset. The 1,000 Bosnian texts have been classified as Bosnian (875), Croatian (61) and Serbian (64).

| **Group** | **Language/Variety** | **Code** |
|---|---|---|
| A | Bosnian | *bs* |
| | Croatian | *hr* |
| | Serbian | *sr* |
| B | Indonesian | *id* |
| | Malay | *my* |
| C | Czech | *cz* |
| | Slovak | *sk* |
| D | Brazilian Portuguese | *pt-BR* |
| | European Portuguese | *pt-PT* |
| E | Argentine Spanish | *es-AR* |
| | European Spanish | *es-ES* |
| F | British English | *en-GB* |
| | American English | *en-US* |

Table 5: Languages and varieties groups and codes.

outperform character n-grams. Given that datasets are not identical, it is difficult to draw any conclusion from the 1.2% difference in accuracy between DSLRAE and Zampieri et al. (2013). Manual inspection of misclassified news suggests some textual properties that are specially challenging: a) high density of foreign proper names (*Russian*, *Baby*, *Pony*, *Jack*, ...) may dilute the evidence provided by vernacular words; b) conversely, low density of features specific to any variant (such as place or family names[5], demonyms, lexical choices) may be insufficient to drive the text to the right class; this is also the case of some perfectly neutral sentences where a trained linguist could not spot any clue about their origin; c) certain syntactical idiosyncrasies (for example Argentinian idioms *la pasas bien*, *tal como muchas veces*, *en exceso de*) are not captured by bigrams; d) there are instances of cross-information, e. g., Argentinian news about Spain and vice versa where maybe more of a topic rather than a variety is being detected (e. g., news about Urdangarín or Fernández de Kirchner); e) there are some typos and misspellings (*carabanas*, *dosco*) whose role remains unclear; e) finally, there is at least one text misclassified in the gold standard: it is labeled as Argentinian but it was written by the Spanish EFE news agency. Some of these difficulties cross-cut all language groups and are not specific to Spanish but rather to DSL as a task.

In contrast to what Zampieri and Gebre (2012) found, ten-fold cross-validation on the training dataset for different feature settings on the DSL dataset did not find character n-grams to outperform word n-grams for group D (Portuguese). It could be hypothesized that they used a unique source (newspaper) for each variety and therefore rigid editorial conventions could be at play; moreover, the collections were

[5]Zampieri and Gebre (2012) highlight the importance of proper nouns when using word n-grams.

three years distant, so topic consistency could also be compromised[6]. Manual inspection of mislabeled sentences shows some already known categories: evidence diluted by foreign words (*Red Brick Warehouse*, *Mészáros*, *Fat Duck*), poor evidence (*Valongo*, *Sao Paulo*) or cross-information (*TAP*, *Brasília*). There is, however, a Portuguese-specific issue: some texts obey the 1990 Orthographic Agreement[7] which blurs the orthographic distinctions regarding diacritics or consonant clusters; in fact, one sentence contains words following both standards (*perspectiva* and *reprodução*). It remains unexplained why word bigrams did not capture the Brazilian preference for passive voice (*foram rebaixados*), auxiliary + gerund chunks (*estamos utilizando*) or clitic dropping (*lembro*).

Despite findings by Tiedemann and Ljubešić (2012), character n-grams performed better during ten-fold cross-validation on the training dataset for different feature settings on the DSL dataset for group A (Bosnian, Croatian and Serbian). Misclassified sentences involve failing to capture adapted place names (*Belgiji*, *Švedskoj*) or derivational choices (*organiziranog*).

Results of ten-fold cross-validation on the training dataset for different feature settings for group B (Indonesian and Malay) top ranked word unigrams. Ranaivo-Malançon (2006) uses number formatting and exclusive word lists. It can be hypothesized that lexical overlap is low (see Table 2) and/or frequency distributions are dissimilar thus allowing word unigrams to perform as well as 'white lists'.

Languages of group C (Czech and Slovak) are dissimilar both orthographically and lexically. These dissimilarities are surprisingly well captured by the top 10,000 most frequent words.

## 5 Conclusions and Future Work

In this paper, we have shown that a hierarchical classifier is well suited to discriminate among different language groups and languages or varieties therein. Different features are shown to better suit typological traits of supported languages. A comparison to previous approaches is provided, when available.

In a multilingual setting, the effect of adding Galician to group D could be investigated. Focusing on Spanish language, we plan to geographically expand the classifier to deal with all national varieties, a much harder task as both Baldwin and Lui (2010) and Zampieri et al. (2013) remark. Moreover, the classifier could be used, as Tiedemann and Ljubešić (2012) suggest, to learn varieties discriminators to label texts beyond national classes (e.g. both Caribbean and Andean Spanish cross-cut national borders and, conversely, nations involved are known not to be dialectally uniform). Given that error analysis showed that word bigrams fail to capture certain syntactical idiosyncrasies, a model with longer n-grams and/or knowledge-richer features such as POS sequences could also be explored, although Zampieri et al. (2013) report lower performance than knowledge-poor features. Finally, classification techniques such as those described in Gyawali et al. (2013) may be used to discard translations when building monolingual, vernacular corpora.

A diachronic expansion, such as Trieschnigg et al. (2012), is also in mind. Medieval Castilian coexisted with other Romance varieties such as Leonese or Aragonese whose features permeated Castilian texts. Researchers are in need of a tool to properly classify diachronic texts to accurately describe older stages of Spanish. Following the suggestion of Tiedemann and Ljubešić (2012), we envisage the use of parallel texts such as versions of the Bible from different areas to learn the differences among varieties.

## References

Timothy Baldwin and Marco Lui. 2010. Language identification: The long and the short of the matter. In *HLT-NAACL*, pages 229–237.

Kenneth Beesley. 1988. Language identifier: A computer program for automatic natural-language identification of on-line text. In *Language at Crossroads: Proceedings of the Annual Conference of the American Translators Association*, pages 47–54.

A. L. Berger, S. A. Della Pietra, and V. J. Della Pietra. 1996. A maximum entropy approach to natural language processing. *Computational Linguistics*, 22(1):39–71.

[6]Ljubešić et al. (2007) warn against corpus-specific features.

[7]http://www.portaldalinguaportuguesa.org/acordo.php

Leonard Bloomfield. 1935. *Language*. Allen & Unwin, London.

William B. Cavnar and John M. Trenkle. 1994. N-gram-based text categorization. In *Proceedings of 3rd Annual Symposium on Document Analysis and Information Retrieval (SDAIR 94)*, pages 161–175.

J. N. Darroch and D. Ratcliff. 1972. Generalized iterative scaling for log-linear models. *The Annals of Mathematical Statistics*, 43(5):1470–1480.

Ted Dunning. 1994. Statistical identification of language. Technical report, Computing Research Laboratory. New Mexico State University.

E. Mark Gold. 1967. Language identification in the limit. *Information and Control*, 10(5):447–474.

Gregory Grefenstette. 1995. Comparing two language identification schemes. In *Proceedings of the 3rd International Conference on Statistical Analysis of Textual Data (JADT 95)*, pages 263–268.

Cyril Grouin, Dominic Forest, Lyne Da Sylva, Patrick Paroubek, and Pierre Zweigenbaum. 2014. Présentation et résultats du défi fouille de texte DEFT2010 : où et quand un article de presse a-t-il été écrit ? In *Proceedings Atelier de clôture de la sixième édition du Défi Fouille de Textes (DEFT-2010)*, pages 1–15.

Binod Gyawali, Gabriela Ramirez, and Thamar Solorio. 2013. Native language identification: a simple n-gram based approach. In *Proceedings of the Eighth Workshop on Innovative Use of NLP for Building Educational Applications*, pages 224–231.

Chu-Ren Huang and Lung-Hao Lee. 2008. Contrastive approach towards text source classification based on top-bag-of-word similarity. In *PACLIC*, pages 404–410.

Norman C. Ingle. 1978. *Language identification table*. The author, Shoreham-by-Sea.

Heinz Kloss. 1967. Abstand languages and Ausbau languages. *Anthropological Linguistics*, 9(7):29–41.

Zhang Le, 2004. *Maximum Entropy Modeling Toolkit for Python and C++*, December.

Nikola Ljubešić, Nives Mikelić, and Damir Boras. 2007. Language identification: How to distinguish similar languages. In *Proceedings of the 29th International Conference on Information Technology Interfaces*, pages 541–546.

Marco Lui and Timothy Baldwin. 2011. Cross-domain feature selection for language identification. In *IJCNLP*, pages 553–561.

Marco Lui and Timothy Baldwin. 2012. `langid.py`: An off-the-shelf language identification tool. In *Proceedings of the ACL 2012 System Demonstrations*, pages 25–30.

Marco Lui and Paul Cook. 2013. Classifying English documents by national dialect. In *Proceedings of the Australasian Language Technology Association Workshop 2013 (ALTA 2013)*, pages 5–15.

Bruno Martins and Mário J. Silva. 2005. Language identification in web pages. In *Proceedings of the 2005 ACM Symposium on Applied Computing*, pages 764–768.

Paul McNamee. 2005. Language identification: A solved problem suitable for undergraduate instruction. *Journal of Computing Sciences in Colleges*, 20(3):94–101.

Muntsa Padró and Lluís Padró. 2004. Comparing methods for language identification. *Procesamiento del Lenguaje Natural*, 33:155–162.

S. A. Della Pietra, V. J. Della Pietra, and J. Lafferty. 1997. Inducing features of random fields. *IEEE Transactions on Pattern Analysis and Machine Intelligence*, 19(4):1–13.

Bali Ranaivo-Malançon. 2006. Automatic Identification of Close Languages – Case study: Malay and Indonesian. *ECTI Transactions on Computer and Information Technology*, 2(2):126–134.

Liling Tan, Marcos Zampieri, Nikola Ljubešić, and Jörg Tiedemann. 2014. Merging comparable data sources for the discrimination of similar languages: The DSL corpus collection. In *Proceedings of the 7th Workshop on Building and Using Comparable Corpora (BUCC)*.

Joel Tetreault, Daniel Blanchard, and Aoife Cahill. 2013. A report on the first native language identification shared task. In *Proceedings of the Eighth Workshop on the Innovative Use of NLP for Building Educational Applications*, pages 48–57.

Jörg Tiedemann and Nikola Ljubešić. 2012. Efficient discrimination between closely related languages. In *Proceedings of COLING 2012*, pages 2619–2634.

R.B. Trieschnigg, D. Hiemstra, M. Theune, F.M.G. de Jong, and T. Meder. 2012. An exploration of language identification techniques for the Dutch folktale database. In *Proceedings of the Workshop on Adaptation of Language Resources and Tools for Processing Cultural Heritage (LREC 2012)*, pages 47–51.

Peter Trudgill. 2004. Glocalisation and the Ausbau sociolinguistics of modern Europe. In Anna Duszak and Urszula Okulska, editors, *Speaking from the Margin: Global English from a European Perspective*, pages 35–49. Peter Lang, Frankfurt am Main.

Marcos Zampieri and Binyam Gebre. 2012. Automatic identification of language varieties: The case of Portuguese. In *Proceedings of KONVENS 2012*, pages 233–237.

Marcos Zampieri, Binyam Gebrekidan Gebre, and Sascha Diwersy. 2013. N-gram language models and POS distribution for the identification of Spanish varieties. In *Proceedings of TALN2013*, pages 580–587.

Marcos Zampieri, Liling Tan, Nikola Ljubešić, and Jörg Tiedemann. 2014. A report on the DSL shared task 2014. In *Proceedings of the 1st Workshop on Applying NLP Tools to Similar Languages, Varieties and Dialects (VarDial)*.

Marcos Zampieri. 2013. Using bag-of-words to distinguish similar languages: How efficient are they? In *Proceedings of the 14th IEEE International Symposium on Computational Intelligence and Informatics (CINTI2013)*, pages 37–41.

# Exploring Methods and Resources for Discriminating Similar Languages

**Marco Lui[♡♣], Ned Letcher[♡], Oliver Adams[♡], Long Duong[♡♣], Paul Cook[♡] and Timothy Baldwin[♡♣]**

[♡] Department of Computing and Information Systems
The University of Melbourne
[♣] NICTA Victoria

mhlui@unimelb.edu.au, ned@nedletcher.net, oadams@student.unimelb.edu.au, lduong@student.unimelb.edu.au, paulcook@unimelb.edu.au, tb@ldwin.net

**Abstract**

The *Discriminating between Similar Languages (DSL)* shared task at VarDial challenged participants to build an automatic language identification system to discriminate between 13 languages in 6 groups of highly-similar languages (or national varieties of the same language). In this paper, we describe the submissions made by team UniMelb-NLP, which took part in both the closed and open categories. We present the text representations and modeling techniques used, including cross-lingual POS tagging as well as fine-grained tags extracted from a deep grammar of English, and discuss additional data we collected for the open submissions, utilizing custom-built web corpora based on top-level domains as well as existing corpora.

## 1 Introduction

Language identification (LangID) is the problem of determining what natural language a document is written in. Studies in the area often report high accuracy (Cavnar and Trenkle, 1994; Dunning, 1994; Grefenstette, 1995; Prager, 1999; Teahan, 2000). However, recent work has shown that high accuracy is only achieved under ideal conditions (Baldwin and Lui, 2010), and one area that needs further work is accurate discrimination between closely-related languages (Ljubešić et al., 2007; Tiedemann and Ljubešić, 2012). The problem has been explored for specific groups of confusable languages, such as Malay/Indonesian (Ranaivo-Malancon, 2006), South-Eastern European languages (Tiedemann and Ljubešić, 2012), as well as varieties of English (Lui and Cook, 2013), Portuguese (Zampieri and Gebre, 2012), and Spanish (Zampieri et al., 2013). The *Discriminating Similar Language (DSL)* shared task (Zampieri et al., 2014) was hosted at the VarDial workshop at COLING 2014, and brings together the work on these various language groups by proposing a task on a single dataset containing text from 13 languages in 6 groups, drawn from a variety of news text datasets (Tan et al., 2014).

In this paper, we describe the entries made by team UniMelb NLP to the DSL shared task. We took part in both the closed and the open categories, submitting to the main component (Groups A-E) as well as the separate English component (Group F). For our closed submissions, we focused on comparing a conventional LangID methodology based on individual words and language-indicative letter sequences (Section 2.1) to a methodology that uses a de-lexicalized representation of language (Section 2.3). For Groups A-E we use cross-lingual POS-tagger adaptation (Section 2.3.1) to convert the raw text to a POS stream using a per-group tagger, and use $n$-grams of POS tags as our de-lexicalized representation. For English, we also use a de-lexicalized representation based on lexical types extracted from a deep grammar (Section 2.3.2), which can be thought of as a very fine-grained tagset. For the open submissions, we constructed new web-based corpora using a standard methodology, targeting per-language top-level domains (Section 2.4.2). We also compiled additional training data from existing corpora (Section 2.4.1).





*Proceedings of the First Workshop on Applying NLP Tools to Similar Languages, Varieties and Dialects*, pages 129–138, Dublin, Ireland, August 23 2014.

## 2 Overview

Our main focus was to explore novel methods and sources of training data for discriminating similar languages. In this section, we describe techniques and text representations that we tested, as well as the external data sources that we used to build language identifiers for this task.

### 2.1 Language-Indicative Byte Sequences

Lui and Baldwin (2011) introduced the $\mathcal{LD}$ feature set, a document representation for LangID that is robust to variation in languages across different sources of text. The $\mathcal{LD}$ feature set can be thought of as language-indicative byte sequences, i.e. sequences of 1 to 4 bytes that have been selected to be strongly characteristic of a particular language or set of languages regardless of the text source. Lui and Baldwin (2012) present `langid.py`,[1] an off-the-shelf LangID system that utilizes the $\mathcal{LD}$ feature set. In this work, we re-train `langid.py` using the training data provided by the shared task organizers, and use this as a baseline result representative of the state-of-the-art in LangID.

### 2.2 Hierarchical LangID

In LangID research to date, systems generally do not take into account any form of structure in the class space. In this shared task, languages are explicitly grouped into 6 disjoint groups. We make use of this structure by introducing a two-level LangID model. The first level implements a single group-level classifier, which takes an input sentence and identifies the language group (A–F) that the sentence is from. The output of this group-level classifier is used to select a corresponding per-group classifier, that is trained only on data for languages in the group. This per-group classifier is applied to the input sentence and the output thereof is the final label for the sentence.

### 2.3 De-Lexicalized Text Representation for DSL

One of the challenges in a machine learning approach to discriminating similar languages is to learn differences between languages that are truly representative of the distinction between varieties, rather than differences that are merely representative of peculiarities of the training data (Kilgarriff, 2001). One possible confounding factor is the topicality of the training data — if the data for each variety is drawn from different datasets, it is possible that a classifier will simply learn the topical differences between datasets. Diwersy et al. (2014) carried out a study of colligations in French varieties, where the variation in the grammatical function of noun lemmas was studied across French-language newspapers from six countries. In their initial analysis the found that the characteristic features of each country included the name of the country and other country-specific proper nouns, which resulted in near 100% classification accuracy but do not provide any insight into national varieties from a linguistic perspective.

One strategy that has been proposed to mitigate the effect of such topical differences is the use of a de-lexicalized text representation (Lui and Cook, 2013). The de-lexicalization is achieved through the use of a Part-Of-Speech tagger, which labels each word in a sentence according to its word class (such as Noun, Verb, Adjective etc). De-lexicalized text representations through POS tagging were first considered for native language identification (NLI), where they were used as a proxy for syntax in order to capture certain types of grammatical errors (Wong and Dras, 2009). Syntactic structure is known to vary across national dialects (Trudgill and Hannah, 2008), so Lui and Cook (2013) investigated POS plus function word $n$-grams as a proxy for syntactic structure, and used this representation to build classifiers to discriminate between Canadian, British and American English. They found that classifiers using such a representation achieved above-baseline results, indicating some systematic differences between varieties could be captured through the use of such a de-lexicalized representation. In this work, we explore this idea further — in particular, we examine (1) the applicability of de-lexicalized text representations to other languages using automatically-induced crosslingual POS taggers, and (2) the difference in accuracy for discriminating English varieties between representations based on a coarse-grained universal tagset (Section 2.3.1) as compared to a very fine-grained tagset used in deep parsing (Section 2.3.2).

[1]`http://github.com/saffsd/langid.py`

| | Sandy | quit | on | Tuesday | Sandy | quit | Tuesday |
|---|---|---|---|---|---|---|---|
| UT | NOUN | VERB | ADP | NOUN | NOUN | VERB | NOUN |
| LTT | n_-_pn | v_np* | p_np_i-tmp | n_-_c-dow | n_-_pn | v_np* | n_-_c-dow |
| | British English | | | | American English | | |

Table 1: Example of tags assigned with coarse-grained Universal Tagset (UT) and fine-grained lexical type tagset (LTT).

### 2.3.1 Crosslingual POS Tagging

A key issue in generating de-lexicalized text representations based on POS tags is the lack of availability of POS taggers for many languages. While some languages have some tools available for POS tagging (e.g. Treaties (Schmid, 1994) has parameter files for Spanish and Portuguese), the availability of POS taggers is far from universal. To address this problem for the purposes of discriminating similar languages, we draw on previous work in unsupervised cross-lingual POS tagging (Duong et al., 2013) to build a POS tagger for each group of languages, a method which we will refer to hereafter as "UMPOS".

UMPOS employs a 12-tag Universal Tagset introduced by Petrov et al. (2012), which consists of the tags *NOUN, VERB, ADJ* (adjective), *ADV* (adverb), *PRON* (pronoun), *DET* (determiner or article), *ADP* (preposition or postposition), *NUM* (numeral), *CONJ* (conjunction), *PRT* (particle), *PUNCT* (punctuation), and *X* (all other categories, e.g., foreign words or abbreviations). These twelve basic tags constitute a "universal" tagset in that they can be used to describe the morphosyntax of any language at a coarse level.

UMPOS generates POS taggers for new languages in an unsupervised fashion, by making use of parallel data and an existing POS tagger. The input for UMPOS is: (1) parallel data between the source and target languages; and (2) a supervised POS tagger for the source language. The output will be the tagger for the target language. The parallel data acts as a bridge to transfer POS annotation information from the source language to the target language.

The steps used in UMPOS are as follow. First, we collect parallel data which has English as the source language, drawing from Europarl (Koehn, 2005) and EUbookshop (Skadiņš et al., 2014). UMPOS word-aligns the parallel data using the Giza++ alignment tool (Och and Ney, 2003). The English side is POS-tagged using the Stanford POS tagger (Toutanova et al., 2003), and the POS tags are then projected from English to the target language based solely on one-to-one mappings. Using the sentence alignment score, UMPOS ranks the "goodness" of projected sentences and builds a seed model for the target language on a subset of the parallel data. To further improve accuracy, UMPOS builds the final model by applying self-training with revision to the rest of the data as follows: (1) the parallel corpus data is divided into different blocks; (2) the first block is tagged using the seed model; (3) the block is revised based on alignment confidence; (4) a new tagger is trained on the first block and then used to tag the second block. This process continues until all blocks are tagged. In experiments on a set of 8 languages, Duong et al. (2013) report accuracy of 83.4%, which is state-of-the-art for unsupervised POS tagging.

### 2.3.2 English Tagging Using ERG Lexical Types

Focusing specifically on language Group F — British English and American English — we leveraged linguistic information from the analyses produced by the English Resource Grammar (ERG: Flickinger (2002)), a broad-coverage, handcrafted grammar of English in the HPSG framework (Pollard and Sag, 1994) and developed within the DELPH-IN[2] research initiative. In particular, we extracted the lexical types assigned to tokens by the parser for the best analysis of each input string. In accordance with the heavily lexicalized nature of HPSG, lexical types are the primary means of distinguishing between different morphosyntactic contexts in which a given lexical entry can occur. They can be thought of as fine-grained POS tags, containing subcategorisation information in addition to part of speech information, and semantic information in cases that it directly impacts on morphosyntax. The version of the ERG we used (the "1212" release) has almost 1000 lexical types.

Table 1 illustrates an example of the type of syntactic variation that can be captured with the finer-

[2]http://www.delph-in.net

| Group | Language | Code | Web Corpora | | Existing Corpora | |
|---|---|---|---|---|---|---|
| | | | TLD | # words | # datasets | # words |
| A | Bosnian | bs | .ba | 817383 | 4 | 715602 |
| A | Croatian | hr | .hr | 43307311 | 5 | 1536623 |
| A | Serbian | sr | .rs | 1374787 | 4 | 1204684 |
| B | Indonesian | id | .id | 23812382 | 3 | 564824 |
| B | Malaysian | my | .my | 2596378 | 3 | 535221 |
| C | Czech | cz | .cz | 17103140 | 8 | 2181486 |
| C | Slovakian | sk | .sk | 17253001 | 8 | 2308083 |
| D | Brazilian Portuguese | pt-BR | .br | 27369673 | 4 | 860065 |
| D | European Portuguese | pt-PT | .pt | 22620401 | 8 | 2860321 |
| E | Argentine Spanish | es-AR | .ar | 45913651 | 2 | 619500 |
| E | Peninsular Spanish | es-ES | .es | 30965338 | 9 | 3458462 |
| F | British English | en-GB | .uk | 20375047 | 1 | 523653 |
| F | American English | en-US | .us | 21298230 | 1 | 527915 |

Table 2: Word count of training data used for open submissions.

grained lexical types, that would be missed with the coarse-grained universal tagset. In American English, both *Sandy resigned on Tuesday* and *Sandy resigned on Tuesday* are acceptable whereas British English does not permit the omission of the preposition before dates. In the coarse-grained tagset, the American English form results in a sequence VERB : NOUN, which is not particularly interesting as we expect this to occur in both English varieties, whereas the fine-grained lexical types allow us to capture the sequence `v_np*_ntr` : `n_-_c-dow` (verb followed by count noun [day of week]), which we expect to see in American English but not in British English.

Since the ERG models a sharp notion of grammaticality, not all inputs receive an analysis — whether due to gaps in the coverage of the grammar or genuinely ungrammatical input. The ERG achieved a coverage of 86% over the training data across both British English and American English. Sentences which failed to parse were excluded from use as input into the classifier. However the inability to classify any sentence which we cannot parse is unsatisfactory. We solved this problem by generating lexical type features for sentences which failed to parse using the ERG-trained übertagger of Dridan (2013), which performs both tokenisation and supertagging of lexical types and improves parser efficiency by reducing ambiguity in the input lattice to the parser.

### 2.4 External Corpora

The DSL shared task invited two categories of participation: (1) Closed, using only training data provided by the organizers (Tan et al., 2014); and (2) Open, using any training data available to participants. To participate in the latter category, we sourced additional training data through: (1) collection of data relevant to this task from existing text corpora; and (2) automatic construction of web corpora. The information about the additional training data is shown in Table 2.

#### 2.4.1 Existing Corpora

We collected training data from a number of existing corpora, as shown in Table 3. Many of the corpora that we used are part of OPUS (Tiedemann, 2012), which is a collection of sentence-aligned text corpora commonly used for research in machine translation. The exceptions are: (1) `debian`, which was constructed using translations of message strings from the Debian operating system,[3]; (2) BNC — the British National Corpus (Burnard, 2000); (3) OANC — the open component of the Second Release of the American National Corpus (Ide and Macleod, 2001), and (4) Reuters Corpus Volume 2 (RCV2);[4] a corpus of news stories by local reporters in 13 languages. We sampled approximately 19000 sentences from each of the BNC and OANC, which we used as training data to generate ERG lextype features (Section 2.3.2) for British English (en-GB) and American English (en-US), respectively. From RCV2 we

[3] http://www.debian.org

[4] http://trec.nist.gov/data/reuters/reuters.html

| | bs | hr | sr | pt-PT | pt-BR | id | my | cz | sk | es-ES | es-AR | en-US | en-GB |
|---|---|---|---|---|---|---|---|---|---|---|---|---|---|
| BNC | | | | | | | | | | | | | ✓ |
| debian | ✓ | ✓ | ✓ | ✓ | ✓ | ✓ | ✓ | ✓ | ✓ | ✓ | ✓ | | |
| ECB | | | | ✓ | | | | ✓ | ✓ | ✓ | | | |
| EMEA | | | | ✓ | | | | ✓ | ✓ | ✓ | | | |
| EUconst | | | | ✓ | | | | ✓ | ✓ | ✓ | | | |
| Europarl | | | | ✓ | | | | ✓ | ✓ | ✓ | | | |
| hrenWaC | | ✓ | | | | | | | | | | | |
| KDE4 | | ✓ | ✓ | ✓ | ✓ | ✓ | ✓ | ✓ | ✓ | ✓ | | | |
| KDEdoc | | | | ✓ | ✓ | | | | ✓ | ✓ | | | |
| OANC | | | | | | | | | | | | ✓ | |
| OpenSubtitles | ✓ | ✓ | ✓ | ✓ | ✓ | ✓ | ✓ | ✓ | ✓ | ✓ | | | |
| RCV2 | | | | | | | | | | ✓ | ✓ | | |
| SETIMES2 | ✓ | ✓ | ✓ | | | | | | | | | | |
| Tatoeba | ✓ | | | | | | | ✓ | | | | | |

Table 3: Training data compiled from existing corpora.

used the Latin American Spanish news stories as a proxy for Argentine Spanish (es-AR). Note that, for a given text source, we didn't necessarily use data for all available languages. For example, `debian` contains British English and American English translations, which we did not use.

### 2.4.2 Web Corpus Construction

Each existing corpus we describe in Section 2.4.1 provides incomplete coverage over the set of languages in the shared task dataset. In order to have a resource that covers all the languages in the shared task drawn from a single source, we constructed web corpora for each language. Our approach was strongly inspired by the approach used to create ukWaC (Ferraresi et al., 2008), and the creation of each sub-language's corpus involved crawling the top level domains of the primary countries associated with those sub-languages. Based on the findings of Cook and Hirst (2012), the assumption underlying this approach is that text found in the top-level domains (TLDs) of those countries will primarily be of the sub-language dominant in that country. For instance, we assume that Portuguese text found when crawling the `.pt` TLD will primarily be European Portuguese, while the Portuguese found in `.br` will be primarily Brazilian Portuguese.

The process of creating a corpus for each sub-language involved translating a sample of 200 of the original ukWaC queries into each language using Panlex (Baldwin et al., 2010).[5] These queries were then submitted to the Bing Search API using the BootCaT tools (Baroni and Bernardini, 2004), constraining results to the relevant TLD. For each query, we took the first 10 URLs yielded by Bing and appended them to a list of seed URLs for that language. After deduplication, the seed URLs were then fed to a Heritrix 3.1.1[6] instance with default settings other than constraining the crawled content to the relevant TLD.

Corpora were then created from the data gathered by Heritrix. Following the ukWaC approach, only documents with a MIME type of HTML and size between 5k and 200k bytes were used. Justext (Pomikálek, 2011) was used to extract text from the selected documents. `langid.py` (Lui and Baldwin, 2012) was then used to discard documents whose text was not in the relevant language or language group. The corpus was then refined through deduplication. First, near-deduplication was done at the paragraph level using Onion (Pomikálek, 2011) with its default settings. Then, exact-match sentence-level deduplication, ignoring whitespace and case, was applied.

## 3 Results and Discussion

Table 4 summarizes the runs submitted by team UniMelb NLP to the VarDial DSL shared task. We submitted the maximum number of runs allowed, i.e. 3 closed runs and 3 open runs, to both the "general" Groups A–E subtask as well as the English-specific Group F subtask. We applied different methods to Group F, as some of the tools (the ERG) and resources (BNC/OANC) were specific to English. For clarity in discussion, we have labeled each of our runs according to a 3-letter code: the first letter indicates the

[5] A sample of the queries was used because of time and resource limitations.

[6] `https://webarchive.jira.com/wiki/display/Heritrix`

| Run | Description | Macro-avg F-Score | |
|---|---|---|---|
| | | dev | tst |
| | Grp A-E closed | | |
| AC1 | langid.py 13-way | 0.822 | 0.817 |
| AC2 | langid.py per-group | 0.923 | 0.918 |
| AC3 | POS features | 0.683 | 0.671 |
| | Grp F closed | | |
| FC1 | Lextype features | 0.559 | 0.415 |
| FC2 | langid.py per-group | 0.548 | 0.403 |
| FC3 | POS features | 0.545 | 0.435 |
| | Grp A-E open | | |
| AO1 | Ext Corpora (word-level model) | 0.705 | 0.703 |
| AO2 | Web Corpora (word-level model) | 0.771 | 0.767 |
| AO3 | 5-way voting | 0.881 | 0.878 |
| | Grp F open | | |
| FO1 | Lextype features using BNC/OANC training data | 0.491 | 0.572 |
| FO2 | Web Corpora (word-level model) | 0.490 | 0.581 |
| FO3 | 5-way voting | 0.574 | 0.442 |

Table 4: Summary of the official runs submitted by UniMelbNLP. "dev" indicates scores from our internal testing on the development partition of the dataset.

subtask (A for Groups A–E, F for Group F), the second indicates Closed ("C") or Open ("O"), and the final digit indicates the run number.

AC1 represents a benchmark result based on the LangID system (Lui and Baldwin, 2012). We used the training tools provided with `langid.py` to generate a new model using the training data provided by the shared task organizers, noting that as only data from a single source is used, we are not able to fully exploit the cross-domain feature selection (Lui and Baldwin, 2011) implemented by `langid.py`. The macro-averaged F-score across groups is substantially lower than that on standard LangID datasets (Lui and Baldwin, 2012).

AC2 and FC2 are a straightforward implementation of hierarchical LangID (Section 2.2), using mostly-default settings of `langid.py`. A 6-way group-level classifier is trained, and well as 6 different per-group classifiers. We increase the number of features selected per class (i.e. group or language) to 500 from the default of 300, to compensate for the smaller number of classes (`langid.py` off-the-shelf supports 97 languages). In our internal testing on the provided development data, the group-level classifier achieved 100% accuracy in classifying sentences at the group level, essentially reducing the problem to within-group disambiguation. Despite being one of the simplest approaches, overall this was our best-performing submission for Groups A–E. It also represents a substantial improvement on AC1, further emphasizing the need to implement hierarchical LangID in order to attain high accuracy in discriminating similar languages.

AC3 and FC3 are based solely on POS-tag sequences generated by UMPOS, and implement a hierarchical LangID approach similar to AC2/FC2. Each sentence in the training data is mapped to a POS-tag sequence in the 12-tag universal tagset, using the per-group POS tagger for the language group. Each tag was represented using a single character, allowing us to make use of `langid.py` to train 6 per-group classifiers based on *n*-grams of POS-tags. We used *n*-grams of order 1–6, and selected 5000 top-ranked sequences per-language. To classify test data, the same group-level classifier used in AC2 was used to map sentences to language groups, and then the per-group POS tagger was applied to derive the corresponding stream of POS tags for each sentence. The corresponding per-group classifier trained on POS tag sequences was then applied to produce the final label for the sentence. For Groups A–E, we find that

| | bs | hr | sr | | id | my | | cz | sk |
|---|---|---|---|---|---|---|---|---|---|
| T | 53.0 | 23.2 | 60.0 | VHN | 0.9 | 1.3 | .1.1 | 1.0 | 1.2 |
| TV | 32.4 | 13.2 | 43.3 | DHN | 0.1 | 0.1 | 1.1. | 2.0 | 2.2 |
| NT | 31.5 | 13.9 | 43.2 | N.1. | 12.1 | 3.1 | 1.1 | 4.0 | 4.4 |
| TVN | 24.8 | 9.8 | 34.3 | N.N | 63.3 | 48.0 | .N.1 | 0.5 | 0.7 |
| VT | 19.4 | 6.1 | 27.1 | .DNV | 1.8 | 1.1 | .C | 39.0 | 33.5 |
| TN | 29.1 | 10.9 | 29.6 | DH | 1.7 | 2.1 | .1.. | 0.7 | 1.0 |
| NTV | 18.6 | 8.4 | 29.4 | N.DN | 3.2 | 2.0 | .P | 51.2 | 41.8 |
| TVNN | 16.8 | 6.9 | 23.7 | VH | 11.3 | 14.9 | 1. | 14.0 | 13.9 |
| NVT | 11.2 | 2.9 | 15.5 | PNV1 | 0.5 | 0.4 | 1.. | 1.2 | 1.6 |
| VTV | 11.0 | 3.2 | 17.0 | .1. | 13.2 | 3.8 | .R | 44.0 | 30.0 |

| | pt-BR | pt-PT | | es-AR | es-ES | | en-GB | en-US |
|---|---|---|---|---|---|---|---|---|
| X | 3.4 | 2.8 | .. | 22.6 | 43.3 | NNN | 48.2 | 43.2 |
| N.NN | 22.2 | 15.3 | N.. | 16.4 | 31.7 | HV | 41.5 | 46.4 |
| .NN | 29.9 | 22.9 | .P | 52.2 | 68.3 | NN | 86.3 | 83.0 |
| XN | 0.4 | 0.4 | P. | 6.6 | 16.8 | H | 61.8 | 65.9 |
| NNNN | 6.2 | 3.2 | D. | 4.4 | 12.6 | R | 61.5 | 65.5 |
| D | 99.2 | 99.5 | ..$ | 0.0 | 0.0 | RR | 7.2 | 9.4 |
| NNN | 28.3 | 18.6 | J.. | 5.0 | 12.6 | NNNN | 21.7 | 18.5 |
| .NNN | 6.7 | 4.0 | ..VV | 0.9 | 5.2 | .C | 15.8 | 18.8 |
| N.D | 58.6 | 47.8 | DN.. | 4.2 | 11.0 | ... | 0.8 | 0.3 |
| NX | 0.8 | 0.5 | .PD | 24.5 | 36.3 | N.C | 11.3 | 13.6 |

Table 5: Top 10 POS features per-group by Information Gain, along with percentage of sentences in each language in which the feature appears. The notation used is as follows: . = punctuation, J = adjective, P = pronoun, R = adverb, C = conjunction, D = determiner/article, N = noun, 1 = numeral, H = pronoun, T = particle, V = verb, and X = others

the POS-tag sequence features are not as effective as the character *n*-grams used in AC2. Nonetheless, the results attained are above baseline, indicating that there are systematic differences between languages in each group that can be captured by an unsupervised approach to POS-tagging using a coarse-grained tagset. This extends the similar observation made by Lui and Cook (2013) on varieties of English, showing that the same is true for the other language groups in this shared task. Also of interest is the higher accuracy attained by the POS-tag features on Groups A–E (i.e. AC3) than on English (Group F, FC3). The top-10 sequences per-group are presented in Table 5, where it can be seen that the sequences are often slightly more common in one language in the group than the other language(s). One limitation of the Information Gain based feature selection used in `langid.py` is that each feature is scored independently, and each language receives a binarized score. This can be seen in the features selected for Group A, where all the top-10 features selected involve particles (labelled T). Overall, this indicates that Croatian (hr) appears to use particles much less frequently than Serbian (sr) or Bosnian (bs), which is an intriguing finding. However, most of the top-10 features are redundant in that they all convey very similar information.

Similar to FC3, a hierarchical LangID approach is used in FC1, in conjunction with per-group classifiers based on a sequence of tags derived from the original sentence. The difference between the taggers used for FC3 and FC1 is that the FC3 tagger utilizes the 12-tag universal tagset, whereas the FC1 tagger uses the English-specific lexical types from the ERG (Section 2.3.2), a set of approximately 1000 tags. There is hence a trade-off to be made between the degree of distinction between tags, and the relative sparsity of the data — having a larger tagset means that any given sequence of tags is proportionally less likely to occur. On the basis of the results of FC1 and FC3 on the `dev` data, the lexical type features marginally outperform the coarse-grained universal tagset. However, this result is made harder to interpret by the mismatch between the `dev` and `tst` partitions of the shared task dataset. We will discuss this issue in more detail below, in the context of examining the results on Group F for the open category.

In the open category, we focused primarily on the effect of using different sources of training data. AO1 and AO2 both implement a hierarchical LangID approach, again using the group-level classifier from AC2. For the per-group classifiers, runs AO1 and AO2 use a naive Bayes model on a word-level representation, with feature selection by Information Gain. The difference between the two is that A01 uses samples from existing text corpora (Section 2.4.1), whereas A02 uses web corpora that we prepared specifically for this shared task (Section 2.4.2). In terms of accuracy, both types of corpora perform substantially better than baseline, indicating that at the word level, there are differences between the language varieties that are consistent across the different corpus types. This result is complementary to Cook and Hirst (2012), who found that web corpora from specific top-level domains were representative of national varieties of English. AO2 (web corpora) outperforms AO1 (existing corpora), further highlighting the relevance of web corpora as a source of training data for discriminating similar languages. However, our models trained on external data were not able to outperform the models trained on the official training data for Groups A–E. A03 consists of a 5-way majority vote between results AC1, AC2, AC3, AO1 and AO2. Including the predictions from the closed submissions substantially improves the result with respect to AO1/AO2, but overall our best result for Groups A–E was obtained by run AC2.

For Group F, FO1 utilizes ERG lexical type features in the same manner as FC1, the difference being that FC1 uses the shared task `trn` partition, whereas FO1 uses sentences sampled from existing corpora, specifically `BNC` for en-GB and `OANC` for en-US. FO2 implements the same concept as AO2, namely a word-level naive Bayes model trained using web corpora. For the Group F (i.e. English) subtask, this was our best-performing submission overall. FO3 is a 5-way vote between FC1, FC2, FC3, FO1 and FO2, similar to AO3. Notably, our Group F submissions based on the supplied training data all performed substantially better on the `dev` partition of the shared task dataset than on the `tst` partition. The inverse is true for our submissions based on external corpora, where all our entries performed substantially better on the `tst` partition than on the `dev` partition. Furthermore, the differences are fairly large, particularly since Group F is a binary classification task with a 50% baseline. This implies that, at least under our models, the en-GB portion of the `trn` partition is a better model of the en-US portion of the `tst` partition than the en-GB portion thereof. This is likely due to the manual intervention that was only carried out on the test portion of the dataset (Zampieri et al., 2014).

Our Group F results appear to be inferior to previous work on discriminating English varieties (Lui and Cook, 2013). However, there are a number of differences that make it difficult to compare the results: Lui and Cook (2013) studied differences between Australian, British and Canadian English, whereas the shared task focused on differences between British and American English. Lui and Cook (2013) also draw on training data from a variety of domains (national corpora, web corpora and Twitter messages), whereas the shared task used a dataset collected from newspaper texts (Tan et al., 2014). Consistent with Cook and Hirst (2012) and Lui and Cook (2013), we found that web corpora appear to be representative of national varieties, and consistent with Lui and Cook (2013) we found that de-lexicalized representations of text are able to provide better than baseline discrimination between national varieties. Overall, these results highlight the need for further research into discriminating between varieties of English.

## 4 Conclusion

Discriminating between similar languages is an interesting sub-problem in language identification, and the DSL shared task at VarDial has given us an opportunity to examine possible solutions in greater detail. Our most successful methods implement straightforward hierarchical LangID, firstly identifying the language group that a sentence belongs to, before identifying the specific language. We examined a number of text representations for the per-group language identifiers, including a standard representation for language identification based on language-indicative byte sequences, as well as with de-lexicalized text representations. We found that the performance of de-lexicalized representations was above baseline, however we were not able to fully investigate approaches to integrating predictions from lexicalized and de-lexicalized text representations due to time constraints. We also found that when using external corpora, web corpora constructed by scraping per-country top-level domains performed as well as (if not better than) data collected from existing text corpora, supporting the hypothesis that web corpora are representative of national varieties of respective languages. Overall, our best result was obtained by applying two-level hierarchical LangID, firstly identifying the language group that a sentence belongs to, and then disambiguating within each group. Our best result was achieved by applying an existing LangID method (Lui and Baldwin, 2012) to both the group-level and the per-group classification tasks.

## Acknowledgments

The authors wish to thank Li Wang, Rebecca Dridan and Bahar Salehi for their kind assistance with this research. NICTA is funded by the Australian Government as represented by the Department of Broadband, Communications and the Digital Economy and the Australian Research Council through the ICT Centre of Excellence program.

## References

Timothy Baldwin and Marco Lui. 2010. Language identification: The long and the short of the matter. In *Proceedings of Human Language Technologies: The 11th Annual Conference of the North American Chapter of the Association for Computational Linguistics (NAACL HLT 2010)*, pages 229–237, Los Angeles, USA.

Timothy Baldwin, Jonathan Pool, and Susan M Colowick. 2010. Panlex and lextract: Translating all words of all languages of the world. In *Proceedings of the 23rd International Conference on Computational Linguistics: Demonstrations*, pages 37–40, Beijing, China.

Marco Baroni and Silvia Bernardini. 2004. BootCaT: Bootstrapping corpora and terms from the Web. In *Proceedings of the Fourth International Conference on Language Resources and Evaluation (LREC 2004)*.

Lou Burnard. 2000. *User Reference Guide for the British National Corpus*. Technical report, Oxford University Computing Services.

William B. Cavnar and John M. Trenkle. 1994. N-gram-based text categorization. In *Proceedings of the Third Symposium on Document Analysis and Information Retrieval*, pages 161–175, Las Vegas, USA.

Paul Cook and Graeme Hirst. 2012. Do Web corpora from top-level domains represent national varieties of English? In *Proceedings of the 11th International Conference on Textual Data Statistical Analysis*, pages 281–293, Liège, Belgium.

Sascha Diwersy, Stefan Evert, and Stella Neumann. 2014. A weakly supervised multivariate approach to the study of language variation. In Benedikt Szmrecsanyi and Bernhard Wälchli, editors, *Aggregating Dialectology, Typology, and Register Analysis. Linguistic Variation in Text and Speech*. De Gruyter, Berlin.

Rebecca Dridan. 2013. Ubertagging. Joint segmentation and supertagging for English. In *Proceedings of the 2013 Conference on Empirical Methods in Natural Language Processing*, pages 1201–1212, Seattle, USA.

Ted Dunning. 1994. Statistical identification of language. Technical Report MCCS 940-273, Computing Research Laboratory, New Mexico State University.

Long Duong, Paul Cook, Steven Bird, and Pavel Pecina. 2013. Simpler unsupervised POS tagging with bilingual projections. In *Proceedings of the 51st Annual Meeting of the Association for Computational Linguistics (Volume 2: Short Papers)*, pages 634–639.

Adriano Ferraresi, Eros Zanchetta, Marco Baroni, and Silvia Bernardini. 2008. Introducing and evaluating ukWaC, a very large web-derived corpus of English. In *Proceedings of the 4th Web as Corpus Workshop: Can we beat Google*, pages 47–54, Marrakech, Morocco.

Dan Flickinger. 2002. On building a more efficient grammar by exploiting types. In Stephan Oepen, Dan Flickinger, Jun'ichi Tsujii, and Hans Uszkoreit, editors, *Collaborative Language Engineering*. CSLI Publications, Stanford, USA.

Gregory Grefenstette. 1995. Comparing two language identification schemes. In *Proceedings of Analisi Statistica dei Dati Testuali (JADT)*, pages 263–268, Rome, Italy.

Nancy Ide and Catherine Macleod. 2001. The American National Corpus: A standardized resource of American English. In *Proceedings of Corpus Linguistics 2001*, pages 274–280, Lancaster, UK.

Adam Kilgarriff. 2001. Comparing corpora. *International Journal of Corpus Linguistics*, 6(1):97–133.

Philipp Koehn. 2005. Europarl: A parallel corpus for statistical machine translation. In *Proceedings of the Tenth Machine Translation Summit (MT Summit X)*, pages 79–86, Phuket, Thailand.

Nikola Ljubešić, Nives Mikelić, and Damir Boras. 2007. Language identification : how to distinguish similar languages ? In *29th International Conference on Information Technology Interfaces*, pages 541–546.

Marco Lui and Timothy Baldwin. 2011. Cross-domain feature selection for language identification. In *Proceedings of the 5th International Joint Conference on Natural Language Processing (IJCNLP 2011)*, pages 553–561, Chiang Mai, Thailand.

Marco Lui and Timothy Baldwin. 2012. langid.py: An off-the-shelf language identification tool. In *Proceedings of the 50th Annual Meeting of the Association for Computational Linguistics (ACL 2012) Demo Session*, pages 25–30, Jeju, Republic of Korea.

Marco Lui and Paul Cook. 2013. Classifying English documents by national dialect. In *Proceedings of the Australasian Language Technology Association Workshop 2013*, pages 5–15, Brisbane, Australia.

Franz Josef Och and Hermann Ney. 2003. A systematic comparison of various statistical alignment models. *Computational Linguistics*, 29(1):19–51.

Slav Petrov, Dipanjan Das, and Ryan McDonald. 2012. A universal part-of-speech tagset. In *Proceedings of the 8th International Conference on Language Resources and Evaluation (LREC 2012)*, Istanbul, Turkey, may. European Language Resources Association (ELRA).

Carl Pollard and Ivan A. Sag. 1994. *Head-driven Phrase Structure Grammar.* University of Chicago Press, Chicago, USA.

Jan Pomikálek. 2011. *Removing Boilerplate and Duplicate Content from Web Corpora.* Ph.D. thesis, Masaryk University.

John M. Prager. 1999. Linguini: language identification for multilingual documents. In *Proceedings of the 32nd Annual Hawaii International Conference on Systems Sciences (HICSS-32)*, Maui, Hawaii.

Bali Ranaivo-Malancon. 2006. Automatic Identification of Close Languages - Case study : Malay and Indonesian. *ECTI Transaction on Computer and Information Technology*, 2(2):126–134.

Helmut Schmid. 1994. Probabilistic part-of-speech tagging using decision trees. In *Proceedings of the Conference on New Methods in Natural Language Processing*, Manchester, 1994.

Raivis Skadiņš, Jörg Tiedemann, Roberts Rozis, and Daiga Deksne. 2014. Billions of parallel words for free: Building and using the EU Bookshop corpus. In *Proceedings of the 9th International Conference on Language Resources and Evaluation (LREC-2014)*, Reykjavik, Iceland.

Liling Tan, Marcos Zampieri, Nikola Ljubešić, and Jörg Tiedemann. 2014. Merging comparable data sources for the discrimination of similar languages: The DSL corpus collection. In *Proceedings of the 7th Workshop on Building and Using Comparable Corpora (BUCC)*, Reykjavik, Iceland.

W. J. Teahan. 2000. Text Classification and Segmentation Using Minimum Cross-Entropy. In *Proceedings the 6th International Conference "Recherche dInformation Assistee par Ordinateur" (RIAO00)*, pages 943–961, Paris, France.

Jörg Tiedemann and Nikola Ljubešić. 2012. Efficient discrimination between closely related languages. In *Proceedings of the 24th International Conference on Computational Linguistics (COLING 2012)*, pages 2619–2634, Mumbai, India.

Jörg Tiedemann. 2012. Parallel data, tools and interfaces in OPUS. In *Proceedings of the 8th International Conference on Language Resources and Evaluation (LREC 2012)*, pages 2214–2218, Istanbul, Turkey.

Kristina Toutanova, Dan Klein, Christopher D. Manning, and Yoram Singer. 2003. Feature-rich part-of-speech tagging with a cyclic dependency network. In *Proceedings of the 2003 Conference of the North American Chapter of the Association for Computational Linguistics on Human Language Technology - Volume 1 (NAACL '03)*, pages 173–180, Edmonton, Canada.

Peter Trudgill and Jean Hannah. 2008. *International English: A guide to varieties of Standard English.* Hodder Education, London, UK, 5th edition.

Sze-Meng Jojo Wong and Mark Dras. 2009. Contrastive analysis and native language identification. In *Proceedings of the Australasian Language Technology Workshop 2009 (ALTW 2009)*, pages 53–61, Sydney, Australia.

Marcos Zampieri and Binyam Gebrekidan Gebre. 2012. Automatic identification of language varieties: The case of Portuguese. In *Proceedings of KONVENS 2012*, pages 233–237, Vienna, Austria.

Marcos Zampieri, Binyam Gebrekidan Gebre, and Sascha Diwersy. 2013. N-gram language models and POS distribution for the identification of Spanish varieties. In *Proceedings of TALN 2013*, pages 580–587, Sable d'Olonne, France.

Marcos Zampieri, Liling Tan, Nikola Ljubešić, and Jörg Tiedemann. 2014. A report on the DSL shared task 2014. In *Proceedings of the 1st Workshop on Applying NLP Tools to Similar Languages, Varieties and Dialects (VarDial)*, Dublin, Ireland.

# The NRC System for Discriminating Similar Languages

**Cyril Goutte, Serge Léger and Marine Carpuat**
Multilingual Text Processing
National Research Council Canada
Ottawa, ON K1A0R6
Firstname.Lastname@nrc.ca

**Abstract**

We describe the system built by the National Research Council Canada for the "Discriminating between similar languages" (DSL) shared task. Our system uses various statistical classifiers and makes predictions based on a two-stage process: we first predict the language group, then discriminate between languages or variants within the group. Language groups are predicted using a generative classifier with 99.99% accuracy on the five target groups. Within each group (except English), we use a voting combination of discriminative classifiers trained on a variety of feature spaces, achieving an average accuracy of 95.71%, with per-group accuracy between 90.95% and 100% depending on the group. This approach turns out to reach the best performance among all systems submitted to the open and closed tasks.

## 1 Introduction

Language identification is largely considered a solved problem in the general setting, except in frontier cases such as identifying languages from very little data, from mixed input or when discriminating similar languages or language variants.

The "Discriminating between similar languages" (DSL) shared task proposes such a situation, with an interesting mix of languages, as can be seen in Table 1. Three groups contain similar languages (Bosnian+Croatian+Serbian, Indonesian+Malaysian, Czech+Slovakian); three groups contain variants of the same language (Portuguese, Spanish and English). In addition, instances to classify are single sentences, a more realistic and challenging situation than full-document language identification.

Our motivation for taking part in this evaluation was threefold. First, we wanted to evaluate our in-house implementation of document categorization on a real and useful task in a well controlled experimental setting.[1] Second, classifiers that can discriminate between similar languages can be applied to tasks such as identifying close dialects, and may be useful for training Statistical Machine Translation systems more effectively. For instance, Zbib et al. (2012) show that small amounts of data from the right dialect can have a dramatic impact on the quality of Dialectal Arabic Machine Translation systems. Finally, we view the DSL task as a first step towards building a system that can identify code-switching in, for example, social media data, a task which has recently received increased attention from the NLP community[2] (Elfardy et al., 2013).

The next section reviews the modeling choices we made for the shared task, and section 3 describes our results in detail. Additional analysis and comparisons with other submitted systems are available in the shared task report (Zampieri et al., 2014).

## 2 Modeling

Our approach relies on a two-stage process. We first predict the language group, then discriminate the languages or variants within the group. This approach works best if the first stage (i.e. group) classifier



[1]A previous version of our categorization tool produced good results on a Native Language Identification task in 2013 (Tetreault et al., 2013; Goutte et al., 2013).

[2]http://emnlp2014.org/workshops/CodeSwitch/



*Proceedings of the First Workshop on Applying NLP Tools to Similar Languages, Varieties and Dialects*, pages 139–145,
Dublin, Ireland, August 23 2014.

has high accuracy, because if the wrong group is predicted, it is impossible to recover from that mistake in the second stage. On the other hand, as most groups only comprise two languages or variants, our two-stage process makes it possible to rely on a simple binary classifier within each group, and avoid the extra complexity that comes with multiclass modeling.

We were able to build a high-accuracy, generative group classifier (Section 2.2) and rely on Support Vector Classifiers within each group to predict the language or variant (Section 2.3). Group F was treated in a slightly different way, although the underlying model is identical (Section 2.4). Before describing these classifiers, we briefly describe the features that we extract from the textual data.

### 2.1 Feature Extraction

The shared task uses sentences as basic observations, which is a reasonable granularity for this task. As we want to extract lexical as well as spelling features, we focus on two types of features:

- Word *ngrams*: Within sentence consecutive subsequences of $n$ words. In our experiments we considered unigrams (bag of words) and bigrams (bag of bigrams); performance seems to degrade for higher order *ngrams*, due to data sparsity. For bigrams, we use special tokens to mark the start and end of sentences.

- Character *ngrams*: Consecutive subsequences of $n$ characters. In our experiments we use $n = 2, 3, 4, 5, 6$. We use special characters to mark the start and end of sentences.

For each type of feature, we index all the *ngrams* observed at least once in the entire collection. Although it may seem that we risk having a combinatorial explosion of character *ngram* features for large values of $n$, the number of actually observed *ngrams* is clearly sub-exponential and grows roughly as $\mathcal{O}(n^6)$.

### 2.2 Language Group Classifier

Predicting the language group is a 6-way classification task, for which we use the probabilistic model described in (Gaussier et al., 2002; Goutte, 2008). We consider this model because it is more convenient in a multiclass setting than the multiclass SVM approach described below: only one model is required and training is extremely fast. We ended up choosing it because it provided slightly better estimated performance on the group prediction task.

This is a generative model for co-occurrences of words $w$ in documents $d$. It models the probability of co-occurrence $P(w, d)$ as a mixture model over classes $c$:

$$P(w, d) = \sum_c P(w|c)P(d|c)P(c) = P(d) \sum_c P(w|c)P(c|d), \tag{1}$$

where $P(w|c)$ is the profile for class $c$, ie the probability that each word[3] $w$ in the vocabulary may be generated for class $c$, and $P(c|d)$ is the profile for document $d$, ie the probability that a word from that document is generated from each class.

In essence, this is a supervised version of the *Probabilistic Latent Semantic Analysis* model (Hofmann, 1999). It is similar to the *Naive Bayes* model (McCallum and Nigam, 1998), except that instead of sampling the class once per document and generating all words from that class, this model can resample the class for each word in the document. This results in a much more flexible model, and higher performance.

Given a corpus of documents labelled with class information, and assuming that all co-occurrences in a document belong to the class of that document,[4] the maximum likelihood parameter estimates are identical to *Naive Bayes*. From the counts $n(w, d)$ of the occurences of word $w$ in document $d$, and denoting $|c| = \sum_{d \in c} \sum_w n(w, d)$, the total number of words in class $c$, the maximum likelihood estimates

[3] In the context of this study, a "word" $w$ may be a (word or character) *ngram*, according to Section 2.1.

[4] This means that for a training document $d$ in class $c_d$, $P(c_d|d) \equiv 1$.

for the profile parameters are:

$$\widehat{P}(w|c) = \frac{1}{|c|} \sum_{d \in c} n(w, d). \tag{2}$$

Maximum likelihood estimates for parameters $P(d)$ and $P(c|d)$ may be obtained similarly, but they are not useful for predicting new documents. The model is therefore solely represented by a set of class profile vectors giving lexical probabilities in each class.

Note that this is a generative model for the training collection only. In order to predict class assignment for a new document, we need to introduce the new document $\widetilde{d}$ and associated, unknown parameters $P(\widetilde{d})$ and $P(c|\widetilde{d})$. We estimate the posterior assignment probability $P(c|\widetilde{d})$ by *folding in* $\widetilde{d}$ into the collection and maximizing the log-likelihood of the new document,

$$\widetilde{\mathcal{L}} = \sum_{w} n(w, \widetilde{d}) \log P(\widetilde{d}) \sum_{c} P(c|\widetilde{d}) P(w|c),$$

with respect to $P(c|\widetilde{d})$, keeping the class profiles $P(w|c)$ fixed. This is a convex optimization problem that may be efficiently solved using the iterative Expectation Maximization algorithm (Dempster et al., 1977). The resulting iterative, fixed-point equation is:

$$P(c|\widetilde{d}) \leftarrow P(c|\widetilde{d}) \sum_{w} \frac{n(w, \widetilde{d})}{|\widetilde{d}|} \frac{P(w|c)}{\sum_{c} P(c|\widetilde{d}) P(w|c)}, \tag{3}$$

with $|\widetilde{d}| = \sum_w n(w, \widetilde{d})$ is the length of document $\widetilde{d}$. Because the minimization is convex w.r.t. $P(c|\widetilde{d})$, the EM update converges to the unique maximum.

Given a corpus of annotated documents, we estimate model parameters using the maximum likelihood solution (2). This is extremely fast and ideal for training on the large corpus available for this evaluation. At test time, we initialize $P(c|\widetilde{d})$ with the uniform distribution and run the EM equation (3) until convergence for each test sentence. This is relatively slow (compared to training), but may be easily and efficiently parallelized on, e.g. multicore architecture.

Note that although group prediction is a 6-way classification task, we ended up using a 13-class model predicting the languages or variants, mapping the predictions from the 13 language classes into the 6 groups. This provided slightly better estimated performance on group prediction, although the prediction on the individual languages was weaker than what we obtained with the models described in the following sections.

### 2.3 Language Classifiers within Groups A to E

Setting aside Group A for a moment, within each of the other groups, we need to discriminate between two languages or language variants, as summarized in Table 1. This is the ideal situation for a powerful binary discriminative classifier such as the Support Vector Machines. We use a Support Vector Machine (SVM) classifier, as implemented in $\text{SVM}_{light}$ (Joachims, 1998).

Note that the probabilistic classifier described in the previous section may provide predictions over all 13 classes (11 without English) of the shared task with one single model. However, preliminary experiments showed that the resulting performance was slightly below what we could achieve using binary SVMs within each groups in the two-stage approach.

We trained a binary SVM on each of the feature spaces described in Section 2.1. We used a linear kernel, and set the $C$ parameter in $\text{SVM}_{light}$ to the default value. Prediction with a linear kernel is very fast as it only requires computing the dot product of the vector space representation of a document with the equivalent linear weight vector.

#### Multiclass (Group A)

For group A, we need to handle the 3-way multiclass situation to discriminate between Bosnian, Croatian and Serbian. This is done by first training one linear SVM per class in a one-versus-all fashion. We then apply a calibration step using a Gaussian mixture on SVM prediction scores in order to transform these scores into proper posterior probabilities (Bennett, 2003). We then predict the class with the highest calibrated probability. Once the calibration model has been estimated on a small held-out set, applying the calibration to the three models and picking the highest value is very efficient.

#### Voting

The different *ngram* feature spaces lead to different models with varying performance. We combine these models using a simple voting strategy. Within each group, we rank the models trained on each feature space by performance, estimated by cross-validation (CV). We then perform a majority voting between predictions, breaking possible ties according to the estimated performance of the individual models.

When voting, adding models of lower performance typically improves the voting performance as long as their predictions are not too correlated with models that are already included in the vote. We therefore need to set the number of models to include in the vote carefully: this is also done by maximizing the performance based on the cross-validation estimator.

### 2.4 Classifier for Group F (English)

The specific issue of the English data from Group F is discussed in more details in the shared task report (Zampieri et al., 2014) so we only mention a few points that are specific to our system.

Due to the poor cross-validation performance (distinguishing GB and US english is difficult but obviously not impossible) we suspected early on that there was an issue with the data. We asked two native English speakers to perform a human evaluation on a small sample of the training and development data, which confirmed both our suspicion, and the fact that this was a difficult task. On the sentences that our judges confidently tagged GB or US (60% of the sample), they were wrong slightly more often than chance. We therefore suspected that if the test data was more reliable, a statistical model estimated on the training data may also do worse than chance.

We therefore decided to train a straightforward SVM model on bigrams of words. From this, we submitted two runs: one with the SVM predictions (run1), and the second with the same predictions flipped (run2).

## 3 Experimental Results

### 3.1 Data

The data provided for the evaluation is described in more detail in (Tan et al., 2014). Table 1 summarizes the size of the corpus across groups and languages for the training (including development) and test sets. Training and test data are balanced across languages and variants.

In order to provide an estimate of performance and guide our modeling choices, we use a 10-fold, stratified cross-validation estimator. We split the training examples for each language into ten equal-sized parts, and test on each fold the models trained on the remaining nine folds. The test predictions obtained on all the folds are then used to compute the cross-validation estimator.

### 3.2 Group Prediction

Training the group classifier using the probabilistic model described in section 2.2 on the 260,000 sentences using character 4-grams as features takes 133 seconds on a single, 32-core Linux workstation. Predicting the group for the 11,000 test documents (groups A-E) takes just 18 seconds, approximately 1.6ms/sentence.

The performance of the group predictor is near perfect: a single document is predicted incorrectly (Spanish instead of Portuguese) out of the 11,000 test sentences. This matches the excellent performance estimated by 10-fold cross-validation to an error of 0.038%.

### 3.3 Language Prediction in Groups A to E

For each group from A to E, we submitted:

| | | # sentences | |
|---|---|---|---|
| Group | Language | Train | Test |
| A | Bosnian | 20,000 | 1000 |
| | Croatian | 20,000 | 1000 |
| | Serbian | 20,000 | 1000 |
| B | Indonesian | 20,000 | 1000 |
| | Malaysian | 20,000 | 1000 |
| C | Czech | 20,000 | 1000 |
| | Slovak | 20,000 | 1000 |
| D | Brazil Portuguese | 20,000 | 1000 |
| | Portugal Portuguese | 20,000 | 1000 |
| E | Argentine Spanish | 20,000 | 1000 |
| | Spain Spanish | 20,000 | 1000 |
| F | GB English | 20,000 | 800 (∗) |
| | US English | 20,000 | 800 (∗) |

Table 1: Number of training (including development) and test sentences accross groups and languages. (*): the English test data was available separately.

**run1**: The single best SVM model obtained on a single feature space (no voting), according to the 10-fold cross-validation. Depending on the group, the best feature space is either character 5grams or 6grams.

**run2**: Same model as run1, with additional tuning of the prediction threshold to ensure balanced predictions on the cross-validated data. On groups B to E, run1 uses a natural threshold of 0 to predict the language or variant. When the SVM score is positive, run1 predicts one class, when it is negative, run1 predicts the other. In constrast, run2 uses the fact that we know that the classes are balanced, and adjusts the threshold to force predictions to be balanced across classes.

**run3**: The best voting combination. It is obtained by ranking the various feature spaces by decreasing 10-fold CV performance, and picking the number of votes that yields the highest cross-validation estimate for the voting combination. Depending on the group, the best combination involves between 1 and 7 models.

Training the SVM models for group A, including calibration, on the 60,000 training sentences takes 7 minutes and 33 seconds for the best model (character 5grams), and 31 minutes overall for the 7 feature spaces. Prediction for the best model takes 16 seconds, approximately 1.5ms/sentence; for all 7 models used in the vote, prediction requires a total of 1 minute and 16 seconds.

Training on groups B to E is faster because we only need one SVM model per feature space. In addition, for group C, only one model is necessary because no vote outperforms the best model. Training the best model on each group (character 6gram) requires between 242 and 721 seconds depending on the group. Training all models used in the vote requires up to 29 minutes. Prediction with the best model takes 1.4 to 2.1ms/sentence, while computing all predictions used in the vote requires up to 8ms/sentence.

Table 2 summarizes the performance for our three runs on the 5 target groups. We give the cross-validation estimator computed before submission, as well as the test error obtained from the gold standard data released with the official results. Although there are small differences between actual test results and the CV estimates, the CV estimates are fairly reliable. They always indicate that run3 is best, which is only incorrect on Group D, where the actual test performance of run1 is only very slightly better.[5]

According to the official results (Zampieri et al., 2014), this allowed our system to get the best per-group accuracy on all groups, as well as the best overall accuracy with 95.71%. This is also higher than the two open submissions.

[5]The difference corresponds to only 2 sentences.

| | Group A | | Group B | | Group C | | Group D | | Group E | |
|---|---|---|---|---|---|---|---|---|---|---|
| | CV | Test | CV | Test | CV | Test | CV | Test | CV | Test |
| run1 (1-best) | 6.12 | 6.70 | 0.720 | 0.600 | **0.0075** | **0.00** | 4.85 | **4.40** | 10.59 | 9.85 |
| run2 (thresh.) | 6.12 | 6.70 | 0.720 | 0.600 | **0.0075** | **0.00** | 4.87 | 4.50 | 10.57 | 10.05 |
| run3 (vote) | **5.54** | **6.40** | **0.642** | **0.450** | **0.0075** | **0.00** | **4.47** | 4.50 | **9.91** | **9.05** |

Table 2: Cross-validated (CV) and test error (1-accuracy), in %, on Groups A to E.

| (Group F) | CV | Test |
|---|---|---|
| run1 (bag-of-bigrams) | **44.67** | 52.37 |
| run2 (flipped) | 55.33 | **47.63** |

Table 3: Cross-validated (CV) and test error (1-accuracy), in %, on Group F (English).

### 3.4 Group F (English)

Because of the data issue in that group, our submission used one of the simpler models. As a consequence, training and test times are of less relevance. Training the bigram model on 40,000 sentences took 2 minutes while prediction on the 1600 English test sentences took 4 seconds, i.e. 2.5ms/sentences.

Table 3 shows the cross-validation and test errors of our two runs on the English data. This illustrates that the cross-validated estimate for accuracy was poor for our system. As suspected, the more reliable test data shows that our system (**run1**) was in fact not learning the right task. As a result, our submission with flipped predictions (**run2**) yields better accuracy on the test set.

In fact it appears from official evaluation results that our run2 was the only close task submission that performed better than chance on the test data.

## 4 Summary

Using fairly straightforward modeling tools, a probabilistic document classifier and linear Support Vector Machines, we built a two stage system that classifies language variants in the shared task with an average accuracy of 95.71%, providing the best overall performance for both open and closed task submissions. The individual language group performance varies from 91% to 100% depending on the group. This systems seems like a good baseline for experimenting with dialect identification, or code-switching in social media data. We are especially interested in investigating how performance evolves with smaller segments of texts.

## References


Paul N. Bennett. 2003. Using asymmetric distributions to improve text classifier probability estimates. In *Proceedings of the 26th Annual International ACM SIGIR Conference on Research and Development in Informaion Retrieval*, SIGIR '03, pages 111–118, New York, NY, USA. ACM.

A. P. Dempster, N. M. Laird, and D. B. Rubin. 1977. Maximum likelihood from incomplete data via the EM algorithm. *Journal of the Royal Statistical Society, Series B*, 39(1):1–38.

Heba Elfardy, Mohamed Al-Badrashiny, and Mona Diab. 2013. Code switch point detection in arabic. In *18th International Conference on Applications of Natural Language to Information Systems*, pages 412–416.

Éric Gaussier, Cyril Goutte, Kris Popat, and Francine Chen. 2002. A hierarchical model for clustering and categorising documents. In *Proceedings of the 24th BCS-IRSG European Colloquium on IR Research: Advances in Information Retrieval*, pages 229–247, London, UK, UK. Springer-Verlag.

Cyril Goutte, Serge Léger, and Marine Carpuat. 2013. Feature space selection and combination for native language identification. In *Proceedings of the Eighth Workshop on Innovative Use of NLP for Building Educational Applications*, pages 96–100, Atlanta, Georgia, June. Association for Computational Linguistics.

Cyril Goutte. 2008. A probabilistic model for fast and confident categorization of textual documents. In Michael W. Berry and Malu Castellanos, editors, *Survey of Text Mining II*, pages 187–202. Springer London.

Thomas Hofmann. 1999. Probabilistic latent semantic analysis. In *Proc. of Uncertainty in Artificial Intelligence, UAI'99*, pages 289–296.

Thorsten Joachims. 1998. Text categorization with Suport Vector Machines: Learning with many relevant features. In Claire Nédellec and Céline Rouveirol, editors, *Proceedings of ECML-98, 10th European Conference on Machine Learning*, volume 1398 of *Lecture Notes in Computer Science*, pages 137–142. Springer.

Andrew McCallum and Kamal Nigam. 1998. A comparison of event models for Naive Bayes text classification. In *AAAI-98 Workshop on Learning for Text Categorization*, pages 41–48. AAAI Press.

Liling Tan, Marcos Zampieri, Nikola Ljubešić, and Jörg Tiedemann. 2014. Merging comparable data sources for the discrimination of similar languages: The DSL corpus collection. In *Proceedings of the 7th Workshop on Building and Using Comparable Corpora (BUCC)*, Reykjavik, Iceland.

Joel Tetreault, Daniel Blanchard, and Aoife Cahill. 2013. A report on the first native language identification shared task. In *Proceedings of the Eighth Workshop on Innovative Use of NLP for Building Educational Applications*, pages 48–57, Atlanta, Georgia, June. Association for Computational Linguistics.

Marcos Zampieri, Liling Tan, Nikola Ljubešić, and Jörg Tiedemann. 2014. A report on the DSL shared task 2014. In *Proceedings of the 1st Workshop on Applying NLP Tools to Similar Languages, Varieties and Dialects (VarDial)*.

Rabih Zbib, Erika Malchiodi, Jacob Devlin, David Stallard, Spyros Matsoukas, Richard Schwartz, John Makhoul, Omar F. Zaidan, and Chris Callison-Burch. 2012. Machine translation of arabic dialects. In *Proceedings of the 2012 Conference of the North American Chapter of the Association for Computational Linguistics: Human Language Technologies*, pages 49–59, Montréal, Canada, June. Association for Computational Linguistics.

# Experiments in Sentence Language Identification with Groups of Similar Languages

**Ben King**
Department of EECS
University of Michigan
Ann Arbor
benking@umich.edu

**Dragomir Radev**
Department of EECS
School of Information
University of Michigan
Ann Arbor
radev@umich.edu

**Steven Abney**
Department of Linguistics
University of Michigan
Ann Arbor
abney@umich.edu

## Abstract

Language identification is a simple problem that becomes much more difficult when its usual assumptions are broken. In this paper we consider the task of classifying short segments of text in closely-related languages for the Discriminating Similar Languages shared task, which is broken into six subtasks, (A) Bosnian, Croatian, and Serbian, (B) Indonesian and Malay, (C) Czech and Slovak, (D) Brazilian and European Portuguese, (E) Argentinian and Peninsular Spanish, and (F) American and British English. We consider a number of different methods to boost classification performance, such as feature selection and data filtering, but we ultimately find that a simple naïve Bayes classifier using character and word $n$-gram features is a strong baseline that is difficult to improve on, achieving an average accuracy of 0.8746 across the six tasks.

## 1 Introduction

Language identification constitutes the first stage of many NLP pipelines. Before applying tools trained on specific languages, one must determine the language of the text. It is also is often considered to be a solved task because of the high accuracy of language identification methods in the canonical formulation of the problem with long monolingual documents and a set of mostly dissimilar languages to choose from. We consider a different setting with much shorter text in the form of single sentences drawn from very similar languages or dialects.

This paper describes experiments related to and our submissions to the Discriminating Similar Languages (DSL) shared task. This shared task has six subtasks, each a classification task in which a sentence must be labeled as belonging to a small set of related languages:

- Task A: Bosnian *vs.* Croatian *vs.* Serbian
- Task B: Indonesian *vs.* Malay
- Task C: Czech *vs.* Slovak
- Task D: Brazilian *vs.* European Portuguese
- Task E: Argentinian *vs.* Peninsular Spanish
- Task F: American *vs.* British English

The first three tasks involve classes that could be rightly called separate languages or dialects. The classes of each of the final three tasks have high mutual intelligibility and are so similar that some linguists may not even classify them as separate dialects. We will use the term "language variant" to refer to such classes.

In this paper we experiment with several types of methods aimed at improving the classification accuracy of these tasks: machine learning methods, data pre-processing, feature selection, and additional training data. We find that a simple naïve Bayes classifier using character and word $n$-gram features is a strong baseline that is difficult to improve on. Because this paper covers so many different types of methods, its format eschews the standard "Results" section, instead providing comparisons of methods as they are presented.





*Proceedings of the First Workshop on Applying NLP Tools to Similar Languages, Varieties and Dialects*, pages 146–154, Dublin, Ireland, August 23 2014.

## 2 Related Work

Recent directions in language identification have included finer-grained language identification (King and Abney, 2013; Nguyen and Dogruoz, 2013; Lui et al., 2014), language identification for microblogs (Bergsma et al., 2012; Carter et al., 2013), and the task of this paper, language identification for closely related languages.

Language identification for closely related languages has been considered by several researchers, though it has lacked a systematic evaluation before the DSL shared task. The problem of distinguishing Croatian from Serbian and Slovenian is explored by Ljubešić et al. (2007), who used a list of most frequent words along with a Markov model and a word blacklist, a list of words that are not allowed to appear in a certain language. A similar approach was later used by Tiedemann and Ljubešić (2012) to distinguish Bosnian, Croatian, and Serbian. They further develop the idea of a blacklist classifier, loosening the binary restriction of the earlier work's blacklist and considering the frequencies of words rather than their absolute counts. This blacklist classifier is able to outperform a naïve Bayes classifier with large amounts of training data. They also find training on parallel data to be important, as it allows the machine learning methods to pick out features relating to the differences between the languages themselves, rather than learning differences in domain.

Zampieri et al. consider classes that would be most often classified as language varieties rather than separate languages or dialects (Zampieri et al., 2012; Zampieri and Gebrekidan, 2012; Zampieri et al., 2013). A similar problem of distinguishing among Chinese text from mainland China, Singapore, and Taiwan is considered by Huang and Lee (2008) who approach the problem by computing similarity between a document and a corpus according to the size of the intersection between the sets of types in each.

A similar, but somewhat different problem of automatically identifying lexical variants between closely related languages is considered in (Peirsman et al., 2010). Using distributional methods, they are able to identify Netherlandic Dutch synonyms for words from Belgian Dutch.

## 3 Data

This paper's training data and evaluation data both come from the DSL corpus collection (DSLCC) (Tan et al., 2014). We use the training section of this data for training and the development section for evaluation. The training section consists of 18,000 labeled instances per class, while the development section has 2,000 labeled instances per class.

In order to try to increase classifier accuracy (and to avoid the problems with the task F training data), we decided to collect additional training data for each open-class task. For each task, we collected newspaper text from the appropriate websites for each of the 2–3 languages. We used regular expressions to split the text into sentences, and created a set of rules to filter out strings that were unlikely to be good sentences. Because the pages on the newspaper websites tended to have some boilerplate text, we collated all the sentences and only kept one copy of each sentence.

| Task | Language/Dialect | Newspaper | Sentences | Words |
|---|---|---|---|---|
| A | Bosnian | *Nezavisne Novine* | 175,741 | 3,250,648 |
| | Croatian | *Novi List* | 231,271 | 4,591,318 |
| | Serbian | *Večernje Novosti* | 239,390 | 5,213,507 |
| B | Indonesian | *Kompas* | 114,785 | 1,896,138 |
| | Malay | *Berita Harian* | 36,144 | 695,597 |
| C | Czech | *Deník* | 160,972 | 2,432,393 |
| | Slovak | *Denník SME* | 62,908 | 970,913 |
| D | Brazilian Portuguese | *O Estado de S. Paulo* | 558,169 | 11,199,168 |
| | European Portuguese | *Correio da Manhã* | 148,745 | 2,979,904 |
| E | Argentinian Spanish | *La Nación* | 333,246 | 7,769,941 |
| | Peninsular Spanish | *El País* | 195,897 | 4,329,480 |
| F | American English | *The New York Times* | 473,350 | 10,491,641 |
| | British English | *The Guardian* | 971,097 | 20,288,294 |

Table 1: Sources and amounts of training data collected for the open track for each task.

In order to create balanced training data, for each task we downsampled the number of sentences of the larger collection(s) to match the number of sentences in the smaller collection. For example, we downsampled the British English collection to 473,350 sentences and combined it with the American English sentences to create the training data for English. Figure 1 shows results of training using this external data.

### 3.1 Features

We use many types of features that have been found to be useful in previous language identification work: word unigrams, word bigrams, and character $n$-grams ($2 \leq n \leq 6$). Character $n$-grams are simply substrings of the sentence and may include in addition to letters, whitespace, punctuation, digits, and anything else that might be in the sentence. Words, for the purpose of word unigrams and bigrams, are simply maximal tokens not containing any punctuation, digit, or whitespace.

When instances are encoded into feature vectors, each feature has a value equal to the number of times it occured in the corresponding sentence, so the majority of features have a value of 0 for any given instance, but it is possible for a feature to occur multiple times in a sentence and have a value greater than 1.0 in the feature vector. Table 2 below compares the performance of a naïve Bayes classifier using each of the different feature groups below.

| | | Word | | Character | | | | |
|---|---|---|---|---|---|---|---|---|
| **Task** | **All** | **1** | **2** | **2** | **3** | **4** | **5** | **6** |
| Bosnian/Croatian/Serbian | 0.9348 | 0.9290 | 0.8183 | 0.7720 | 0.8808 | 0.9412 | 0.9338 | 0.9323 |
| Indonesian/Malay | 0.9918 | 0.9943 | 0.9885 | 0.8545 | 0.9518 | 0.9833 | 0.9908 | 0.9930 |
| Czech/Slovak | 0.9998 | 1.0000 | 0.9985 | 0.9980 | 0.9998 | 0.9998 | 1.0000 | 1.0000 |
| Portuguese | 0.9535 | 0.9468 | 0.9493 | 0.7935 | 0.8888 | 0.9318 | 0.9468 | 0.9570 |
| Spanish | 0.8623 | 0.8738 | 0.8625 | 0.7673 | 0.8273 | 0.8513 | 0.8610 | 0.8660 |
| English | 0.4970 | 0.4948 | 0.5005 | 0.4825 | 0.4988 | 0.5010 | 0.5048 | 0.4993 |
| Average | 0.8732 | 0.8731 | 0.8529 | 0.7780 | 0.8412 | 0.8681 | 0.8729 | 0.8746 |

Table 2: Accuracies compared for different sets of features compared. The classifier used here is naïve Bayes.

## 4 Methods

Our baseline method against which we compare all other models is a naïve Bayes classifier using word unigram features trained on the DSL-provided training data. The methods we compare to it can be broken into three classes: other machine learning methods, feature selection methods, and data filtering methods.

The classification pipeline used here has the following stages: (1) data filtering, (2) feature extraction, (3) feature selection, (4) training, and (5) classification.

### 4.1 Machine Learning Methods

We will use the following notation throughout this section. An instance $x$, that is, a sentence to be classified, with a corresponding class label $y$ is encoded into a feature vector $\mathbf{f}(x)$, where each entry is an integer denoting how many times the feature corresponding to that entry's index occurred in the sentence. The class label here is a language and it's drawn from a small set $y \in \mathcal{Y}$.

In addition to the naïve Bayes classifier, we also experiment with two versions of logistic regression and a support vector machine classifier. The MALLET machine learning library implementations are used for the first three classifiers (McCallum, 2002) and SVMLight is used for the fourth (Joachims, ).

**Naïve Bayes** A naïve Bayes classifier models the class label as an independent combination of input features.

$$P(y|\mathbf{f}(x)) = \frac{1}{P(\mathbf{f}(x))} P(y) \prod_{i=1}^{n} P(\mathbf{f}(x)_i|y) \tag{1}$$

As naïve Bayes is a generative classifier, it has been shown to be able to outperform discriminative classifiers when the number of training instances is small compared to the number of features (Ng and Jordan, 2002). This classifier is additionally advantageous in that it has a simple closed-form solution for maximizing its log likelihood.

**Logistic Regression** A logistic regression classifier is a discriminative classifier whose parameters are encoded in a vector $\theta$. The conditional probability of a class label over an instance $(x, y)$ is modeled as follows:

$$P(y|x;\theta) = \frac{1}{Z(\mathbf{x};\theta)} \exp\{\mathbf{f}(x,y)\cdot\theta\} \quad ; \quad Z(\mathbf{x},\theta) = \sum_{y\in\mathcal{Y}} \exp\{\mathbf{f}(x,y)\cdot\theta\} \tag{2}$$

The parameter vector $\theta$ is commonly estimated by maximizing the log-likelihood of this function over the set of training instances $(x, y) \in \mathcal{T}$ in the following way:

$$\theta = \text{argmax}_{\theta} \sum_{(x,y)\in\mathcal{T}} \log P(y_i|x_i;\theta) - \lambda R(\theta) \tag{3}$$

The term $R(\theta)$ above is a regularization term. It is common for such a classifier to overfit the parameters to the training data. To keep this from happening, a regularization term can be added which keeps the parameters in $\theta$ from growing too large. Two common choices for this function are L2 and L1 normalization:

$$R_{L2} = ||\theta||_2^2 = \sum_{i=1}^{n} \theta_i^2 \quad , \quad R_{L1} = ||\theta||_1 = \sum_{i=1}^{n} |\theta_i| \tag{4}$$

L2 regularization is well-grounded theoretically, as it is equivalent to a model with a Gaussian prior on the parameters (Rennie, 2004). But L1 regularization has a reputation for enforcing sparsity on the parameters. In fact, it has been shown to be quite effective when the number of irrelevant dimensions is greater than the number of training examples, which we expect to be the case with many of the tasks in this paper (Ng, 2004).

**Support Vector Machines** A support vector machine (SVM) is a type of linear classifier that attempts to find a boundary that linearly separates the training data with the maximum possible margin. SVMs have been shown to be a very efficient and high accuracy method to classify data across a wide variety of different types of tasks (Tsochantaridis et al., 2004).

Table 3 below compares these machine learning methods. Because of its consistently good performance across tasks, we use a naïve Bayes classifier throughout the rest of the paper.

### 4.2 Feature Selection Methods

We expect that the majority of features are not relevant to the classification task, and so we experimented with several methods of feature selection, both manual and automatic.

**Information Gain** As a fully automatic method of feature extraction, we used information gain to score features according to their expected usefulness. Information gain (IG) is an information theoretic concept that (colloquially) measures the amount of knowledge about the class label that is gained by having access to a specific feature. If $f$ is the occurence an individual feature and $\bar{f}$ the non-occurence of a feature, we measure its information gain by the following formula:

$$G(f) = P(f)\left[\sum_{y\in\mathcal{Y}} P(y|f)\log P(y|f)\right] + P(\bar{f})\left[\sum_{y\in\mathcal{Y}} \log P(y|\bar{f})\log P(y|\bar{f})\right] \tag{5}$$

| Task | Logistic Regression (L2-norm) | Logistic Regression (L1-norm) | Naïve Bayes | SVM |
|---|---|---|---|---|
| Bosnian/Croatian/Serbian | 0.9138 | 0.9135 | 0.9290 | 0.9100 |
| Indonesian/Malay | 0.9878 | 0.9810 | 0.9943 | 0.9873 |
| Czech/Slovak | 0.9983 | 0.9958 | 1.0000 | 0.9985 |
| Portuguese | 0.9383 | 0.9368 | 0.9468 | 0.9325 |
| Spanish | 0.8843 | 0.8770 | 0.8738 | 0.8768 |
| English | 0.5000 | 0.4945 | 0.4948 | 0.4958 |
| Average | 0.8704 | 0.8648 | 0.8731 | 0.8668 |

Table 3: Comparison of different machine learning methods using word unigram features on the six tasks.

To reduce the number of features being used in classification (and to hopefully remove irrelevant features), we choose the 10,000 features with the highest IG scores. IG considers each feature independently, so it is possible that redundant feature sets could be chosen. For example, it might happen that both the quadrigram `ther` and the trigram `the` score highly according to IG and are both selected, even though they are highly correlated with one another.

**Parallel Text Feature Selection** Because IG feature selection often seemed to choose features more related to differences in domain than to differences in language (see Table 7), we wanted to try to isolate features that are specific to language differences. It has been shown in previous work that training on parallel text can help to isolate language differences since the domains of the languages are identical (Tiedemann and Ljubešić, 2012). For each of the tasks,[1] we use translations of the complete Bible as a parallel corpus, running IG feature selection exactly as above. Table 4 below gives more details about the texts used.

| Task | Language/Dialect | Bible |
|---|---|---|
| B | Indonesian | *Alkitab dalam Bahasa Indonesia Masa Kini* |
| | Malay | *2001 Today's Malay Version* |
| C | Czech | *Ceský studijní preklad* |
| | Slovak | *Slovenský Ekumenický Biblia* |
| D | Brazilian Portuguese | *a BÍBLIA para todos* |
| | European Portuguese | *Almeida Revista e Corrigida (Portugal)* |
| E | Argentinian Spanish | *La Palabra (versión hispanoamericana)* |
| | Peninsular Spanish | *La Palabra (versión española)* |
| F | American English | *New International Version* |
| | British English | *New International Version Anglicized* |

Table 4: Bibles used as parallel corpora for feature selection.

**Manual Feature Selection** We also used manual feature selection, selecting features to use in the classifiers from lists published on Wikipedia comparing the two languages. Of course some of the features in lists like these are features that are quite difficult to detect using NLP (especially before the language has been identified) such as characteristic passive or genitive constructions. But there are many features that we are able to detect and use in a list of manually selected features, such as character $n$-grams relating to morphology and spelling and word $n$-grams relating to vocabulary differences.

Table 5 below compares these feature selection methods on each task. Since the manual feature selection suggested all types of features, including character $n$-gram and word unigram and bigram features, the experiments in this section use all features described in Section 3.1. The results show that any type of feature selection consistently hurts performance, though IG hurts the least, and it should be noted that in certain cases with other machine learning methods, IG feature selection actually yielded better

[1]excluding Task A, for which we were unable to find a Bible in Latin-script Serbian or any Bible in Bosnian

performance than all features. That the feature selection methods designed to isolate language-specific features performed so poorly is one indicator that the labeled data has additional differences that are not tied to the languages themselves. We discuss this idea further in Section 5.

| Task | No feature selection | IG | Parallel | Manual |
|---|---|---|---|---|
| Bosnian/Croatian/Serbian | 0.9348 | 0.9300 | – | 0.6328 |
| Indonesian/Malay | 0.9918 | 0.9768 | 0.8093 | 0.8485 |
| Czech/Slovak | 0.9998 | 0.9995 | 0.9940 | 0.8118 |
| Portuguese | 0.9535 | 0.9193 | 0.7215 | 0.6888 |
| Spanish | 0.8623 | 0.8310 | 0.5210 | 0.7023 |
| English | 0.4970 | 0.4978 | 0.5020 | 0.5053 |
| Average | 0.8732 | 0.8590 | – | 0.6982 |

Table 5: Comparison of manual and automatic feature selection methods. IG and parallel feature selection both use the 10,000 features with the highest IG scores.

### 4.3 Data Filtering Methods

**English Word Removal** In looking through the training data for the non-English tasks, we observed that it was not uncommon for sentences in these languages to contain English words and phrases. Because foreign words should be independent of the language/dialect used, English words included in the sentences for other tasks should just be noise that, if removed will improve classification performance.

For each of the non-English tasks (A, B, C, D, and E), we create a new training set for identifying English/non-English words by mixing together 1,000 random English words with 10,000 random task-language words. The imbalance in the classes is a compromise, approximating the actual proportions in the test without leading to a degenerate classifier. Because English and the other classes are so dissimilar, the performance of the English word classifier is very insensitive to the actual ratio. From this data, we train a naïve Bayes classifier using character 3-grams, 4-grams, and 5-grams.

We manually labeled the words of 150 sentences from the five non-English tasks in order to evaluate the English word classifier. Across the five tasks, the precision was 0.76 and the recall was 0.66, leading to an F1-score of 0.70. Any words labeled as English by the classifier were removed from the sentence and it was passed on to the feature extraction, classification, and training stages.

**Named Entity Removal** We also observed another common class of word that could potentially act as a noise source: named entities. Across all the languages listed studied here, it is common for named entities to begin with a capital letter. Lacking named entity recognizers for all the languages here, we instead used the property of having an initial capital letter as a surrogate for recognizing a word as a named entity. Because all the languaes studied here also have the convention of capitalizing the first word of a sentence, we remove all words beginning with a capital letter except for the first and pass this abridged sentence on to the feature extraction, classification, and training stages.

| Task | No data filtering | English Word Removal | Named Entity Removal |
|---|---|---|---|
| Bosnian/Croatian/Serbian | 0.9138 | 0.9105 | 0.9003 |
| Indonesian/Malay | 0.9878 | 0.9885 | 0.9778 |
| Czech/Slovak | 0.9983 | 0.9980 | 0.9973 |
| Portuguese | 0.9383 | 0.9365 | 0.9068 |
| Spanish | 0.8843 | 0.8835 | 0.8555 |
| English | 0.5000 | 0.5000 | 0.5050 |
| Average | 0.8704 | 0.8695 | 0.8571 |

Table 6: Comparison of data filtering methods using word unigram features on the six tasks.

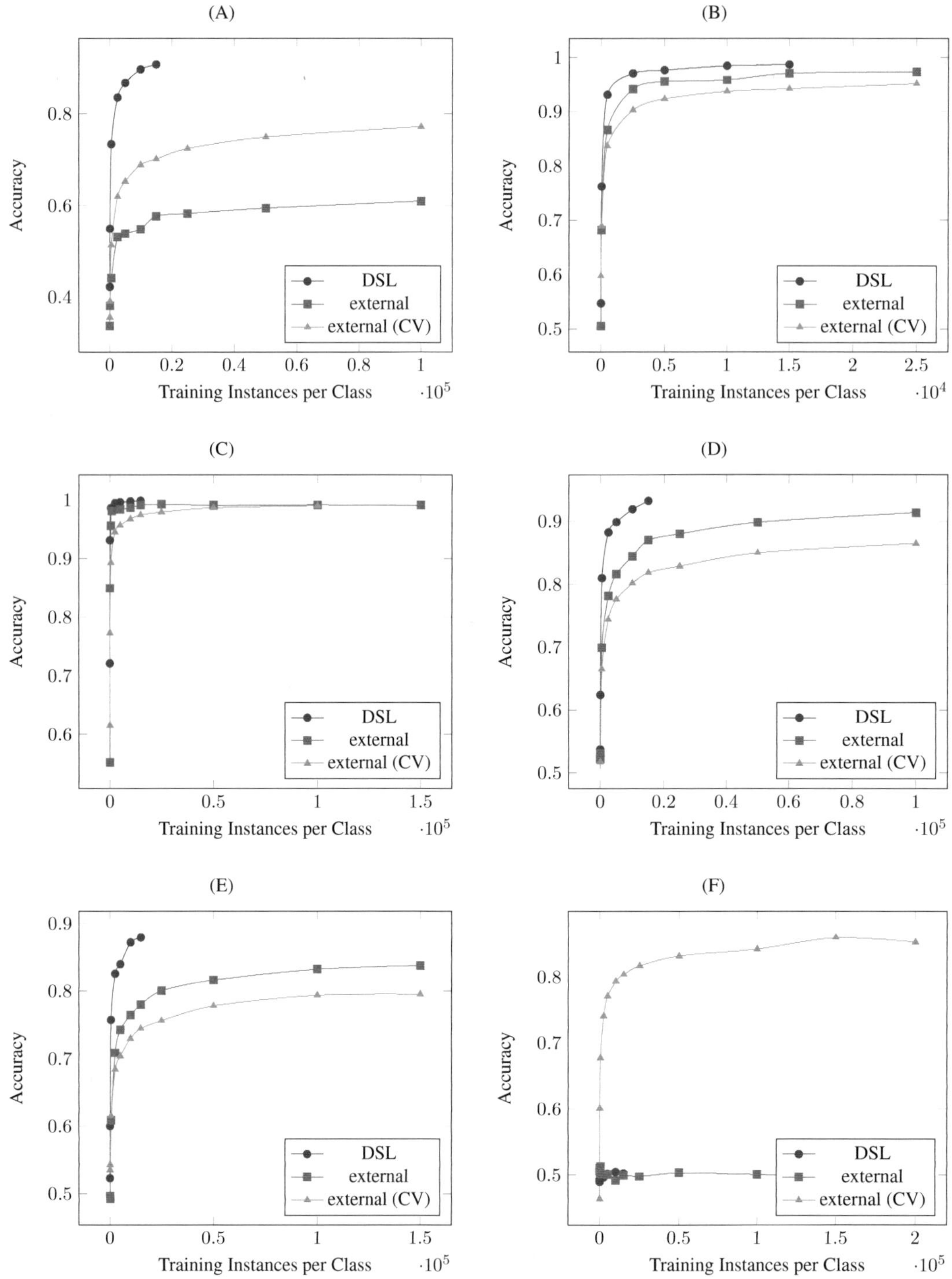


Figure 1: Learning curves for the six tasks as the number of training instances per language is varied. The line marked "DSL" is the learning curve for the DSL-provided training data evaluated against the developement data. The line marked "external" is our external newspaper training data evaluated against the development data. The line marked "external (CV)" is our external training data evaluated using 10-fold cross-validation.

| Bosnian/Croatian/Serbian | Indonesian/Malay | Czech/Slovak | Portuguese | Spanish | English |
|---|---|---|---|---|---|
| da | bisa | sa | Portugal | the | I |
| kako | berkata | se | R | Rosario | you |
| sa | kerana | aj | euros | han | The |
| kazao | karena | ako | Brasil | euros | said |
| takode | daripada | ve | cento | Argentina | Obama |
| rekao | saat | pre | governo | PP | your |
| evra | dari | pro | Lusa | Fe | If |
| tijekom | beliau | ktoré | PSD | Rajoy | that |
| posle | selepas | sú | Ele | España | but |
| posto | bahwa | ktorý | Governo | Madrid | It |

Table 7: The ten word-unigram features given the highest weight by information gain feature selection for each of the six tasks.

## 5 Discussion

Across many of the tasks, there was evidence that performance was tied more strongly to domain-specific features of the two classes rather than to language- (or language-variant-) specific features. For example, Table 7 shows the best word-unigram features selected by information gain feature selection for each of the tasks. The Portuguese, Spanish, and English tasks specifically have as many of their most important features named entities and other non-language specific features.

It seems that for many of the tasks, it is easier to distinguish the subject matter written about than it is to distinguish the languages/dialects themselves. With Portuguese, for example, Brazilian dialect speakers were much more likely to discuss places in Brazil and mention Brazilian reais (currency, abbreviated as R), while European speakers mentioned euros, places in Portugal, and discussed Portuguese politics. While there are definite linguistic differences between Brazilian and European Portuguese, these seem to be less pronounced than the superficial differences in subject matter.

Practically, this is not necessarily a bad thing for this shared task, as the domain information gives extra clues that allow the task to be completed with higher accuracy than would otherwise be possible. This would become problematic if one wanted to apply a classifier trained on this data to general domains, where the classifier may not be able to rely on the speaker talking about a certain subject matter. To address this, the classifier would either need to focus on features specific to the language pair itself or would need to be trained on data that spanned many domains.

Further evidence of domain overfitting comes from the fact that the larger training sets drawn from newspaper text were not able to improve performance on the development set over the provided training data, which is presumably drawn from the same collection as the development data. Figure 1 shows learning curves for each of the six tasks. Though all the external text is self-consistent (cross-validation results in high accuracy), in none of the cases does training on a large amount of external data allow the classifier to exceed the accuracy achieved by training on the DSL data.

## 6 Conclusion

In this paper we experimented with several methods for classification of sentences in closely-related languages for the DSL shared task. Our analysis showed that, when dealing with closely related languages, the task of classifying text according to its language was difficult to untie from the taks of classifying other text characteristics, such as the domain. Across all our types of methods, we found that a naïve Bayes classifier using character $n$-gram, word unigram, and word bigram features was a strong baseline.

In future work, we would like to try to improve on these results by incorporating features that try to capture syntactic relationships. Certainly some of the pairs of languages considered here are close enough that they could be chunked, tagged, or parsed before knowing exactly which variety they belong to. This would allow for the inclusion of features related to transitivity, agreement, complementation, etc. For example, in British English, the verb "provide" is monotransitive, but ditransitive in American English. It is unclear how much features like these would improve accuracy, but it is likely that they would ultimately be necessary to improve classification of similar languages to human levels of performance.

## References


Shane Bergsma, Paul McNamee, Mossaab Bagdouri, Clayton Fink, and Theresa Wilson. 2012. Language identification for creating language-specific twitter collections. In *Proceedings of the Second Workshop on Language in Social Media*, pages 65–74. Association for Computational Linguistics.

Simon Carter, Wouter Weerkamp, and Manos Tsagkias. 2013. Microblog language identification: Overcoming the limitations of short, unedited and idiomatic text. *Language Resources and Evaluation*, 47(1):195–215.

Chu-Ren Huang and Lung-Hao Lee. 2008. Contrastive approach towards text source classification based on top-bag-of-word similarity. pages 404–410.

Thorsten Joachims. Svmlight: Support vector machine. `http://svmlight. joachims. org/`.

Ben King and Steven Abney. 2013. Labeling the languages of words in mixed-language documents using weakly supervised methods. In *Proceedings of NAACL-HLT*, pages 1110–1119.

Nikola Ljubešić, Nives Mikelić, and Damir Boras. 2007. Language identication: How to distinguish similar languages? In *Proceedings of the 29th International Conference on Information Technology Interfaces*, pages 541–546.

Marco Lui, Jey Han Lau, and Timothy Baldwin. 2014. Automatic detection and language identification of multilingual documents. *Transactions of the Association for Computational Linguistics*, 2:27–40.

Andrew K. McCallum. 2002. Mallet: A machine learning for language toolkit. `http://mallet.cs.umass.edu`.

Andrew Y Ng and Michael I Jordan. 2002. On discriminative vs. generative classifiers: A comparison of logistic regression and naive bayes. *Advances in neural information processing systems*, 2:841–848.

Andrew Y Ng. 2004. Feature selection, l 1 vs. l 2 regularization, and rotational invariance. In *Proceedings of the twenty-first international conference on Machine learning*, page 78. ACM.

Dong-Phuong Nguyen and A Seza Dogruoz. 2013. Word level language identification in online multilingual communication. Association for Computational Linguistics.

Yves Peirsman, Dirk Geeraerts, and Dirk Speelman. 2010. The automatic identification of lexical variation between language varieties. *Natural Language Engineering*, 16(4):469–491.

Jason Rennie. 2004. On l2-norm regularization and the gaussian prior. `http://people.csail.mit.edu/jrennie/writing`.

Liling Tan, Marcos Zampieri, Nikola Ljubešic, and Jörg Tiedemann. 2014. Merging comparable data sources for the discrimination of similar languages: The dsl corpus collection. In *Proceedings of The 7th Workshop on Building and Using Comparable Corpora (BUCC)*.

Jörg Tiedemann and Nikola Ljubešić. 2012. Efficient discrimination between closely related languages. In *COLING*, pages 2619–2634.

Ioannis Tsochantaridis, Thomas Hofmann, Thorsten Joachims, and Yasemin Altun. 2004. Support vector machine learning for interdependent and structured output spaces. In *Proceedings of the twenty-first international conference on Machine learning*, page 104. ACM.

Marcos Zampieri and Binyam Gebrekidan. 2012. Automatic identification of language varieties: The case of portuguese. In *Proceedings of KONVENS*, pages 233–237.

Marcos Zampieri, Binyam Gebrekidan Gebre, and Sascha Diwersy. 2012. Classifying pluricentric languages: Extending the monolingual model. In *Proceedings of the Fourth Swedish Language Technlogy Conference (SLTC2012)*, pages 79–80.

Marcos Zampieri, Binyam Gebrekidan Gebre, and Sascha Diwersy. 2013. N-gram language models and pos distribution for the identification of spanish varieties. *Proceedings of TALN2013, Sable dOlonne, France*, pages 580–587.

# A Simple Baseline for Discriminating Similar Languages

**Matthew Purver**
Cognitive Science Research Group
School of Electronic Engineering and Computer Science
Queen Mary University of London
m.purver@qmul.ac.uk

**Abstract**

This paper describes an approach to discriminating similar languages using word- and character-based features, submitted as the Queen Mary University of London entry to the Discriminating Similar Languages shared task. Our motivation was to investigate how well a simple, data-driven, linguistically naive method could perform, in order to provide a baseline by which more linguistically complex or knowledge-rich approaches can be judged. Using a standard supervised classifier with word and character n-grams as features, we achieved over 90% accuracy in the test; on fixing simple file handling and feature extraction bugs, this improved to over 95%, comparable to the best submitted systems. Similar accuracy is achieved using only word unigram features.

## 1 Introduction and Approach

Most approaches to written language detection use character or byte ngram features to capture characteristic orthographic sequences – see e.g. (Cavnar and Trenkle, 1994) to (Lui et al., 2014) and many in between, as well as implementations such as the widely used open-source Chromium Compact Language Detector.[1] Some approaches determine these characteristic features from linguistic properties of the language (e.g. (Lins and Gonçalves, 2004)), while some determine them from data (e.g. (Cavnar and Trenkle, 1994)). A wide range of approaches to modelling and classification can be used, ranging from simple Naïve Bayes models (Grefenstette, 1995) to more complex generative mixture models for tasks with multilingual texts (Lui et al., 2014). Our interest in this task was to see how well a naive, entirely data-driven baseline method would perform in the task of discriminating *similar* languages (DSL) as posed by the DSL Shared Task (Zampieri et al., 2014).

Our approach was intended to capture two basic insights into variation between similar languages. First, that closely related languages often use quite different words for the same concept: e.g. US English *elevator* vs UK English *lift*; Croatian *tjedan* vs Serbian *nedelja* vs Bosnian *sedmica*. Second, that there are often regular variations in the details of a word's orthographic or phonological form: e.g. US English *color, favorite* vs UK English *colour, favourite*; Croatian/Bosnian *rijeka*, *htjeti* vs Serbian *reka*, *hteti*. The former insight can be approximated by use of word ngrams; the latter via character ngrams. While such ngram features cannot capture similarity of meaning or non-sequential dependencies, they may do a reasonable job of capturing similarity of sentential context (often taken to be an indicator of lexical meaning) and sequential phenomena.

Together with simplicity in method, speed and simplicity of implementation was also an objective. We therefore used only the training and development data available in the shared task — see (Tan et al., 2014) — together with a standard freely available discriminative SVM classifier and common text pre-processing methods.



[1] https://code.google.com/p/chromium-compact-language-detector/



*Proceedings of the First Workshop on Applying NLP Tools to Similar Languages, Varieties and Dialects*, pages 155–160,
Dublin, Ireland, August 23 2014.

## 2 Background and Related Work

**Shared Task** The Discriminating Similar Languages (DSL) Shared Task was established as part of the 2014 VarDial workshop.[2] The task provided datasets for 13 different languages in 6 groups of closely related languages, shown in Table 1. Data was divided into training, development and test sets: for each language, 18,000 labelled training instances and 2,000 labelled development instances were provided; an unlabelled and previously unseen test set containing 1,000 instances per language was then used for evaluation by the organisers – see (Tan et al., 2014) for full details of the dataset, and (Zampieri et al., 2014) for the task and evaluation.

| | |
|---|---|
| Group A | Bosnian (`bs`), Croatian (`hr`), Serbian (`sr`) |
| Group B | Indonesian (`id`), Malaysian (`my`) |
| Group C | Czech (`cz`), Slovakian (`sk`) |
| Group D | Brazilian Portuguese (`pt-BR`), European Portuguese (`pt-PT`) |
| Group E | Peninsular Spain (`es-ES`), Argentine Spanish (`es-AR`) |
| Group F | American English (`en-US`), British English (`en-GB`) |

Table 1: Languages and groups in the DSL Shared Task.

However, problems were discovered in labelling the languages in Group F, and an evaluation for groups A-E was therefore performed separately; we discuss only this latter task and evaluation here.

**Related Work** Classification approaches based on character or byte sequences have shown success in providing general models of language identification; see e.g. (Lui et al., 2014). In more specific experiments into discriminating between pairs or triples of similar languages, many researchers have found that word-based features can aid accuracy; but classification method and feature choice vary widely.

When distinguishing Malay from Indonesian, Ranaivo-Malançon (2006) combines character n-gram frequencies with heuristics based on number format and lists of words unique to each language. Ljubešić et al. (2007) use a character trigram-based probabilistic language model, again in combination with a unique-word list, to distinguish between Croatian, Serbian and Slovenian, achieving high accuracies (over 99%); Tiedemann and Ljubešić (2012) extend this task to include Bosnian and improve performance by using a Naive Bayes classifier with unigram word features to achieve accuracies over 95%.

Some research suggests that word-based features can even outperform character-based approaches. For Brazilian vs European Portuguese, Zampieri and Gebre (2012) found that word unigrams gave very similar performance to character n-gram features when used in a probabilistic language model; Zampieri et al. (2013) then showed that word 1- or 2-grams outperformed character ngrams of any length from 1 to 5 (and that both outperformed features based purely on syntactic part-of-speech), when distinguishing different varieties of Spanish. Lui and Cook (2013) likewise found that bag-of-words features generally outperformed features based on syntax or character sequences when distinguishing between Canadian, Australian and UK English. However, Zampieri (2013) found that in some cases (e.g French) character n-grams might give benefits above simple word unigram features.

In this work, then our interest was to investigate whether these simple, knowledge-poor approaches can generalise and apply across several language groups, using a single integrated approach to classification incorporating character- and word-based features within one model; and to compare the utility of word and character features.

## 3 Methods

**Processing and training** We tokenise the training texts from (Tan et al., 2014) based on transitions between alphanumeric and non-alphanumeric characters, and remove URLs, email addresses, Twitter usernames and emoticons. We then form feature vectors with entries for all observed word (token) unigrams, and character ngrams of lengths 1-3; feature values are counts (raw term frequencies) normalised

[2] `http://corporavm.uni-koeln.de/vardial/`

by the text length in tokens or characters respectively. We then train a single multi-class linear-kernel support vector machine using LIBLINEAR (Fan et al., 2008) with the language identifiers (`en-US`, `en-UK`, `hr`, `bs`, `sr` etc.) as labels. SVMs are well-suited to high-dimensional feature spaces; and SVMs with ngrams of these lengths have shown good performance in other language identification work (Baldwin and Lui, 2010). Features were given numerical indices corresponding to the unique ngram type (i.e. we used a feature dictionary with no hashing). No feature selection or frequency cutoff was used. No part-of-speech tagging or grammatical analysis was attempted; no external language resources or tools were used other than described above.

**Development and testing** Development and test set texts were tokenised and featurised using the same process; feature indices were taken from the dictionary generated during training, with unseen ngram types ignored. LIBLINEAR was then used to predict the most likely language identifier label.

By re-using a standard set of in-house utilities for tokenisation and featurisation,[3] the code for training and parameter testing (see below) was written and tested for functionality in around 30 minutes. Pre-processing, featurisation and vectorisation then took around 25 minutes over the training and development sets, and writing out LIBLINEAR format files around 15 minutes, running on a MacBook Air with 1.7GHz Intel Core i7 processor and 8Gb memory. Classifier training then takes around 1 minute, depending on exact parameter settings. Testing on the development set or test set takes around 1 second per language group.

## 4 Experiments and Results

**Development** We used 10-fold cross-validation on the training set, and testing on the development set, to choose a suitable SVM cost parameter (tradeoff between error and maximum margin criterion). We cross-validated over the training set to check overall multi-class accuracy while varying the cost over a range from 1 to 100 – see Table 2. We then trained on the full training set, and tested accuracy on the development across each language group – see Table 3. Given reported problems with the group F dataset (`en-UK/en-US`), we focussed on groups A-E.

| Cost: | 1.0 | 3.0 | 10.0 | 30.0 | 50.0 | 100.0 |
|---|---|---|---|---|---|---|
| Overall A-E | 91.36 | 93.24 | 94.44 | 94.83 | 94.86 | 94.85 |

Table 2: 10-fold cross-validation accuracy on training set with varying SVM cost.

| | Cost: | 1.0 | 3.0 | 10.0 | 30.0 | 50.0 | 100.0 |
|---|---|---|---|---|---|---|---|
| Group A | `bs/hr/sr` | 88.93 | 91.96 | 93.20 | 93.56 | 93.46 | 93.26 |
| Group B | `id/my` | 97.11 | 97.72 | 98.14 | 98.28 | 98.31 | 98.42 |
| Group C | `cz/sk` | 99.90 | 99.92 | 99.95 | 99.97 | 99.97 | 99.95 |
| Group D | `pt-BR/pt-PT` | 89.83 | 91.99 | 93.52 | 94.12 | 94.00 | 94.05 |
| Group E | `es-AR/es-ES` | 82.72 | 85.82 | 87.78 | 89.26 | 89.24 | 89.01 |
| Overall A-E | | 91.34 | 93.28 | 94.34 | 94.86 | 94.81 | 94.73 |

Table 3: Accuracy on development set with varying SVM cost.

A cost parameter value of 30 to 50 appeared to perform best across all groups, so these two values were used for separate runs in the shared task test. Note though that performance appears relatively stable over a cost range of 10-100 (perhaps 30-100 for group E). The classifier performs worst for group E (`es-AR/es-ES`), with only this language group failing to reach 90% accuracy. Group C (`cz/sk`) performs best with almost perfect accuracy; this may be due to the existence of characters which are highly discriminative on their own (e.g. ô is used in Slovak, but not in Czech, ů in Czech but not in Slovak – although a few dozen examples appear labelled as Slovak in this dataset).

[3]Tools with equivalent functionality are widely available e.g. as part of NLTK, `http://www.nltk.org/`.

**Test – Shared Task** A blind run on the test set was then performed and submitted as part of the shared task. Overall accuracy was 90.61% (macro-averaged F-score 92.51%), placing us 5th amongst the task entrants; results per group are shown in Table 4.

| | Cost: | 30.0 |
|---|---|---|
| Group A | bs/hr/sr | 87.87 |
| Group B | id/my | 93.50 |
| Group C | cz/sk | 96.20 |
| Group D | pt-BR/pt-PT | 90.45 |
| Group E | es-AR/es-ES | 86.45 |
| Overall A-E | | 90.61 |

Table 4: Accuracy on test set as submitted for the shared task.

**Corrected Test** However, after submission of the test run, a bug was discovered in the code which paired test sentences with predictions; predictions had been omitted for about 500 of the 11,000 test texts (i.e. 4.5% of the data) due to an unfortunate combination of unpaired double-quote characters in the test data with the use of a standard CSV-file handling library. After release of the gold-standard test set labels, the classifier was therefore re-run, with resulting accuracies as shown in Table 5.

| | Cost: | 1.0 | 3.0 | 10.0 | 30.0 | 50.0 | 100.0 |
|---|---|---|---|---|---|---|---|
| Group A | bs/hr/sr | 87.97 | 90.70 | 92.40 | 92.90 | 93.00 | 93.17 |
| Group B | id/my | 98.30 | 98.85 | 99.05 | 99.15 | 99.15 | 99.15 |
| Group C | cz/sk | 99.90 | 99.95 | 99.95 | 99.95 | 99.95 | 99.95 |
| Group D | pt-BR/pt-PT | 88.50 | 91.45 | 93.25 | 93.95 | 93.90 | 93.80 |
| Group E | es-AR/es-ES | 83.65 | 86.70 | 88.45 | 89.35 | 89.45 | 89.45 |
| Overall A-E | | 91.33 | 93.27 | 94.42 | 94.86 | 94.90 | 94.93 |

Table 5: True accuracy on test set after restoring omitted predictions.

Accuracies are very similar to those on the development set. Overall accuracy at the chosen cost parameter range of 30-50 is 94.9%, slightly worse than the 1st and slightly better than the 2nd-placed systems in the official test (95.71% and 94.68% respectively). Increasing the cost parameter setting could perhaps give a very slight boost to performance. Again, group E performs worst, and Group C best; per-group and overall accuracies are very similar to those achieved on the development set.

A second unintended feature of the feature generation code was subsequently discovered: character n-grams were being extracted spanning word boundaries (including the whitespace characters separating words). These were removed, leaving only the intended character n-grams within words, and accuracies are shown in Table 6. Again, overall performance increases slightly, now to over 95%, although Group A accuracy shows a slight decrease (0.1%). Group E accuracy improves by over 1% and is now over 90% at the chosen cost parameter.

| | Cost: | 1.0 | 3.0 | 10.0 | 30.0 | 50.0 | 100.0 |
|---|---|---|---|---|---|---|---|
| Group A | bs/hr/sr | 89.83 | 92.13 | 92.73 | 92.77 | 92.63 | 92.67 |
| Group B | id/my | 98.55 | 99.15 | 99.25 | 99.35 | 99.35 | 99.35 |
| Group C | cz/sk | 99.95 | 99.95 | 99.95 | 99.95 | 99.95 | 99.95 |
| Group D | pt-BR/pt-PT | 91.00 | 93.25 | 94.80 | 95.15 | 95.10 | 95.15 |
| Group E | es-AR/es-ES | 86.10 | 88.35 | 90.30 | 90.85 | 90.95 | 91.15 |
| Overall A-E | | 92.79 | 94.35 | 95.16 | 95.35 | 95.33 | 95.37 |

Table 6: Accuracy on test set after removing spurious character n-grams.

**Effect of features** To investigate the utility of our chosen feature sets and their insights into lexical and orthographic distinctions, we then compared the overall performance to that achieved when removing certain features. Table 7 shows the accuracies achieved without word unigram features (i.e. using only character ngrams of lengths 1-3); Table 8 shows accuracies without character ngram features (i.e. using only word unigrams).

| | Cost: | 1.0 | 3.0 | 10.0 | 30.0 | 50.0 | 100.0 |
|---|---|---|---|---|---|---|---|
| Group A | `bs/hr/sr` | 81.43 | 85.40 | 88.03 | 89.77 | 90.10 | 90.70 |
| Group B | `id/my` | 91.80 | 94.15 | 96.05 | 96.95 | 97.20 | 97.50 |
| Group C | `cz/sk` | 99.90 | 99.95 | 99.95 | 99.95 | 99.95 | 99.95 |
| Group D | `pt-BR/pt-PT` | 82.75 | 86.70 | 89.15 | 90.80 | 91.50 | 91.80 |
| Group E | `es-AR/es-ES` | 77.80 | 80.95 | 83.50 | 85.20 | 85.10 | 85.65 |
| Overall A-E | | 86.25 | 89.06 | 91.04 | 92.28 | 92.53 | 92.90 |

Table 7: Accuracy on test set without word unigrams.

| | Cost: | 1.0 | 3.0 | 10.0 | 30.0 | 50.0 | 100.0 |
|---|---|---|---|---|---|---|---|
| Group A | `bs/hr/sr` | 86.83 | 89.63 | 91.73 | 92.20 | 92.43 | 92.07 |
| Group B | `id/my` | 97.70 | 98.65 | 98.85 | 99.10 | 99.15 | 99.10 |
| Group C | `cz/sk` | 99.70 | 99.70 | 99.80 | 99.90 | 99.90 | 99.90 |
| Group D | `pt-BR/pt-PT` | 86.65 | 90.55 | 92.55 | 93.25 | 93.40 | 93.20 |
| Group E | `es-AR/es-ES` | 85.10 | 87.10 | 88.35 | 89.35 | 89.35 | 89.45 |
| Overall A-E | | 90.80 | 92.81 | 94.02 | 94.53 | 94.63 | 94.50 |

Table 8: Accuracy on test set using only word unigrams.

Neither system performs as well as the classifier with the full, combined feature set (Table 6). However, the system with only word unigrams does almost as well as the full system, losing a maximum of 2% performance at the extreme range of cost parameter values, and less than 1% at the chosen optimal values. The system with only character ngrams, however, loses noticably more performance, with around 3% lost even at optimal cost values.

## 5 Conclusions

A simple approach using ngram features and discriminative classification achieves competitive results on the task of discriminating similar languages, and the availability of existing language processing and machine learning tools makes setting up and training such a system easy and extremely quick. Simple word unigram features perform well on their own, although combination with character n-gram features improves performance; the choice of classifier parameters is important but seems to generalise well across different languages. Future extensions of this work could include features which take into account longer word or character sequences and/or more flexible characterisations and combinations of those features, for example via the convolutional neural network approach of (Kalchbrenner et al., 2014).

## References

Timothy Baldwin and Marco Lui. 2010. Language identification: The long and the short of the matter. In *Human Language Technologies: The 2010 Annual Conference of the North American Chapter of the Association for Computational Linguistics*, pages 229–237, Los Angeles, California, June. Association for Computational Linguistics.

William B. Cavnar and John M. Trenkle. 1994. N-gram-based text categorization. In *Proceedings of the 3rd Symposium on Document Analysis and Information Retrieval*, pages 161–175, Las Vegas.

Rong-En Fan, Kai-Wei Chang, Cho-Jui Hsieh, Xang-Rui Wang, and Chih-Jen Lin. 2008. LIBLINEAR: A library for large linear classification. *Journal of Machine Learning Research*, 9:1871–1874.

Gregory Grefenstette. 1995. Comparing two language identification schemes. In *Proceedings of Analisi Statistica dei Dati Testuali (JADT)*, pages 263–268, Rome.

Nal Kalchbrenner, Edward Grefenstette, and Phil Blunsom. 2014. A convolutional neural network for modelling sentences. In *Proceedings of the 52nd Annual Meeting of the Association for Computational Linguistics (Volume 1: Long Papers)*, pages 655–665, Baltimore, Maryland, June. Association for Computational Linguistics.

Rafael Dueire Lins and Paulo Gonçalves. 2004. Automatic language identification of written texts. In *Proceedings of the 2004 ACM Symposium on Applied Computing*, SAC '04, pages 1128–1133, New York, NY, USA. ACM.

Nikola Ljubešić, Nives Mikelić, and Damir Boras. 2007. Language identification: How to distinguish similar languages? In *Proceedings of the 29th International Conference on Information Technology Interfaces (ITI)*, pages 541–546.

Marco Lui and Paul Cook. 2013. Classifying english documents by national dialect. In *Proceedings of the Australasian Language Technology Association Workshop 2013 (ALTA 2013)*, pages 5–15, Brisbane, Australia.

Marco Lui, Jey Han Lau, and Timothy Baldwin. 2014. Automatic detection and language identification of multilingual documents. *Transactions of the Association for Computational Linguistics*, 2:27–40.

Bali Ranaivo-Malançon. 2006. Automatic identification of close languages - case study: Malay and Indonesian. *ECTI Transactions on Computer and Information Technology*, 2(2):126–134, November.

Liling Tan, Marcos Zampieri, Nikola Ljubešić, and Jörg Tiedemann. 2014. Merging comparable data sources for the discrimination of similar languages: The DSL Corpus Collection. In *Proceedings of the 7th Workshop on Building and Using Comparable Corpora (BUCC)*.

Jörg Tiedemann and Nikola Ljubešić. 2012. Efficient discrimination between closely related languages. In *Proceedings of COLING 2012*, pages 2619–2634, Mumbai, India, December.

Marcos Zampieri and Binyam Gebrekidan Gebre. 2012. Automatic identification of language varieties: The case of Portuguese. In *Proceedings of KONVENS2012*, pages 233–237, Vienna, September.

Marcos Zampieri, Binyam Gebrekidan Gebre, and Sascha Diwersy. 2013. N-gram language models and POS distribution for the identification of Spanish varieties. In *Proceedings of TALN2013*, pages 580–587, Sables d'Olonne, France.

Marcos Zampieri, Liling Tan, Nikola Ljubešić, and Jörg Tiedemann. 2014. A report on the DSL Shared Task 2014. In *Proceedings of the 1st Workshop on Applying NLP Tools to Similar Languages, Varieties and Dialects (VarDial)*.

Marcos Zampieri. 2013. Using bag-of-words to distinguish similar languages: How efficient are they? In *Proceedings of the 14th IEEE International Symposium on Computational Intelligence and Informatics (CINTI)*, pages 37–41, Budapest, November.

# Author Index